QUAKE 4

PRIMA OFFICIAL GAME GUIDE

STEPHEN STRATTON
BRYAN STRATTON

Prima Games
A Division of Random House, Inc.
3000 Lava Ridge Court, Suite 100 / Roseville, CA 95661 / 1-800-733-3000 / www.primagames.com

Product Manager: Mario De Govia
Editor: Amanda Peckham
Design: Marc Riegel
Layout: Kim Tran

ISBN: 0-7615-5262-6
Library of Congress Catalog Card Number: 2005908360
Printed in the United States of America

05 06 07 08 GG 10 9 8 7 6 5 4 3 2 1

Contents

WELCOME TO QUAKE 4

THE STORY THUS FAR

In the mid-twenty-first century, a vile, warlike alien race called the Strogg launched a massive invasion of Earth. After years of struggle and suffering unbearable casualties, mankind finally realized that their only chance at survival was to mount a desperate counterassault on the Strogg homeworld, planet Stroggos.

The first assault force was launched from the GDF fleet and encountered massive resistance—most of the dropships were destroyed by the Strogg homeworld's massive defense weapon, known as the "Big Gun." One sole surviving marine broke through and managed to destroy the Big Gun and ultimately defeat the Strogg leader, the Makron. However, the war did not end there.

You are Matthew Kane, a member of the elite GDF Rhino Squad and part of the final colossal invasion that spans across the entire planet of Stroggos. Equipped with high-tech weaponry and vehicles and teamed with a top GDF marine squadron, you soon realize this war is far from over. In fact, your worst nightmares have yet to become realized...

HOW TO USE THIS GUIDE

We've spared no effort to ensure that this guide contains all of the tips, tricks, hints, and strategy you need to destroy every enemy, find every hidden item, and survive the horrors in store for you on planet Stroggos.

BASIC TRAINING

The "Basic Training" section is essential reading for any new Quake 4 recruit; even Quake masters will want to look at it. This section covers every command in the game, from attacking to zooming your viewpoint; it also features detailed strategies applicable to any combat situation. Knowing when and how to strafe can mean the difference between life and death on Stroggos, so don't report for duty until you've completed Basic Training.

WEAPONS AND ITEMS

With all the weapons to wield and items to collect in Quake 4, you need a separate chapter to keep them all straight. Fortunately, that's what the "Weapons and Items" section of the guide is all about. Refer to it for tips and strategies for using the various weapons, as well as information on each item (or pick-up) in the game. Environmental objects of import are also detailed in this section.

VEHICLES

There are many different vehicles in Quake 4. Some you must pilot, others you must battle and destroy. For quick reference, every GDF and Strogg vehicle is covered in complete detail in this section of the guide. Check the vehicle descriptions to learn all about each one, including effective combat tips to employ against hostile vehicles.

CHARACTERS

Stats and bios on every member of Rhino Squad—the principal characters of Quake 4—are presented in this spoiler-free section. Read to acquire new insight into the minds of the GDF's most elite squadron of marines.

ENEMIES

The "Enemies" section tells you everything you need to know and more about the four main classes of foes you'll face: light infantry, heavy infantry, commanders, and generals (bosses). Any creature in *Quake 4* that wants to do you harm is covered in detail in this chapter. Knowing how to deal with different enemies saves you ammunition, health, and armor, so bone up on the strengths and weaknesses of each one.

MULTIPLAYER

As deep and rich as the single-player *Quake 4* experience is, don't overlook the visceral thrill of its five multiplayer modes. The "Multiplayer" section reveals the intricacies of all 13 multiplayer maps, with labeled floor plans for each one. A hefty multiplayer training section is also included to teach newbies the fundamentals of all things multiplayer and refresh the memories of seasoned veterans.

WALKTHROUGH

This is the guide's biggest section. The walkthrough takes you on a waypoint-by-waypoint tour through each level, giving advice on how to handle tough fights, warning you of nasty ambushes, and showing you how to complete each objective in order to progress through the game. Every waypoint in the text relates to its matching waypoint on the maps—this ensures that you'll never get lost. Just scan the maps to find your location and what you must do. The maps are also labeled with enemy and pick-up locations for quick reference.

GAMERSCORE ACHIEVEMENTS

Every Xbox 360 title has its own set of achievements you can complete to add points to your overall Gamerscore. Anyone can view your Gamerscore over Xbox Live to see how many points you've accumulated and thereby judge just how hardcore you really are. This short chapter lists all of the different achievements in *Quake 4*, along with their point values when met.

NOTE

Certain pick-up amounts and locations [such as health packs and ammunition] vary depending upon the game's difficulty level. The walkthrough is written from the "Corporal [Normal]" difficulty, but it's entirely applicable for any difficulty level, as the game's objectives do not change.

WALKTHROUGH MAP ICONS

You'll notice that the walkthrough maps are labeled with a small variety of icons. Here's what each icon represents:

🔋	AMMUNITION	↘	WEAPON
❤	ARMOR	⬡	EXPLOSIVE BARREL
✚	HEALTH	⬡	ENEMY SPAWN
✚	MEDIC	1	WAYPOINT
🔧	TECHNICIAN	A	CONNECTION

⬡ =denotes item below or behind an object

BASIC TRAINING

CUSTOMIZING THE CONTROLS

All of the controls in *Quake 4* are fully customizable, and although just about every player has his or her own control scheme, this guide assumes you're using the default controls.

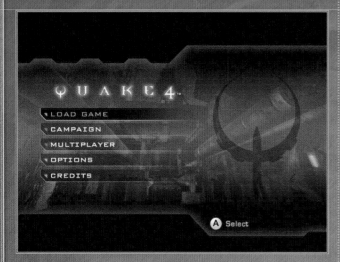

To customize the controls, select "Options" at the Main menu and then select "Controls" from the menu that appears. You can customize three categories of controls: Sticks, Buttons, and Sensitivity. Experiment with the many different control options and find the setup that best suits your unique style of play.

DEFAULT CONTROLS

STICKS

ACTION	BUTTON
Forward	L
Backpedal	L
Strafe Left	L
Strafe Right	L
Look Up	R
Look Down	R
Look/Turn Left	R
Look/Turn Right	R

BUTTONS

ACTION	BUTTON
Jump	A
Use/Interact	B
Reload	X
Flashlight	Y
Pause	START
Objectives/Scores	BACK
Crouch	L3
Center View	R3
Zoom	LT
Attack	RT
Previous Weapon	LB
Next Weapon	RB
Change Weapon	✪

IN-GAME CONTROLS

This section describes the controls and actions you may perform during a single-player or multiplayer game.

LOOKING AROUND

By default, Ⓡ controls your view. Simply move Ⓡ in the direction that you want to look. You move in the direction that you're looking when you press Ⓛ; so by holding Ⓛ down, you can steer yourself with Ⓡ. Press Ⓡ3 to center your view.

When you're carrying a weapon that's equipped with a scope, press ⓁⓉ to get an up-close-and-personal view of the action. This lets you see distant objects more clearly, but it also cuts down on your peripheral vision. Weapon scopes are best used to inspect rooms you're about to enter and to pick off distant enemies.

Tip

When using a scope to attack enemies at range, try to strafe back and fourth a bit. Even a small amount of strafing can reduce the amount of return-fire you sustain.

MOVEMENT

Movement is absolutely the most vital skill you need to master in *Quake 4*. All the fancy weapons and walkthroughs in the world won't help you if you can't keep from running into walls.

At the most basic end of the movement spectrum is traveling forward and backpedaling. Press Ⓛ to move in the direction you're facing. Press Ⓛ to move away from the direction you're facing. Simple enough, right?

SURVIVING ON STROGGOS, PART 1: BE PATIENT

If you try to use your Deathmatch strategies in *Quake 4's* single-player mode, you won't make it out of the second level alive. *Quake 4* is not a run-'n'-gun game—it requires strategy, observational skills, and most of all, patience.

When entering an area for the first time (or when returning to an area after accomplishing an objective), proceed slowly and cautiously. Listen for the sounds of nearby enemies and to what your squadmates tell you. Scan the area for objects to use as cover in the event of an attack. Anticipate ambushes.

Quake 4 often throws you into intense battles with little warning, attempting to cause you to make careless mistakes. Your best weapons are your wits—keep them about you at all times.

STRAFING

"Strafing" is the term used to describe moving left or right while facing forward. It is most commonly used to dodge enemy fire while returning some of your own, although it has other uses (see the "Surviving on Stroggos, Part 2: Rounding Corners" sidebar). Use ⓛ and ⓛ to strafe left and right.

We've said it before and we'll say it again: Standing still during a firefight is masochistic at best and suicidal at worst. Use ⓡ to keep your targeting reticle fixed on your enemy, and strafe from side to side to avoid his attacks while returning fire.

You can close the distance between you and an enemy more safely by running toward the enemy while simultaneously strafing from side to side.

CIRCLE-STRAFING

If you're facing an enemy in an open area, especially in multiplayer games, you must master the art of circle-strafing. While keeping your targeting reticle fixed on the enemy, strafe right and left in a circle around him while backpedaling or moving forward to maintain your preferred distance. Change direction randomly to prevent your enemy from predicting your moves.

SURVIVING ON STROGGOS, PART 2: ROUNDING CORNERS

This simple trick will save you some pain: As you approach a blind corner, turn to face it and then strafe around it. That way, if there's anything nasty waiting for you around the corner, you're already facing it.

JUMPING

Jumping is another basic movement with a variety of uses. Press Ⓐ while moving to hop over obstacles, leap across gaps, reach an elevated area, or dodge enemy fire.

CAUTION

Jumping or falling long vertical distances can injure or kill you. Look before you leap!

You can jump onto just about any solid object of waist height or shorter. Some objects, such as barrels and tables, can be pushed into strategic positions that allow you to jump onto them and reach areas or items that were previously out of reach.

CROUCHING AND CRAWLING

At several points in the game, you come to narrow tunnels that you can only enter by crouching down and then crawling. To crawl, press and hold ⑬ and press ⓛ or ⓛ to crawl forward or backward. You can also use ⑬ to hide behind objects.

SURVIVING ON STROGGOS, PART 3: TAKE COVER!

Standing out in the open throughout a gunfight is a very bad idea. You're not bulletproof, so conceal as much of your body as possible behind cover—this minimizes your risk of being hit by enemy fire.

Stand behind pillars and crates as you attack. Duck completely behind them when bullets start flying in your direction and every time you need to reload. If enemies swarm in, back up through doorways, strafe to one side, and then blast your foes as they line up to follow you— the shotgun is particularly useful for this tactic.

JUMP-CROUCHING

An advanced movement technique is jump-crouching. You use this when you need to enter a narrow opening that's too far off the ground to crouch and crawl into. To execute a jump-crouch, jump while moving forward, then immediately crouch ⓛ+Ⓐ,⑬. While this can be a tricky maneuver to master, it allows you to access areas you otherwise couldn't.

CLIMBING LADDERS

Many Strogg are human-shaped and sized, so you'll see several utility ladders as you infiltrate their bases and bunkers. To climb up a ladder, just look at it and then move forward. To climb down one, approach the ladder, turn around, look downward, and then backpedal.

INTERACTING WITH CONTROL PANELS

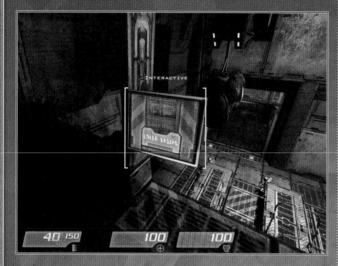

You can interact with many control panels in the Strogg's bases and facilities, usually ones found near sealed doors and elevators. Useable control panels become highlighted by an "Interact" reticle when you approach. Press **Ⓑ** to activate the control panel and see what happens.

SPEAKING WITH CHARACTERS

Though you encountered a few living, breathing characters in *Doom 3*, you get to fight alongside many more in *Quake 4*. Approach a character and move your targeting reticle over him to view his name, rank, and GDF squadron affiliation.

Some characters will strike up a conversation with you upon seeing you, and you can speak to just about anyone you meet by approaching them and pressing **Ⓑ**. Speak to characters several times by repeatedly pressing **Ⓑ** to get additional information. Not everyone will have something useful to tell you, but you never know until you try.

NOTE

Don't worry if you accidentally fire at characters you meet—you can't hurt friendlies.

MEDICS

GDF medics can heal you. You can easily identify medics by their unique body armor and by the icon displayed next to their rank when you target one.

When your health is low, approach a medic and press **Ⓑ** to speak with him. The medic then quickly heals you to full health. Needless to say, medics are extremely valuable squadmates, and you should strive to protect them.

TECHNICIANS

GDF technicians can restore your armor. Identify technicians by their unique body armor and by the icon displayed next to their rank when you target one.

When your armor is low, approach a technician and press **Ⓑ** to speak with him. The technician then completely restores your body armor.

Technicians can also hack Strogg control panels to oper sealed doors and the like. Like medics, technicians are extremely valuable squadmates who you should defend against harm.

NOTE

Medics and technicians never run out of healing ability, but they won't assist you when they're preoccupied.

ENTERING/EXITING VEHICLES

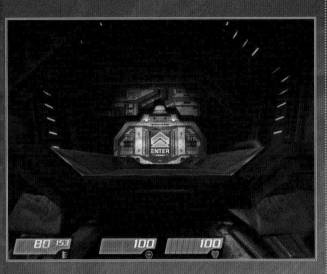

You can enter certain vehicles in *Quake 4*'s single-player campaign. Approach a vehicle; when the yellow "enter arrows" appear on your HUD, press Ⓑ to climb in. Press Ⓑ to exit a vehicle when you're finished with it. If the words "Vehicle Locked" appear on your screen's lower-left corner, you cannot exit the vehicle.

Your controls change to allow you to steer a vehicle after you enter one. Each vehicle has its own unique controls. Please refer to the "Vehicles" section of this guide for complete details on each one.

ATTACKING

Attacking is the second most important skill to master in *Quake 4*. When you aren't targeting a character or a control panel, simply press Ⓡⓣ to fire your currently equipped weapon. Different weapons have different effective ranges—consult the "Weapons and Items" section of this guide for complete details on each one.

SURVIVING ON STROGGOS, PART 4: WORK WITH YOUR SQUADMATES

You're often accompanied by one or more GDF marines throughout most of *Quake 4*'s single-player campaign. Exercising sound combat tactics will help you survive the waves of enemies you must combat in your quest to destroy the Strogg. Don't let your pals take all the heat in every fight— back them up whenever you can to keep them alive and able to assist you down the road.

Your squadmates will do their best to hold off enemies and secure each area you explore. Watch where they position themselves during firefights and then look for suitable places to make your stand alongside them. For example: If enemies are coming at you from multiple angles and your teammates aren't defending your flanks, make sure you do so.

Finally, when you're joined by new group of marines, look at the weapons they're carrying and use this information to help you determine which of your weapons will be most helpful. Versatile weapons, such as the machine gun, are fine, but if no one is armed with a shotgun, enemies that draw near will have their way with you.

CHANGING WEAPONS

There are two ways to change your equipped weapon. You may scroll through each of your weapons by pressing ⓛ and ⓡ, or you may directly switch to a weapon using ✪. When you don't have many weapons, such as in the early stages of the single-player campaign, it's fastest to use ⓛ and ⓡ. But as you accumulate more weaponry, ✪ becomes the fastest way to bring up the firearm you wish to use.

Whenever you change weapons, icons depicting each weapon you currently carry are displayed near the screen's bottom. This lets you quickly take stock of which weapons you currently carry and is quite helpful, as there are numerous points in the game where you gain or lose weaponry.

THE FLASHLIGHT

Unlike *Doom 3*, you cannot simply hold your flashlight—the flashlight is attached to your blaster and machine gun. Pressing ⓨ while either of these weapons is equipped toggles the flashlight on 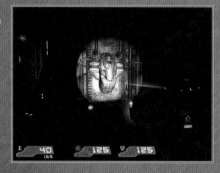 and off. If you're currently wielding a different weapon, pressing ⓨ instantly brings up the machine gun with its flashlight turned on (or the blaster, if you don't have the machine gun). If you don't have either of these weapons, you cannot turn on the flashlight.

SURVIVING ON STROGGOS, PART 5: LET THERE BE LIGHT

Doom 3 repeatedly tested your resolve with the terror-inducing quandary of whether you should hold your flashlight or ready a weapon when entering a new area. This is not a factor in *Quake 4*. Instead, both your blaster and machine gun feature a flashlight, which you should use just as often as you did in *Doom 3*.

Unless you need another weapon, always keep your machine gun equipped and leave its flashlight on. Scour the shadowy nooks and crannies of every room for enemies and for  pick-ups you would otherwise walk right past.

RELOADING

On each firearm you carry, there are two numbers to pay attention to: The first is the amount of ammunition that's currently loaded into the weapon (referred to as the weapon's "clip," even for weapons that don't use ammo magazines). The second is the total amount of extra ammunition you have for the weapon. When the clip runs dry, you must reload the weapon from your cache of extra ammunition before you can fire it again. You can manually reload your weapon at any time by pressing ⓧ.

If you've set "Auto Weapon Reload" to YES at the Game Settings screen, you automatically reload your weapon when the clip runs dry. This has its advantages and drawbacks. On the bright side, it prevents you from accidentally trying to fire an empty weapon. However, reloading takes at least a few seconds, which can mean the difference between life and death during combat.

Tip

You can switch weapons while you reload. Do this if you're suddenly engaged by an enemy while reloading.

Note

When you manually reload a weapon that still has some ammo left in its clip, you don't discard the remainder of the clip's ammo. For example, if your machine gun (which has a standard clip capacity of 40 rounds) is down to 8 rounds when you reload it, your machine-gun ammo cache is only depleted by 32 rounds—you don't lose the 8 rounds from the previous clip.

Surviving on Stroggos, Part 6: Ammo Management

Careless mistakes can cost you your life in *Quake 4*. One of the easiest oversights to make (and avoid) is forgetting to check through and reload your weaponry after a skirmish with the Strogg. Walking into a gunfight with a half-empty clip just isn't the way an GDF marine carries himself, so be sure to reload after every battle.

However, it is possible to reload a bit *too* frequently. After securing an area, stand still and wait a few seconds to make sure nothing else pops out to attack you. Remain stationary as you reload to avoid drawing the attention of foes that might be lying in wait ahead.

Finally, learn which weapons are better suited to different combat scenarios to help you conserve ammo. If one of your weapons is low on spare ammo, use a weapon for which you have a large cache of ammo. You acquire many versatile weapons throughout the game, so experiment and use a variety of them.

Viewing Objectives/Scores

Press **BACK** to call up your current mission objectives in single-player mode or to view the current score during multiplayer matches. Be careful, though—viewing either of these *does not* pause the action, and you can still be attacked by enemies.

Miscellaneous Controls

The following control doesn't fit into a convenient category but it is still important.

Pause Menu

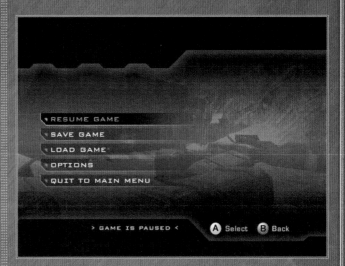

Press **START** to pause the game and switch to the Pause menu. Here you can save your game, load a saved game, quit the game, or view and adjust various options and settings. You can save your game at any time during the single-player campaign.

WEAPONS AND ITEMS

WEAPONS

BLASTER (SP ONLY)

WHAT IS IT?

The blaster is the only weapon in the single-player game that isn't found in multiplayer mode. This small yet reliable weapon uses no clips and never runs out of ammo. Press ⓡ to fire energy projectiles from the blaster, which inflict minor damage to enemies when they land. Pressing ⓡ rapidly allows you to squeeze off multiple blasts in short order.

The blaster also features a flashlight, which you may turn on and off by pressing ⓥ. While the blaster features no ⓛ function, pressing and holding ⓡ for a few seconds charges up a powerful shot, which is unleashed when you release ⓡ. This potent blast causes splash damage to nearby foes when it impacts—don't use it against close-range enemies.

WHERE DO YOU GET IT?

You begin the single-player game with the blaster. For a short time, it's the only weapon at your disposal.

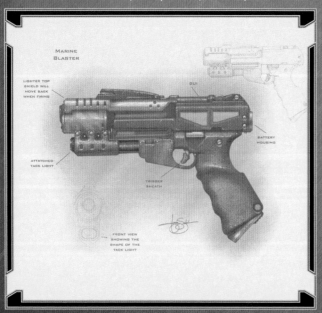

MARINE
BLASTER

LIGHTER TOP
SHIELD WILL
MOVE BACK
WHEN FIRING

GUI

ATTATCHED
TACK LIGHT

BATTERY
HOUSING

TRIGGER
SHEATH

FRONT VIEW
SHOWING THE
SHAPE OF THE
TACK LIGHT

WHEN TO USE IT

You must use the blaster for your first few battles in the single-player campaign, as you don't have access to any other weapon until you find the machine gun. After you obtain the machine gun, use the blaster only when you're trying to conserve ammo or when you want to fire at something in the environment to see if it's destructible.

DRAWBACKS

The blaster is effective in the early stages of the single-player game, but it won't do you much good against the hoards of powerful foes you face later. Its damage output isn't very impressive compared to other weaponry you acquire as you progress. And no matter how fast you are at pressing ⓡ, the blaster will never match the rapid autofire of the machine gun, hyper-blaster, or nailgun.

DARK MATTER GUN

Ammo Type: Dark Matter Cores
Max. Ammo Capacity: 25

WHAT IS IT?

The dark matter gun is the most powerful weapon in the *Quake 4* arsenal. When fired, a large ball of pure "dark matter" slowly flies toward your target(s), passes through them, and finally explodes when it contacts a wall or other solid object in the environment.

A quick science lesson: "Dark matter" is the term scientists use to define superdense objects in the universe that we cannot see even on the most powerful telescope (hence "dark"). We know objects of dark matter must exist, however, and we know they must be extremely dense due to their incredible gravimetric pull—the effect of which we *can* see on other celestial bodies in the universe, such as planets and stars.

If dark matter can push (or rather, pull) planets and stars about the universe, then you can imagine its effect when you unleash it against your enemies in *Quake 4*. The gravitational pull of a DMG projectile yanks all nearby enemies toward it and crushes them, inflicting severe (and in most cases, lethal) damage. When the projectile finally contacts a wall or other solid object, it explodes, causing massive splash damage to all foes within range.

WHERE DO YOU GET IT?

You obtain the dark matter gun during the Data Storage Terminal level. You must destroy the Strogg repair bots that examine it to claim the awesome DMG.

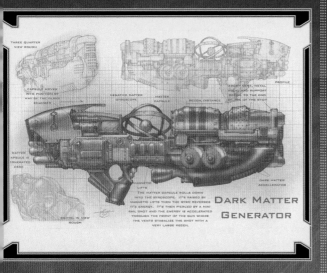

DARK MATTER GENERATOR

WHEN TO USE IT

The dark matter gun is extremely powerful and should be treated with respect. Use it against large groups of Strogg infantry to quickly defeat them all in a shot or two. Otherwise, save the dark matter gun for use in supertough combat situations such as boss fights. Ammo for this weapon is scarce and highly valuable—don't waste it on small groups of enemies you could defeat with more appropriate weaponry.

DRAWBACKS

The main drawback to the dark matter gun is its incredibly low rate of fire. After launching a projectile, you must wait about 5 seconds before the next shot becomes ready.

Unfortunately, you cannot fire the DMG and then switch to another weapon to circumvent its long recharge period—you must keep the DMG equipped in order to ready another of its devastating blasts. However, after firing, you can switch to another weapon and forgo the DMG for the time being if you like.

Finally, as we previously mentioned, ammo pick-ups for the DMG are few and far between. This, combined with its painfully low rate of fire, means you cannot afford to miss with this weapon. Make each shot count!

GAUNTLET (MP ONLY)

WHAT IS IT?

The gauntlet is a motorized buzzsaw affixed to a glove worn on your arm. It's the only weapon found in multiplayer mode that isn't featured in the single-player campaign. Press and hold Ⓡ to activate the gauntlet and slice into nearby enemies. The gauntlet uses no ammo and never runs out of cutting ability.

WHERE DO YOU GET IT?

You begin each multiplayer match with the gauntlet. You never lose this weapon, either—each time you die and respawn, the gauntlet is there with you.

WHEN TO USE IT

Use the gauntlet only when you have no other weapon at your disposal. It's a fallback that's always there for you so that you're never completely defenseless.

DRAWBACKS

The gauntlet inflicts significant damage over time, but you must maintain contact with an enemy for it to work—and that's nearly impossible due to the gauntlet's extremely short range of effect. You must practically pin an enemy against a wall in order to hit him with the gauntlet—a situation you'll rarely encounter in multiplayer matches.

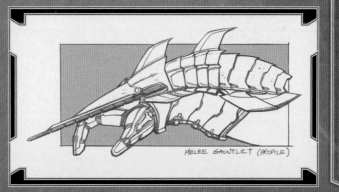

MELEE GAUNTLET (PROFILE)

WEAPONS

PICK-UPS

ENVIRONMENTAL OBJECTS

GRENADE LAUNCHER

Ammo Type: Grenades
Clip Size: 8
Max. Ammo Capacity: 50

WHAT IS IT?

The grenade launcher is a versatile weapon that rapidly fires fragmentation grenades a relatively short distance ahead of you. The grenades you fire bounce and roll along the ground and bounce off of walls and other objects until they stop or detonate. If a grenade strikes an enemy, it explodes instantly and inflicts heavy damage. Since grenades are explosive weapons, they also deal severe splash damage to anything nearby when they blow.

The grenade launcher has a surprisingly high rate of fire for a weapon that's capable of inflicting so much destruction. Its reload time is also quite short, and thanks to its generous clip capacity, there won't be many times when you'll need to reload it during combat. All in all, the grenade launcher is a true benefit to your arsenal and shouldn't be underestimated.

WHERE DO YOU GET IT?

Lieutenant Voss (Rhino Squad) hands you the grenade launcher when you first meet him near the beginning of the MCC Landing Site level. You become a serious threat to the Strogg once you acquire this powerful weapon.

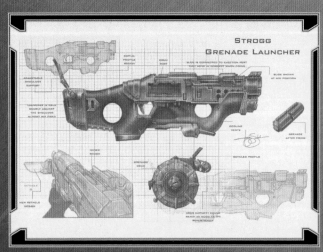

STROGG
GRENADE LAUNCHER

WHEN TO USE IT

With a bit of creativity, the grenade launcher can be used effectively in nearly every combat scenario. Launch grenades at tight groups of Strogg—you'll kill or critically wound all of them if you manage to strike one. Even if you miss, grenades tend to flush enemies out from behind cover, which exposes them to your comrades' gunfire. Since grenades bounce off of walls and objects, wily players will learn to fire them around corners and such.

You're given plenty of ammo for the grenade launcher as you progress through the single-player game, so use this weapon when the need arises. The grenade launcher serves you well against bosses and other tough enemies. It is particularly useful against tele droppers—score a few direct hits on one to quickly kill it, and the splash damage also defeats the enemies it spawns.

DRAWBACKS

The grenade launcher's main drawback is its relatively short range of effect—it won't do you much good against distant enemies unless you charge toward them, which exposes you to hostile fire. Don't use the grenade launcher against quick enemies that like to rush you, such as berserkers and grunts—they can close in on you fast, and the splash damage from your grenades could end up harming you. Finally, the grenades you fire take a while to detonate if they don't strike an enemy, which can give your foes just enough time to move out of harm's way.

HYPERBLASTER

Ammo Type: Batteries
Clip Size: 60
Max. Ammo Capacity: 400
Upgrade: Bounce Shot Mod

WHAT IS IT?

The hyperblaster is the Strogg's version of the GDF machine gun. Think of it as a mix between the blaster and the machine gun—it spits out energy projectiles at a high rate of fire as you hold down Ⓡ.

WHERE DO YOU GET IT?

You obtain the hyperblaster as you navigate a series of crawlspaces near the end of the Nexus Hub Tunnels level.

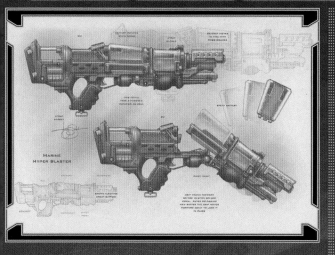

When to Use It

The hyperblaster is very versatile and can be used in many battle scenarios. Use it to quickly clear rooms full of Strogg marines and other weaker enemies. Employ the hyperblaster against tough-to-kill enemies that like to charge you, such as grunts, berserkers, and light tanks. The hyperblaster has a higher damage output and features a standard clip capacity and spare ammo cache that's larger than the machine gun's. Don't underestimate its ability to cut down tough foes in short order.

After you acquire the bounce shot mod during the Data Storage Terminal (Revisited) level, your hyper-blaster's projectiles will bounce off of walls and objects until they strike an enemy. This lets you decimate groups of enemies in tight, cluttered areas, so take full advantage.

Drawbacks

The hyperblaster's only real drawback is found in its projectiles' speed. Though the blasts travel quite fast, they're not as swift as the machine gun's bullets, which instantly strike targets the moment they're fired. This minor drawback makes the hyperblaster unsuitable for use against agile, long-range enemies, as the majority of your shots will often miss.

Lightning Gun

Ammo Type: Lightning Coils
Clip Size: 400
Upgrade: Chain Lightning Mod

What Is It?

The lightning gun is an advanced Strogg-developed weapon of remarkable power. When fired, a stream of pure lightning is shot directly ahead. This lightning stream inflicts heavy damage to enemies it strikes and also has a chance to immobilize them. Hold down (RT) to maintain a steady current of lightning that quickly shocks a foe into oblivion.

The lightning gun has no spare ammo cache—all of its ammo is stored in its clip, so you never need to reload. However, the lightning gun's ammo drains quickly and steadily as you hold down (RT)—you can burn through a whole clip in short order if you aren't careful.

After you acquire the chain lightning mod during the Tram Hub Station level, your lightning gun's stream will "jump" to strike enemies in close proximity to your main target. This allows you to damage multiple enemies at once and is highly effective against tight groups of foes.

Where Do You Get It?

You acquire the lightning gun during the Recomposition Center level. The Strogg are testing its usefulness against an unfortunate GDF marine—use the control panel near the weapon to stop the test and claim it.

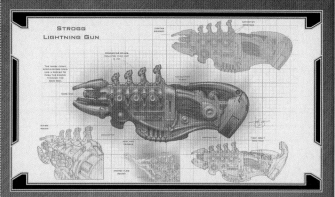

When to Use It

Due to its high damage output and fast rate of ammo consumption, it's best to save the lightning gun for use against the challenging enemies you often encounter in the game's later stages. Since the lightning gun is capable of stunning your foes with its powerful current, it's the perfect weapon to use against tough, agile foes that sport strong offensive capabilities, such as iron maidens and light tanks. The lightning gun will also rapidly disrupt the energy shields carried by gladi-ators, which can help you quickly defeat them.

Drawbacks

The lightning gun's most glaring drawback lies in its relatively short range of effect—its potent current cannot strike enemies at distances greater than medium-range. The lightning gun also chews through its ammo quite rapidly, and you aren't supplied with much until you reach the game's later levels.

WEAPONS

PICK-UPS

ENVIRONMENTAL OBJECTS

MACHINE GUN

Ammo Type: Clips
Clip Size: 40 (80 with upgrade)
Max. Ammo Capacity: 300
Upgrade: Extended Clip Mod

WHAT IS IT?

The machine gun is the most versatile weapon in the game. It has two fire functions: Hold down ⓇⓉ for primary autofire that can quickly shred enemies at close- and medium-range. Hold ⓁⓉ to use the machine gun's scope and pick off distant targets with improved accuracy. (You must press ⓇⓉ each time you wish to fire a shot when using the scope.)

The machine gun is the most powerful weapon to feature the flashlight—simply press Ⓨ to toggle the light on and off. Pressing Ⓨ when you have any other weapon equipped (other than the blaster) instantly brings up the machine gun with its flashlight turned on. (If you don't have the machine gun, the blaster is brought up instead.)

Your machine gun's clip capacity becomes doubled once you acquire the extended clip mod during the Operation: Advantage level—it can hold 80 rounds in a single clip from that point onward. (The upgrade does not increase the weapon's maximum ammo capacity, however.)

WHERE DO YOU GET IT?

You start the single-player campaign with your standard-issue blaster, but the machine gun is the first weapon you acquire as you progress through the game. Your first chance to obtain it comes shortly after the first fight in the first level—take it from the corpse of an GDF marine inside the Air Defense Bunker.

WHEN TO USE IT

Unless you need a more powerful weapon, always keep the machine gun equipped and make sure its flashlight is turned on. This lets you see in dark areas to ensure you don't miss hidden goodies or stumble unaware into an ambush. And while the machine gun's scope greatly increases your aim against distant foes, you can also use it to scan distant areas for pick-ups and enemies—another great reason to keep this weapon equipped at all times. Finally, the machine gun is so versatile that it'll serve you well in many common battle scenarios—there's often no better weapon to walk into an ambush with.

DRAWBACKS

The machine gun's two primary drawbacks lie in its initially small clip size and its moderate damage output. (The weapon's small clip size isn't a factor after you gain the extended clip mod, however.) Though the machine gun can quickly kill groups of Strogg marines and tacticals, its effectiveness becomes limited when you're faced with more resilient enemies such as gladiators. Rely heavily on the machine gun in the game's early stages, but employ more powerful weaponry as you reach tougher combat situations in later levels.

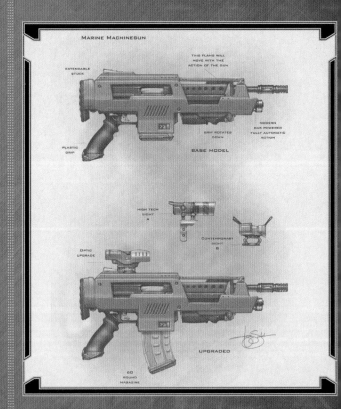

NAILGUN

Ammo Type: Nails
Clip Size: 50 (100 after first upgrade)
Max. Ammo Capacity: 300
First Upgrade: Firepower Mod
Second Upgrade: Nail Seeker Mod

WHAT IS IT?

The nailgun was developed by the Strogg and can be thought of as a heavier version of the hyperblaster. It fires large nail-like projectiles at high velocity and can quickly chop down heavily armored targets. Press and hold ⓇⓉ to fire a steady volley of nails at your foes. These nails are fired with such force that they shred apart when they strike walls or solid objects, causing splash damage to any nearby enemies.

The nailgun's first upgrade—the firepower mod—is acquired right at the start of the Aqueducts level. This enhancement doubles your nailgun's clip capacity by allowing it to hold two clips instead of one. It also greatly increases the nailgun's rate of fire.

You gain the nailgun's second upgrade—the nail seeker mod—near the start of the Recomposition Center level. Press and hold ⓁⓉ after acquiring this upgrade to zoom in with a scope. Enemies you view with the nailgun's scope become targeted by circular reticles, and the nails you fire at these enemies will track them.

WHERE DO YOU GET IT?

You're handed the nailgun at the start of the Perimeter Defense Station level. It's the first Strogg-developed weapon you acquire.

WHEN TO USE IT

The nailgun is the most powerful rapid-fire weapon available and becomes a true weapon of destruction once you gain its upgrades. Ammo is scarce at first, so use it only against powerful enemies in the early stages of the game—it works quite well against gladiators (aim to fire around their energy shields or at their feet to inflict splash damage). Use the nailgun more often as its ammunition becomes more plentiful, but try to keep a sizable spare ammo cache built up in case of emergencies.

DRAWBACKS

The nailgun's projectiles travel slower than your other rapid-fire weaponry (the machine gun and hyperblaster), and until you receive the firepower mod, the nailgun's rate of fire is slower than the machine gun and hyperblaster's. These two drawbacks make it easier for smaller, faster enemies to dodge your long-range fire, so use your nails against larger, slower enemies, such as gladiators and light tanks.

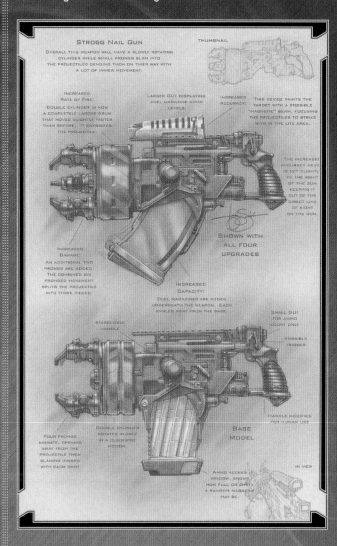

RAILGUN

Ammo Type: Slugs
Clip Size: 3
Max. Ammo Capacity: 51
Upgrade: Rail Penetration Mod

WHAT IS IT?

The railgun is a highly lethal weapon capable of killing lightly armored enemies in a single shot. Developed by the Strogg for use in ranged firefights, this fearsome weapon unleashes a slug at superhigh velocity each time you press ⓇⓉ. Each slug inflicts severe damage on anything it hits and will instantly kill a Strogg marine or tactical. Press ⓁⓉ to utilize the railgun's scope and increase its accuracy against distant targets.

The railgun becomes even more useful after you acquire the rail penetration mod during the Data Processing Security level. With this upgrade, each slug you fire is capable of tearing straight through your target to strike any foes that are lined up behind them. This can let you kill multiple Strogg marines and tacticals with just a few slugs.

WHERE DO YOU GET IT?

Your first chance to acquire the railgun is at the start of the Dispersal Facility level—one of the tacticals that ambushes you is armed with a railgun and drops it after you kill him. Collect the weapon and then use it to quickly defeat the remaining tacticals.

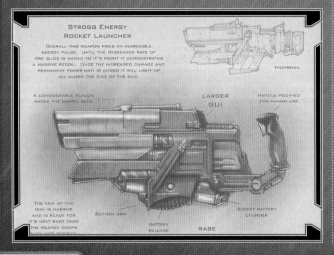

STROGG ENERGY
ROCKET LAUNCHER

WHEN TO USE IT

The railgun is best used against lightly armored foot soldiers such as Strogg marines and tacticals. It can kill either of these types of enemies in a single shot. Avoid using the railgun against tough-to-kill enemies, as it takes multiple hits to drop them (though each hit usually causes the enemy to stumble backward). Try to stay behind cover when using the railgun—this allows you to pop out, rail an enemy, and then immediately duck for cover again.

DRAWBACKS

Some people will hate the railgun due to its extremely low rate of fire—each powerful shot provokes massive recoil and you must wait a few seconds before you can fire another slug. This drawback can leave you open and vulnerable to return fire, making the railgun one of the least versatile weapons in the game. The worst thing you can do is ignore the railgun, however. Practice with it and you'll quickly improve your aim. Once you've grown accustomed to the railgun, you'll find it's the best weapon to use against light infantry threats.

ROCKET LAUNCHER

Ammo Type: Rockets
Clip Size: 40
Upgrade: Rocket Homing Mod

WHAT IS IT?

The rocket launcher is a handheld, portable tool of mass destruction. Press ⓇⓉ to fire a powerful rocket at your target or hold ⓇⓉ to launch rockets at a steady rate. Rockets explode when they contact an enemy (or any object in the environment) and inflict heavy damage. Any foes standing near a rocket when it explodes suffer significant splash damage as well.

The rocket launcher has a maximum clip capacity of 40 rockets and uses no spare ammo cache. All of its rockets are stored in its magazine, and a new rocket is quickly and automatically loaded each time you fire.

After you acquire the rocket homing mod during the Waste Processing Facility level, hold ⓁⓉ and use ® to steer rockets toward enemies around corners and such. Your rocket launcher also gains the capacity to fire three rockets in quick succession with this upgrade— simply hold ⓇⓉ to fire them off.

WHERE DO YOU GET IT?

You obtain the rocket launcher during the Strogg Medical Facilities level—lift it off the corpse of a fallen GDF marine.

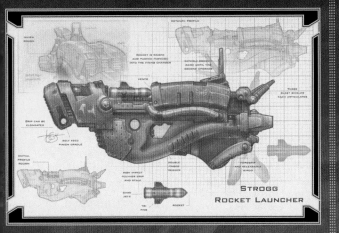

STROGG
ROCKET LAUNCHER

WHEN TO USE IT

The rocket launcher is one of the most powerful weapons in the game and is also quite versatile—you can easily kill tough enemies and wipe out groups of weaker foes with just a few shots. Ammo is fairly scarce, however, so try not to use the rocket launcher too often until you've amassed a large supply. Don't use the rocket launcher against close-range enemies or you'll suffer splash damage.

Implement the rocket launcher's ability to inflict heavy splash damage into your combat strategies. You don't need spot-on accuracy to devastate enemies with this weapon—aim for the ground near their feet to wreck them with splash damage.

DRAWBACKS

The rocket launcher's biggest drawback lies in its rockets' slow movement speed. It's practically useless against distant enemies, especially agile ones—they'll easily move out of harm's way before the rocket impacts. Due to this drawback, you must often "lead" your targets when attacking them with the rocket launcher, a skill that takes a bit of getting used to.

SHOTGUN

Ammo Type: Shells
Clip Size: 8 (10 after upgrade)
Max. Ammo Capacity: 50
Upgrade: Clip Extension Mod

WHAT IS IT?

The shotgun is a powerful weapon suited to close-range combat. Press ⓇⓉ to unleash a devastating blast of shot and cripple nearby targets. Hold down ⓇⓉ to fire one shell after the next in quick succession.

Your shotgun utilizes a cliplike magazine after you acquire the clip extension mod during the Operation: Last Hope level. This dramatically reduces the weapon's reload time and also adds two shells to its maximum clip capacity.

WHERE DO YOU GET IT?

A member of Viper Squad hands you the shotgun when you meet up with them early in the Hangar Perimeter level.

WHEN TO USE IT

Bring out your shotgun whenever enemies swarm in. It can drop heavy infantry such as a berserker or a grunt in two to three blasts and will kill a Strogg marine or a tactical in one or two. If you're fast on your feet and seasoned at circle-strafing, you can use your shotgun at close range to defeat just about any enemy.

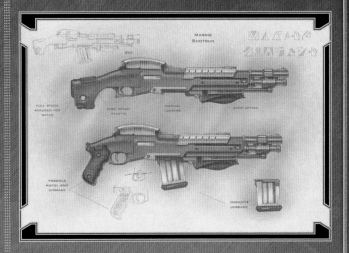

MARNIE
SHOTGUN

DRAWBACKS

The shotgun's effectiveness drops sharply when it's used against long-range targets—numerous shots are required to defeat distant foes; don't use the weapon in this manner. Reloading the shotgun is a time-consuming process until you gain its clip extension mod, as you must load each shell individually. Make sure to reload after each battle.

WEAPONS

PICK-UPS

ENVIRONMENTAL OBJECTS

PICK-UPS

AMMUNITION

Ammo pick-ups are the most plentiful, as there's a different type for every ammunition-consuming weapon in the game. Collect ammo pick-ups to increase your weapons' spare ammo caches. Search every nook and cranny for ammunition—hidden supplies are all over the place. Refer to the weapon sections to learn which pick-ups supply ammo to each weapon.

ARMOR

Armor protects you from harm. When you're attacked, your armor absorbs some of the damage and therefore reduces the amount of health you lose by a significant degree. Collect armor shards and armor vests to restore your armor and survive longer in the heat of battle. You can have a maximum of 100 armor until you reach the Strogg Medical Facilities level—you may then protect yourself with a maximum of 125 armor.

Here's how much armor you gain when you collect each type of armor pick-up:

Armor Shards: Each armor shard you grab increases your total armor value by 5 points.
Small Armor Vest: Collect one of these to add 50 points to your total armor value.
Large Armor Vest: Each of these adds 100 points to your total armor value.

TIP

Large armor vests are easy to distinguish from small ones—if there's a helmet near the vest, it's a large armor vest.

HEALTH PACKS

You inevitably lose health as you take damage from enemy attacks, long falls, and environmental hazards. You die when you run completely out of health.

Collect health packs to restore your health and stay in the fight. You can have a maximum of 100 health until you reach the Strogg Medical Facilities level; you then have a maximum of 125 health from that point onward. Small health packs restore your health by 25 points, and large health packs heal you by 50 points.

ENVIRONMENTAL OBJECTS

BARRELS/CRATES

Crates, barrels, and the like are abundant objects in *Quake 4*. This is fortunate because you can crouch behind a crate or barrel to take cover from hostile fire. Crates are always stationary and cannot be moved, while barrels can be pushed about by shooting them or bumping into them. Duck behind these objects to get out of harm's way when no better cover is available.

CONTROL PANELS

Control panels are common objects found in many levels. Use them to open doors, activate lifts, and so on.

To use a control panel, simply approach it, target it with your reticle, and press ⓑ. Some control panels have multiple buttons—use ✪ to select the button you wish to activate and then press ⓑ to activate it.

DOORS

Doors separate rooms and corridors. Every door opens automatically as you approach them (if they're unlocked). If a door is locked, you must usually activate a nearby control panel or complete a mission objective to unlock it. Some doors never become unlocked and are therefore never used. Others lock behind you and can never be reopened.

CAUTION

Enter doors cautiously—you never know what's waiting for you on the other side.

EXPLODING BARRELS

Exploding barrels are either red or green in color and are easy to distinguish from regular barrels once you learn to recognize them. Fire at an explosive barrel to set it ablaze. The barrel detonates a few seconds later and damages anything nearby. You can speed up their detonation with additional fire if you like.

Tip

Learn to spot explosive barrels and use them to your advantage. Be careful not to use them as cover—hostile fire can detonate them.

FIRE/ACID

Fire and acid are similar in that both substances will harm you if you touch them. Prolonged contact with fire or acid inflicts additional damage that continues to harm you for a short time even after you move away. Keep away from tongues of flame and pools of acid.

LADDERS

Like lifts and stairs, ladders let you move between floors. Approach a ladder and continue to press Ⓛ to climb onto it and up. You must be facing the "climbable" side of the ladder to grab on. Once you're on a ladder, press Ⓛ or Ⓐ to climb up and press Ⓛ or Ⓛ3 to climb down. You can also move side to side by pressing Ⓛ and Ⓛ.

The safest way to climb down a ladder is to approach it, turn around, look down at the floor, and then backpedal onto the ladder. Continue to press Ⓛ or use Ⓛ3 to climb down.

Tip

You may fire your weapon, switch weapons, and reload while climbing a ladder.

STROGG HEALTH STATIONS

When you reach the Strogg Medical Facilities level, you're able to heal at Strogg Health Stations. Simply approach a Strogg Health Station and activate its control panel to start recovering health. A Strogg Health Station's resources are depleted as you use them—the green bar on their control panels indicates how much juice they have left.

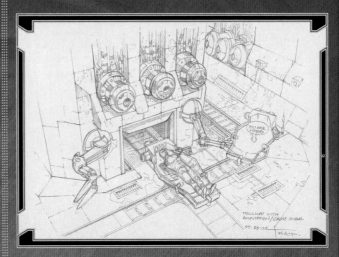

TELEPORTERS

Teleporters are amazing devices developed by the Strogg that can instantly transport matter from one location to another. You encounter these objects in the game's later levels— Strogg infantry use them to spawn into rooms and ambush you.

You can quickly destroy a teleporter with a well-placed rocket or two. When no enemies are about, use charged shots from your blaster (hold down Ⓡ and then release) to destroy them instead of expending rockets. Learn to recognize teleporters and make their destruction your top priority; otherwise you battle many more enemies than you must.

Tip

Enemies that spawn through teleporters make a very distinct sound when they appear. Find the source and destroy it.

WEAPONS / PICK-UPS / ENVIRONMENTAL OBJECTS

VEHICLES

GDF Vehicles

Convoy Trucks

- Used to transport ground troops and cargo
- Multiple marines can ride on back but are exposed to attacks
- Feature roof-mounted heavy machine guns with infinite ammo
- Recover lost armor over time

GDF convoy trucks are used to transport ground troops and heavy cargo over long distances. You ride on a convoy truck throughout most of the Canyon level and must protect it from all hostile threats you encounter. You never get a chance to drive a convoy truck, however.

You are exposed to incoming fire and attacks while you ride in the back of the convoy truck—the truck doesn't absorb damage for you like most other vehicles unless you're manning the roof-mounted machine gun. Furthermore, you must use your own weaponry to eliminate nearby threats and defend yourself from enemies.

Each convoy truck has a heavy machine gun mounted to its roof, and you get to man one during the last half of the Canyon level. You can't be directly attacked while manning a convoy truck's heavy machine gun—instead, the convoy truck absorbs damage. You must use the truck's heavy machine gun to quickly destroy hostile targets and prevent the truck from being destroyed by their fire. The truck's armor indicator is shown at your screen's lower-left corner. If the indicator loses all of its coloring, the truck is destroyed and you must try again.

NOTE

Convoy trucks recover their lost armor if they aren't damaged for a time.

Hover Tanks

- Heavily armored mobile powerhouses
- GDF's most formidable ground vehicles
- Feature devastating cannons and heavy machine guns, both with infinite ammo
- Protected by heavy shields that slowly recharge over time
- Slowly recover lost armor over time
- Has headlights (activate with Ⓨ)

GDF hover tanks utilize cutting-edge technology and can quickly decimate both ground and air forces when used with skill. Each hover tank is operated by one man who both drives the tank and fires its weaponry. You get to pilot a hover tank during the Aqueducts and Aqueducts Annex levels.

WALKERS

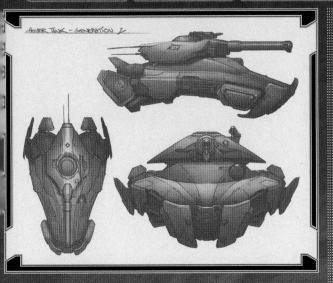

Hover Tank - Generation 2

Hover tanks are surprisingly fast and maneuverable—you can move and strafe about with ease using the same controls as you do on foot. Take advantage of the hover tank's agility and move about to dodge hostile fire.

The hover tank features two weapons: a cannon that fires powerful explosive shells and a heavy machine gun. Use the cannon to combat enemies; the shells it fires travel quickly and create massive splash damage upon impact. Employ the tank's heavy machine gun whenever you must shoot incoming missiles out of the sky. Press Ⓛ and Ⓡ to switch between these two modes of attack.

TIP

Press Ⓛ to use the cannon's scope when targeting distant enemies.

Hover tanks have both armor and shields—indicators along your screen's bottom show the status of both. Attacks damage your hover tank's armor only after its shields have been completely destroyed. Your hover tank is destroyed when its armor indicator loses all of its coloring.

TIP

Your hover tank's shields and armor recharge over time as long as you aren't attacked. Pause to let them recharge after each fight.

- Lightly armored mobile ground units
- Feature shoulder-mounted heavy machine guns and missile launchers, both with infinite ammo
- Protected by light shields that quickly recharge over time
- Slowly recover lost armor over time
- Has headlights (activate with Ⓨ)

GDF walkers are versatile land units used to support friendly ground troops and pummel enemy foot soldiers. They're quite versatile and can effectively combat light airborne threats, such as Strogg hornets. You get to pilot a walker during the Construction Zone level.

TIP

Move diagonally Ⓛ or Ⓛ to make your walker strafe more quickly.

Walkers feature two weapon systems: a heavy machine gun and a missile launcher. Use your walker's heavy machine gun to destroy enemy infantry and other lightly armored threats. Fire missiles at more powerful enemies, such as heavy tanks. Press Ⓛ and Ⓡ to toggle between these two weapon systems.

A walker's missile launcher holds a maximum of six missiles at a time. Another six missiles are automatically reloaded after you fire them all—this process takes a few seconds. You can switch to the walker's heavy machine gun to attack as the missiles reload.

Like hover tanks, GDF walkers have both armor and shields, and the indicators along your screen's bottom show the status of both. Attacks damage your walker's armor only after its shields have been completely destroyed. Your walker is destroyed when its armor indicator loses all of its coloring.

CAUTION

Your walker's shields and armor aren't nearly as sturdy as the hover tank's—pause and let them recharge after each fight.

STROGG VEHICLES

DROP TURRETS

- Deployed by Strogg dropships
- Stick into ground and then fire heavy machine guns
- Protected by a light shield system
- Lightly armored

Drop turrets are deployed by Strogg dropships. They fall from the sky, imbed themselves in the ground, and then open fire with heavy machine guns. Though drop turrets are stationary, their heavy machine guns can rotate 360 degrees to track moving targets.

TIP

Drop turrets make a distinct sound as they fall. Use this noise to detect their presence.

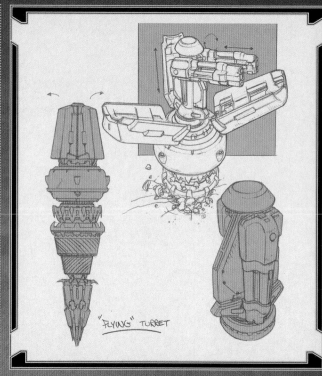

"FLYING" TURRET

Drop turrets are usually encountered during vehicular missions. They have weak shields and armor and are quite easy to destroy with any form of weaponry. Their heavy machine guns can inflict significant damage, however, so target them quickly and don't give them a chance to fire at you.

TIP

Drop turrets' shield systems don't activate until they land. Fire at drop turrets as they fall from the sky to quickly destroy them.

DROPSHIPS

- Armored enemy air transports
- Deploy enemy infantry and drop turrets
- Can attack directly by dropping bombs and firing energy projectiles

Strogg dropships have a variety of functions. They're most commonly used to transport and deploy infantry units and drop turrets. However, dropships can also attack ground forces directly by deploying bombs and firing energy projectiles. You encounter these airborne vehicles at many points in the single-player game.

Tip

Take cover when a troop-deploying dropship lands; then fire at the enemies it drops off the moment they touch the ground.

For the most part, there's little you can do about Strogg dropships—they sail overhead and deploy enemies without giving you much chance to stop them. However, during the Tram Rail level, you must fire your tram car's heavy machine gun at dropships and destroy them before they move close enough to hit your tram car with their potent bombs. It takes only a few seconds of sustained fire to destroy one.

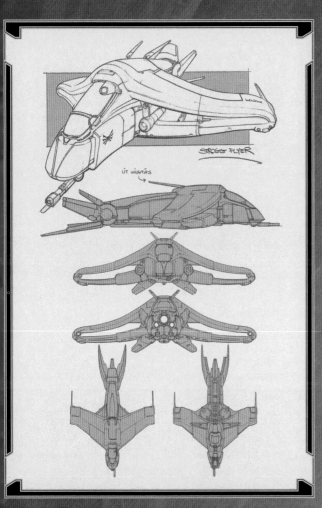

Gun Turrets

- Stationary gun emplacements
- Usually affixed to ceilings (indoors) and structures (outdoors)
- Fire energy projectiles or heavy machine-gun bullets
- Little armor; easily destroyed

Gun turrets pop out of ceilings inside complexes and are also commonly affixed to outdoor structures. Most fire heavy machine guns, but some fire energy projectiles. Gun turrets have weak armor and are easy to destroy with any weapon. Their fire can cause severe damage over time, however, so eliminate them quickly.

Tip

To quickly destroy outdoor gun turrets, fire at their top portion.

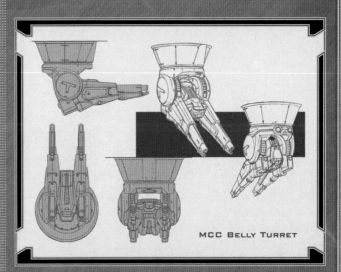

MCC Belly Turret

CHAPTER 1 WELCOME TO QUAKE 4

CHAPTER 2 BASIC TRAINING

CHAPTER 3 WEAPONS AND ITEMS

CHAPTER 4 VEHICLES

CHAPTER 5 CHARACTERS

CHAPTER 6 ENEMIES

CHAPTER 7 WALKTHROUGH

CHAPTER 8 MULTIPLAYER

CHAPTER 9 GAMERSCORE ACHIEVEMENTS

HARVESTERS

- Heavily armored mobile power-houses
- Strogg's most formidable ground vehicles
- Fire devastating mega tracking missiles at distant targets
- Employ powerful twin nailguns against closer foes
- Can impale nearby targets with sharp legs

Harvesters are the Strogg's most fearsome land vehicles. They have heavy armor and walk on four giant legs, which they can use to impale enemy ground forces. Though you only combat harvesters during vehicle-based levels, such as Aqueducts and Construction Zone, they also make appearances in other levels, where they function more like environmental hazards.

Keep your distance at all times when battling a harvester. This prevents them from impaling you with their legs and grants you enough time to dodge their sluggish yet devastating mega tracking missiles. Or, shoot them down with your vehicle's heavy machine gun. Strafe to dodge a harvester's slow-moving nailgun fire.

Blast away at the lower portions of a harvester's legs—a harvester collapses after you blow off two of its legs. You may also target a harvester's twin underbelly nailguns or its pair of drum-shaped, rear-mounted missile launchers to disable their weapon systems. Doing so does not destroy the harvester itself, however.

HORNETS

- Lightly armored airborne attackers
- Commonly encountered during vehicle-based levels
- Fire volleys of low-impact tracking missiles
- Can transport and deploy roller creatures

Hornets are the Strogg's primary fast-attack aircraft. They're extremely agile and are primarily used to lay waste to enemy ground forces. Hornets are protected by light armor and are fairly easy to destroy once you manage to hit them. They fire volleys of low-damage tracking missiles and almost always attack in groups of two or more.

When fighting a hornet with the agile hover tank, use the tank's powerful cannon to destroy each hornet—one direct blast usually does the trick. Hornets often strafe to dodge your first cannon shot, but they usually can't dodge the second—make sure your second shot finds its mark.

When piloting the slow-moving walker, use the walker's heavy machine gun to quickly knock hornets out of the sky. Hornets are fast enough to dodge the walker's missiles but can't escape the rapid fire of its gun.

REPAIR BOTS

- Nonaggressive airborne devices
- Perform a variety of tasks

Repair bots are nonhostile Strogg devices that move through the air and carry out a variety of construction, repair, and maintenance operations. You put these harmless mechanisms to use at certain points in the single-player game in order to progress. If necessary, you can easily destroy a repair bot with small arms.

ROLLER CREATURES

- Well-armored mobile gun turrets
- Commonly encountered during vehicle-based levels
- Can be deployed by Strogg hornets
- Extremely agile
- Must remain motionless to attack

Roller creatures are sphere-shaped mobile gun turrets. They're often deployed by Strogg hornets and can move about very quickly once they hit the ground. In order to attack, a roller creature must stop moving. It then sprouts legs and a heavy machine gun pops out from the roller creature's top. Roller creatures are most vulnerable when they've stopped moving to attack.

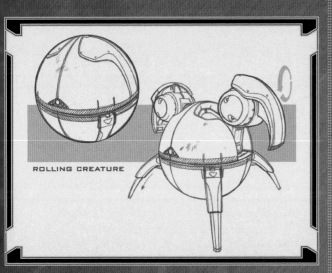

ROLLING CREATURE

When a roller creature stops moving, use the hover tank's cannon or the walker's heavy machine gun to destroy it in short order. It usually takes one blast from the hover tank's cannon or a few seconds of the walker's heavy machine-gun fire to destroy a roller creature.

TRAM CARS

- Lightly armored personnel transports
- Runs on overhead tram rails
- Features heavy machine guns with infinite ammo

Strogg tram cars are mass-transit vehicles affixed to overhead rails. They run on these rails like a train, moving from one station to the next. You must ride tram cars at various points in the single-player game in order to reach new areas.

During the Tram Rail level, you must use your tram car's heavy machine gun to fend off attackers. Fire at each threat in turn as they approach from behind. Your primary targets are Strogg dropships. The bombs they drop when they enter close proximity are lethal, so don't give them the chance. Other tram cars that carry tacticals are your secondary targets. To quickly destroy them, fire at the top portions of their tram cars, which connect their cars to the overhead rail. Don't bother firing at the tacticals themselves.

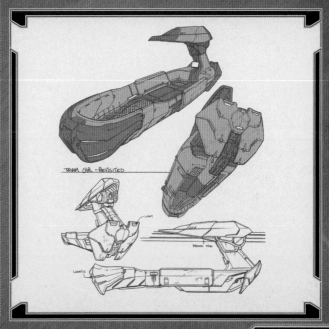

TRAM CAR - REVISITED

CHARACTERS

RHINO SQUAD

Rhino Squad is one of most highly trained Marine Units in the Earth Armed Forces. They are sent into the worst situations that are of the highest priority—situations where failure is not an option. Each member is an expert in his respective field and is trained to the peak of his abilities.

Several months ago the squad lost its former commander, Lieutenant Daily. But he was replaced by the extremely capable Lieutenant Voss. Now Rhino Squad is part of the invasion force that's about to be dropped onto the bleak and forbidding planet Stroggos, home of mankind's greatest enemy, the Strogg. The result of this battle could very well determine whether mankind will flourish or become just another extinct race in the history of the cosmos.

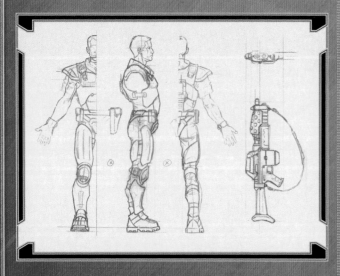

CORPORAL MATTHEW KANE

Age: 23
Place of Birth: Lunar Colony, New Hope
Height: 5' 11"
Weight: 180 lb.
Squad Role: Scout

Above all else, Corporal Matthew Kane is a survivor. He was involved with the disaster on Space Station Armstrong and was the only one to emerge alive. But exactly what happened there may never be known—he is under the strictest orders to remain silent.

After several months of recuperation, Kane was assigned to Rhino Squad. This was due to Lt. Voss who saw in Kane the potential to be a truly valuable asset to the team. But the squad only knows him from his mysterious reputation. They don't trust him and believe he might be too much of a loose cannon. But with their mission on Stroggos, they will quickly find out just what Matthew Kane is capable of.

CORPORAL ALEJANDRO "ALEX" CORTEZ

Age: 22
Place of Birth: Mexico City, Mexico
Height: 5' 7"
Weight: 145 lb.
Squad Role: Sniper

CORPORAL WILLIAM "BILLY" RHODES

Age: 25
Place of Birth: Fort Worth, Texas
Height: 6' 1"
Weight: 180 lb.
Squad Role: Demolitions

Growing up on his family's ranch, Cortez took to guns while very young. His father still brags about how, at the age of eight, young Alejandro could kill a jackrabbit from 150 yards out. After his sister was killed during the first Strogg attack on Earth, Cortez joined the Marine Corps determined to have his revenge.

Extremely cool in a firefight, he has a way of getting to vantage points no one else could find. Silent as darkness and swift as the hand of death, Cortez was assigned to Rhino Squad after he single-handedly defended a communications outpost armed only with a depleted pistol—14 charges against 14 Strogg. Oddly enough, at the end of the fight he still had one charge left.

William Rhodes knew from a very early age he wanted to be a Marine. He entered the corps as soon as he was old enough, and he quickly showed a gift for demolitions. Where anyone else would require a detailed blueprint of a structure to know where best to place a bomb, Rhodes knows instinctively where the weak points are. Be it a heavily fortified dam or a reinforced bunker, Rhodes can reduce it to rubble with a minimal amount of explosives.

Hailing from Fort Worth, Texas, Rhodes plays as hard as he works. He's been demoted twice due to altercations with MPs while out on R&R.

QUAKE 4

WELCOME TO QUAKE 4

CHAPTER 2 BASIC TRAINING

WEAPONS AND ITEMS

CHAPTER 4 VEHICLES

CHAPTER 5 CHARACTERS

CHAPTER 6 ENEMIES

CHAPTER 7 WALKTHROUGH

CHAPTER 8 MULTIPLAYER

GAMERSCORE ACHIEVEMENTS

LANCE CORPORAL NIKOLAI "SLEDGE" SLIDJONOVITCH

Age: 25
Place of Birth: St. Petersburg, Russia
Height: 6' 3"
Weight: 240 lb.
Squad Role: Heavy Weapons

The son of a former Olympic weightlifter for Russia, Nikolai was raised on a farm where he spent most of his childhood doing intense physical labor. He eventually grew to dwarf even his father's huge physique. While his family had expected him to go to college to study chemical engineering, Nikolai surprised everyone by choosing to join the Marine Corps. After his first two days in boot camp, he was given the nickname "Sledge"— a moniker that has stuck with him ever since.

Soft-spoken and a man of few words, Sledge is a welcome addition to Rhino Squad. He can easily handle equipment that would take two normal men to lift. His strength has become the stuff of legend—Sledge is the only human who fought a Strogg in hand-to-hand combat and won. Admittedly, he required three weeks in a hospital afterward.

LIEUTENANT SCOTT VOSS

Age: 30
Place of Birth: Mars Colony, Kingsland
Height: 5' 10"
Weight: 170 lb.
Squad Role: Leader

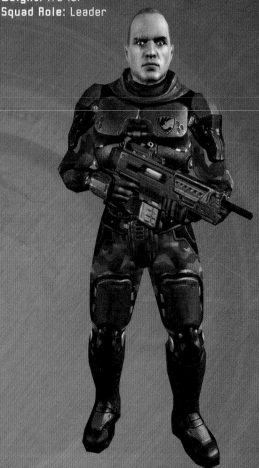

After the death of their former commander, Lieutenant Daily, Rhino Squad wasn't sure they'd ever find someone capable of leading them. Then they met Lt. Scott Voss. He epitomizes the old saying, "It's not so much the size of the dog in the fight as it is the size of the fight in the dog." He's not physically large or overtly demanding, but there is something about his demeanor that demands respect from even the most reckless Marine.

Rhino Squad knows very little about Voss because he never speaks of his past. But were he to talk, they would hear tales of the horrors he endured after being captured during the Mars riots—he was tortured for six months before being freed. He still suffers nightmares and is highly claustrophobic after having been placed in a coffin and buried for days at a time.

Voss knows Rhino Squad questions his reasoning for bringing this newcomer, Matthew Kane, into their group. But Voss has a sneaking suspicion this new kid just might prove to be the most valuable asset Rhino Squad has to offer in their battle against the Strogg.

MASTER SERGEANT MARIAN BIDWELL

Age: 28
Place of Birth: La Grange Point, Space Station McKinley
Height: 6' 3"
Weight: 190 lb.
Squad Role: Second in Command

PRIVATE JEREMIAH ANDERSON

Age: 19
Place of Birth: Chicago, Illinois
Height: 6'
Weight: 160 lb.
Squad Role: Medic

Master Sergeant Marian Bidwell was born in space and plans on dying in space. Both his parents were Marines for life, and he intends on doing the same. He supplied falsified documents in order to join the corps while still 2 years under the legal age limit. He's seen more war and death than most men twice his age, but Bidwell still loves the Marine Corps and all its traditions.

The master sergeant can be extremely brutal during training—he knows the only way a Marine is going to survive under enemy fire is to train under extreme duress. More than one Marine has been severely injured during exercises, but Bidwell will never lessen the training—Rhino Squad is too important to allow anyone but the absolute best out onto the field.

Anderson is the youngest member of Rhino Squad even though he's been with them for over a year. Coming from an affluent family in Chicago, Jeremiah could have easily used his grandfather, General Anderson, to avert serving on the front lines. But instead he requested to be a part of Rhino Squad, hoping to always be in the thick of the action. When Master Sergeant Bidwell heard a general got Anderson assigned to the squad, he made it just that much harder on Jeremiah. Much to Bidwell's surprise, Anderson thrived under the stressful conditions.

Although Jeremiah considers himself a healer, he isn't afraid of using a gun. And with his knowledge of Strogg physiology, he is an expert at stopping the enemy with a minimum of shots.

RHINO SQUAD

CHAPTER 1
WELCOME TO
QUAKE 4

CHAPTER 2
BASIC TRAINING

CHAPTER 3
WEAPONS AND
ITEMS

CHAPTER 4
VEHICLES

CHAPTER 5
CHARACTERS

CHAPTER 6
ENEMIES

CHAPTER 7
WALKTHROUGH

CHAPTER 8
MULTIPLAYER

CHAPTER 9
GAMESCORE
ACHIEVEMENTS

PRIVATE JOHANN STRAUSS

Age: 21
Place of Birth: Düsseldorf, Germany
Height: 5' 8"
Weight: 130 lb.
Squad Role: Technician

Johann Strauss possesses one of the most gifted minds of our age. By the time he was 4 years old, Strauss could perform complex trigonometry equations in his head. At the age of 8 he was fluent in 6 languages and could recite all of Shakespeare's works from memory. He was part of the research team who discovered how the Strogg used black holes to travel across the vast distances of space. He currently holds PhDs in Advanced Computer Science and Biotechnology and is one of eight people fluent in the Strogg language.

In keeping with his genius status, Strauss also has a tremendous ego and can be extremely brash. He would have remained in research were it not for a run-in with General Nathaniel Hastings. Strauss so insulted the general, he found himself on the front lines a week after the argument. While in the field, Strauss found he excelled in working with Strogg technology. Because of his talents, he was assigned to Rhino Squad. Now they receive missions deep in enemy territory that require interaction with Strogg security and computer systems.

SERGEANT DELL MORRIS

Age: 24
Place of Birth: Toronto, Canada
Height: 6' 1"
Weight: 175 lb.
Squad Role: Communications

Sergeant Dell Morris has been with Rhino Squad for over three years, which makes him second in seniority only to Sergeant Bidwell. He is highly skilled at hand-to-hand combat, having achieved black belts in Tae Kwon Do, Jeet Kune Do, and Aikido.

Gifted with a quick wit and boundless energy, Morris likes nothing better than to give a running commentary as he mows down Strogg. While his chatter can be a bit trying on his squadmates, Morris is a complete professional in a firefight. The team has come to look to him for guidance when the lieutenant or master sergeant aren't around.

ENEMIES

NOTE

Unless otherwise noted, all enemies are vulnerable to headshots, which cause them severe damage.

STROGG LIGHT INFANTRY

FAILED AND SLIMY TRANSFERS

- Failed attempts at Stroggification
- Low health, lumbering movements
- Dangerous in large groups
- Only encountered at Waste Processing Facility

Failed transfers, slimy transfers, and failed transfer torsos are only encountered at the Waste Processing Facility. These zombielike humanoid enemies are the aborted remains of botched attempts at "Stroggification"—people who didn't take to the horrific process of becoming a member of the Strogg race. Though they each have unique attacks, all of these enemies are slow-moving and take little effort to kill—small arms work just fine, so don't use anything bigger. Dangerous only in large groups, these grotesque foes often emerge from drain pipes and barrels, pop out of pools of murk, and so on in an attempt to catch you off guard.

Failed Transfers: Carry and attack with shotguns; drop their shotguns after being killed.
Failed Transfer Torsos: The upper bodies of Failed Transfers; crawl along the ground and try to bite your ankles.
Slimy Transfers: Carry no weapons; attack by vomiting acid; acid inflicts damage over time and remains on ground for 5–10 seconds.

SCIENTISTS

- Airborne enemies
- Medium-low health
- Low agility, poor at dodging
- Dangerous at close range
- Fires poisonous grenades at distant targets
- Very dangerous in large groups
- First encountered at Strogg Medical Facility

Scientists are charged with the duty of performing "Stroggification" on captured enemy soldiers. To help them in their work, scientists have the ability to hover about and also sport multiple appendages onto which a variety of blades and cutting tools have been grafted. This makes combating them at close range extremely dangerous. Scientists are threats at long range as well—they fire acid-filled grenadelike projectiles that inflict significant damage when direct hits are scored. These grenades explode on impact, splashing you with toxic chemicals that blur your vision and cause you to lose health over time. Furthermore, an acid pool remains on the ground at the impact site for a short time afterward and harms you if you touch it.

Though they're apt attackers, scientists aren't skilled at dodging and can't absorb much damage. Kill them fast from range with your machine gun or move in close and drop them with a few shotgun blasts. Either way, strafe constantly to avoid their acidic projectiles.

SENTRIES

- Airborne enemies
- Medium-low health
- No melee attacks
- Twin shoulder-mounted chainguns for ranged attacks
- Dangerous in large groups
- First encountered at Nexus Hub Tunnels

Sentries are slow-moving enemies that hover through the air and fire their twin chainguns at any intruder they detect. These enemies are usually found in pairs or in larger groups and often ambush you by popping up from the sides of elevated walkways and the like. Their chainguns aren't very accurate but can inflict considerable damage if they score several hits.

   Like most other light infantry, sentries have a small amount of health and can be destroyed quite easily with a bit of machine-gun fire. They have no melee attacks, a drawback that opens them up for close-range shotgun blasts (one or two do the job). Strafe to dodge their fire as you return your own.

TIP

Sentries are not vulnerable to headshots. The glass bubble below their torso is their weak spot.

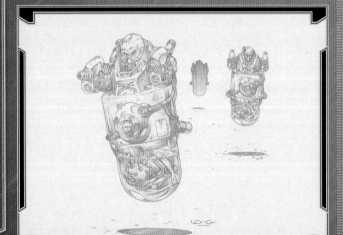

STROGG MARINES

- Low health, poor accuracy
- Agile but unskilled
- Can wield blasters, machine guns, or shotguns
- Dangerous in large groups
- First encountered at Air Defense Bunker

Strogg marines are the backbone of the Strogg army. Quick on their feet but lacking in sound combat tactics, Strogg marines often jump out from behind cover, shout a battle cry, and then open fire with a blaster, machine gun, or shotgun. Their aim is poor, and you can easily dodge their attacks with a bit of strafing.

   You must kill hundreds of these enemies throughout the single-player game, so get used to fighting them early on. Strogg marines are quick but have little health—cut them down with small arms and use more powerful weaponry only when they attack in large numbers. A close-range shotgun blast kills one instantly; a few headshots with the machine gun achieves the same affect.

CHAPTER 1 WELCOME TO QUAKE 4

CHAPTER 2 BASIC TRAINING

CHAPTER 3 WEAPONS AND ITEMS

CHAPTER 4 VEHICLES

CHAPTER 5 CHARACTERS

CHAPTER 6 ENEMIES

CHAPTER 7 WALKTHROUGH

CHAPTER 8 MULTIPLAYER

CHAPTER 9 GAMERSCORE ACHIEVEMENTS

TACTICALS

STROGG HEAVY INFANTRY

BERSERKERS

- Medium-low health, good accuracy
- Less agile than Strogg marines
- Sound combat tactics
- Very dangerous in large groups
- First encountered at Dispersal Facility

Tacticals are unfortunate GDF marines who the Strogg have captured alive and subsequently assimilated into their "culture" through the grotesque process of "Stroggification." Think of tacticals as enhanced versions of Strogg marines—they're fast and have little health, but they wield more powerful weaponry, such as hyperblasters and railguns (many also carry machine guns or shotguns). Furthermore, tacticals employ superb combat strategies—they take cover behind objects and try to pin you down with suppressing fire so their comrades can flank you. Tacticals often attack in groups, and you face scores of them throughout the single-player game, so learn to deal with them fast.

Tacticals are a bit tougher than Strogg marines, but it still doesn't take much effort to kill one. Small arms work well, especially when you score headshots. If a group of tacticals aren't budging from their cover, try firing a grenade to disperse them. Once you acquire the railgun, use it in every fight against tacticals—one rail kills a tactical at any distance.

- Medium health
- Very agile
- Often rush at you
- Powerful melee attacks
- Lightning-based ranged attacks (rarely used)
- Very dangerous in groups
- First encountered at Air Defense Bunker

Berserkers are larger, stronger versions of Strogg marines. Fast and utterly ruthless, berserkers can execute a few lightning-based ranged attacks but prefer to move into close quarters. Once a berserker draws near, it quickly bashes you with its macelike fist and stabs you with its blade-shaped arm. These melee attacks are quite powerful and can kill you in seconds, so keep your distance from berserkers at all times and learn to circle-strafe around them when fighting in tight areas.

Berserkers are tough to kill—it usually takes three up-close shotgun blasts or nearly an entire clip of machine-gun ammo to drop one. Use these arms when you have room to move, but employ heavier weaponry (such as the hyperblaster or nailgun) when facing multiple berserkers or when combating them in confined spaces. When faced with a mixed group of enemies, always kill the berserkers first.

STROGG INFANTRY

STROGG COMMANDERS

STROGG GENERALS (BOSSES)

GRUNTS

- Medium health
- Surprisingly agile
- Often rush at you
- Powerful melee attacks
- Shoulder-mounted chaingun for ranged attacks (rarely used)
- Can power up to become faster and stronger
- Very dangerous in groups
- First encountered at Air Defense Bunker

Grunts are large, monstrous creatures similar in many ways to berserkers. They're very resilient and like to charge you so they can rip you to shreds at close range. While grunts have a shoulder-mounted chaingun for ranged attacks, they almost never use it. Grunts are surprisingly agile and often leap toward you if you're not close enough to strike.

After suffering significant damage, a grunt usually becomes enraged and slams the ground with its fists. Its body glows green afterward, signaling that the grunt has become faster and more powerful. Learn to recognize this change and strive to kill grunts before they power themselves up in this fashion.

Your tactics against grunts are much the same as against berserkers—keep your distance and defeat them with small arms whenever possible, but don't hesitate to pull out stronger weaponry when the need arises. Avoid using explosive weaponry against grunts—they can close in on you fast, and you may catch splash damage. Learn to circle-strafe around grunts so you can combat them effectively in tight areas.

GUNNERS

- Medium health
- Low agility
- Arm-mounted nailgun/grenade launcher for ranged attacks
- Strong melee attacks (rarely used)
- Often used as long-range firefight support
- Very dangerous in groups
- First encountered at Hangar Perimeter

Gunners are large, well-armored soldiers that are often used as long-range combat support. They can execute powerful melee attacks if you move in close, but gunners prefer to combat distant targets. Their arm-mounted combination nailgun/grenade launcher allows them to punish whole groups of enemies at once, and gunners are quite skilled at their trade.

Gunners almost never attack by themselves—they're commonly found supporting groups of Strogg marines and tacticals. In these situations, make gunners your first targets—you don't want them to rain nails and grenades at you during a fight. Though gunners are covered by thick body armor, their head is always exposed. Use your machine gun's scope and aim to score headshots against gunners; it doesn't take long to kill one in this fashion.

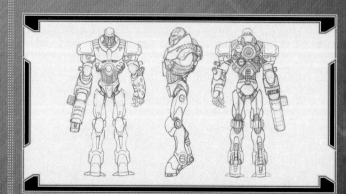

STROGG COMMANDERS

GLADIATORS

- Medium-high health
- Low agility
- Shoulder-mounted railgun for devastating ranged attacks
- Arm-mounted blaster for rapid-fire ranged attacks
- Crushing melee attacks (rarely used)
- Energy shield for extra defense
- First encountered at Perimeter Defense Station

Gladiators are huge, frightening warriors that carry energy shields to help them fend off attacks. Even without their shields, gladiators can withstand a large amount of punishment and never back down from a fight. Their massive shoulder-mounted railgun can inflict tremendous damage—avoid this attack at all costs. Gladiators also carry heavy blasters, which they can fire while protecting themselves with their shields at the same time.

   Though intimidating, gladiators are actually quite easy to defeat once you learn how to deal with them. Dodging their railgun fire is the most important thing to do—you know a shot is coming when their railguns flash, so duck for cover or strafe like crazy. Use moderately heavy weaponry such as the nailgun to drop them, and aim to fire around their energy shields. (You can destroy their shields, but it's an unnecessary waste of ammo.) Gladiators are very slow; you can run circles around them when you have room to operate, so use this to your advantage.

> ## TIP
>
> The lightning gun can quickly disrupt a gladiator's energy shield without costing you too much ammo.

HEAVY TANKS

- Airborne enemy
- High health
- Slow but can perform fast strafing movements
- Arm-mounted nailgun/heavy tracking missile launcher for ranged attacks
- Heavy tracking missiles are slow but devastating
- Crushing melee attacks (rarely used)
- First encountered at Aqueducts

Heavy tanks are perhaps the most powerful nonboss enemies in the single-player game. Though they're large and quite slow, they can withstand a tremendous amount of punishment and can occasionally strafe to dodge slow-moving ranged attacks such as rockets. Heavy tanks are armed with a nailgun, and they also fire heavy tracking missiles at you. While these missiles are quite slow, they chase after you and cause widespread splash damage when they impact—avoid them or pay the price.

   Fortunately, there are few occasions when you must battle heavy tanks on foot. Rapid-fire weaponry, such as the hyperblaster, is a good choice against these enemies, but use your best arms when faced with two heavy tanks at once. Keep moving as you battle these monstrous foes to dodge their potent ranged attacks.

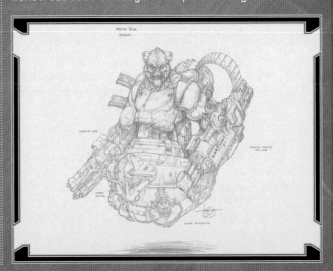

STROGG INFANTRY

STROGG COMMANDERS

STROGG GENERALS (BOSSES)

IRON MAIDENS

- Airborne enemy
- Medium health
- Slow but can perform fast strafing movements
- Can teleport about
- Arm-mounted rocket launcher for ranged attacks
- Bladelike arm for powerful melee attacks
- Can emit a high-pitched scream that deafens and disorients you
- First encountered at Data Storage Security

Iron maidens are terror-inducing enemies that usually emerge from wall-mounted sarcophagi. Ghostly in appearance, iron maidens float about and can perform quick strafing movements to dodge your attacks. When the going gets rough, iron maidens can also teleport to escape your attacks and ambush you from a new angle.

   Iron maidens are about as tough to kill as a berserker or grunt—two or three up-close shotgun blasts do the job. However, iron maidens are wrecking machines—you must kill them fast or they'll tear you apart with their volleys of rockets and brutal melee attacks. The lightning gun is usually the best weapon to use against iron maidens—it kills them quickly and will often immobilize them so they cannot return fire. Strong rapid-fire weaponry, such as the hyperblaster or nailgun, are also sound choices.

LIGHT TANKS

- High health
- Fast-moving but unskilled at dodging
- Often rushes at you
- Powerful melee attacks that can disorient
- Arm-mounted rocket launcher for ranged attacks
- First encountered at Recomposition Center

Light tanks are huge enemies that can absorb an ungodly amount of damage and relentlessly attack you up close or from range. Think of them as berserkers on steroids, except that their ranged attacks are far more potent thanks to their arm-mounted rocket launcher. While light tanks enjoy firing at distant targets, they usually prefer to charge into close quarters and use their macelike fists to bash you with tremendous force.

No matter which weapon you use, it takes plenty of ammo to drop a light tank. Backpedal and circle-strafe to keep your distance at all times. Sidestep their rockets and pepper them with heavy rapid-fire weaponry, or use your grenade launcher if they're not charging at you. If a light tank manages to close in, switch to your shotgun as you continue to backpedal and unload at its head.

NEXUS PROTECTORS

- High health
- Slow moving, poor at dodging
- Flamethrower for both melee and ranged attacks
- Tracking missiles for ranged attacks
- Twin shoulder-mounted hyperblasters for ranged attacks
- First encountered at Nexus Hub

Nexus protectors are large, spiderlike creatures that can whittle away your health in seconds with their crippling ranged attacks. Though they're slow and can rarely dodge your attacks, Nexus protectors have an enormous amount of health, and it takes loads of ammo to slay one. They unleash lethal flamethrowers when you're within relatively close range and fire tracking missiles or energy projectiles when you keep your distance. Their twin shoulder-mounted hyperblasters are extremely powerful and must be avoided at all costs.

Combating Nexus protectors is easy so long as you have room to move and cover to utilize. Keep your distance to negate their lethal flamethrower attacks, and chop them down with heavy rapid-fire weaponry such as the hyperblaster or nailgun. Strafe constantly or move out of sight to avoid their other ranged attacks. Nexus protectors are very slow and can't dodge your attacks—lob grenades or fire rockets if you need to kill one fast.

TELE DROPPERS

- Medium-high health
- Very fast and agile
- No direct attacks
- Spawns weaker enemies, usually Strogg marines
- First encountered at Strogg Medical Facilities

Tele droppers are unique enemies that don't attack you directly. Instead, they run toward you, stop short, and then begin to spawn weaker foes, such as Strogg marines and grunts. After spawning a group of minions, tele droppers run far away and hide to avoid your counterattacks. They return after a few moments to spawn more enemies.

Defeating a tele dropper's spawn is important, but you'll never win the fight if you don't kill the tele dropper itself. The best way to fight a tele dropper is to equip your grenade launcher as it runs toward you; when it stops running, immediately backpedal and start lobbing grenades at it. Direct hits explode on impact and severely damage the tele dropper. More importantly, the splash damage from your grenades kills all of the enemies the tele dropper attempts to spawn. Three to four grenades usually does the trick, so repeat this process as necessary.

STROGG GENERALS (BOSSES)

CYBER-VOSS

- Very high health
- Slow movements, poor at dodging
- Rechargeable shields
- Crushing melee attacks
- Variety of powerful ranged attacks
- Spawns weaker enemies to attack you
- Encountered at the end of Waste Processing Facility

You battle Cyber-Voss in a wide chamber at the end of Waste Processing Facility. Voss's ranged weaponry includes volleys of tracking missiles, a powerful lightning gun, and a devastating dark matter gun. He also executes lethal melee attacks if you move too close, so keep your distance at all times to negate these crushing blows. Pound Voss with rockets the moment the fight begins and constantly circle-strafe around him to avoid his ranged attacks.

Tip

Cyber-Voss is not vulnerable to headshots.

Voss's Life meter is displayed at your screen's top center—he has both shields and health. You must eliminate his shields (the gray, outside portion of the meter) in order to erode his health (the orange, inner portion of the meter). The fight ends when you inflict enough damage to empty the health portion of Voss's Life meter.

After you eliminate Voss's shields, he stops attacking you and moves to a nearby electrified console, which he uses to recharge his shields. Keep hitting him with rockets or other powerful weaponry to chop away at his health, which Voss cannot restore.

TIP

There are several health packs in the chamber—grab them while Voss recharges his shields.

While Voss recharges his shields, he spawns multiple Strogg marines and grunts to engage you. Stop attacking Voss and switch to a powerful rapid-fire weapon (such as the hyperblaster or nailgun) each time he spawns his underlings. Stay far away from Voss, let his faster minions chase after you, and then defeat them.

Each time Voss uses a shield recharge station, a new section of the arena opens up to reveal another recharge station and a few additional pick-ups for you to grab. There are three recharge stations in total, so Voss recharges his shields three times throughout the fight. Each time he does so, he spawns additional enemies to keep you off his back. Back off and kill these enemies whenever he spawns them, then return your attention to defeating Voss.

NETWORK GUARDIAN

- Very high health
- Slow movements, poor at dodging
- Can become airborne with jetpack
- Crushing melee attacks
- Variety of powerful ranged attacks
- Encountered at the end of Data Networking Security

NOTE

The network guardian is not vulnerable to headshots.

You battle the network guardian atop the third and final security tower. When the fight begins, equip your dark matter gun and follow the network guardian as he floats toward the rooftop's center. Open fire the moment he lands to inflict heavy damage with your DMG; strafe to avoid his ranged attacks, which include volleys of rockets, heavy tracking missiles, and heavy blaster shots.

TIP

The network guardian is most vulnerable in the early stages of the fight. Hit him hard with your DMG.

After suffering significant damage, the network guardian takes to the air, becoming a harder target to hit. Keep your distance and continue to strafe about as you combat the airborne network guardian. Use your machine gun to ensure you score hits—its projectiles travel faster than any other weapon's. Nail him with your DMG whenever he lands.

TIP

There are rockets, clips, dark matter cores, and several armor-restoring pick-ups at the rooftop's far end.

Eventually, the network guardian begins to fly about the rooftop at low altitude, attempting to burn you with the flames that shoot from his awesome jetpack. Though the damage from this attack isn't too severe, backpedal and strafe to keep your distance. Continue to riddle him with your machine gun as you do so.

CAUTION

Don't accidentally backpedal off the roof!

After executing his jetpack attack, the network guardian lands and fires a missile straight up into the sky. The missile explodes high overhead, and then several smaller rockets streak downward toward you. Keep your eyes to the sky and try to avoid this powerful attack as best you can while you continue to chop away at the network guardian.

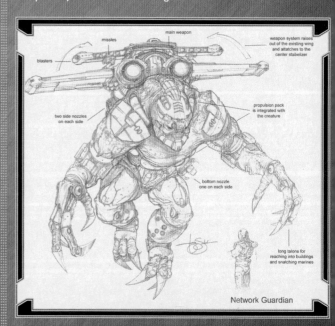

Network Guardian

THE MAKRON

- Final boss; supreme ruler of the Strogg
- Very high health; can recover health
- Slow movements, poor at dodging
- Crushing melee attacks
- Variety of powerful ranged attacks
- Becomes airborne halfway through fight
- Encountered at the end of Nexus Hub and The Nexus

NOTE

You're supposed to lose the first fight against the Makron at the end of Nexus Hub. Survive until he unleashes his dark matter gun on you.

As soon as the Makron crawls out of the Nexus chamber's central pit, fire your DMG at him to immediately inflict heavy damage. Keep your distance from the Makron at all times to nullify his crippling melee blows. The Makron also has a slew of powerful ranged attacks, including:

Triple Blaster: Most common attack. Strafe back and forth to avoid while you return fire.

Dark Matter Gun: Second most common attack. Circle-strafe in one direction to avoid as you return fire.

Dark Matter Beams: Rare attack. Strafe to one side and jump over one of the beams. Circle-strafe behind the Makron and continue to punish him.

Stomp: The Makron leans backward on his hind legs and then slams the ground with his front legs. Jump to avoid the resulting shockwave.

Hyperblaster: Rare attack. Circle-strafe in one direction to dodge as you return fire.

Dark Matter Grenades: Rare attack. Watch the grenades as they fall and move away to reduce splash damage.

NOTE

The Makron is not vulnerable to headshots.

Halfway through the fight, the Makron sheds his lower body and his torso becomes airborne. The Makron utilizes the same ranged attacks while airborne, but he's faster and tougher to hit. Continue to avoid his attacks as you drill him with your DMG.

TIP

When the fight's second stage begins, four teleporters appear, one in each corner of the chamber. Run into one to teleport onto the upper balcony, where several ammo pick-ups and two Strogg Health Stations are located.

After you defeat the Makron's airborne form, the Nexus rises into the chamber's center. An impenetrable energy shield quickly surrounds the Nexus, preventing you from harming it. Multiple enemies then begin to randomly spawn in from the chamber's teleporters. Immediately run to the nearest teleporter to reach the upper balcony—you're an easy target on the ground floor.

Fire a single rocket at the ceiling directly above the Nexus to destroy its energy shield. Switch to your DMG and strafe back and forth as you wait for the energy shield to shatter; then fire your DMG at the Nexus itself. Quickly switch back to your rocket launcher and continue to pound the Nexus until its shield is restored—you don't have enough time to hit it with two DMG blasts. Repeat this process until you achieve victory.

TIP

Bring up your DMG right after you fire a rocket at the ceiling so the DMG can reload as you wait for the Nexus's shield to shatter.

WALKTHROUGH

AIR DEFENSE BUNKER

OVERVIEW

Air Defense Bunker is a short introductory level designed to familiarize you with nearly every facet of *Quake 4*'s gameplay mechanics. Completing this area won't be a walk in the park, however—you're drawn into several skirmishes against a variety of Strogg infantry as you navigate the bunker in search of your fellow squad members. Prove your worth to your squadmates by surviving this intense first level.

ENEMIES ENCOUNTERED
- Grunts
- Berserkers
- Strogg marines

WEAPONS ACQUIRED
- Machine gun

UPGRADES ACQUIRED
- None

AMMUNITION ACQUIRED
- Clips

ITEMS ACQUIRED
- Armor vest, small
- Health packs, small

CRASH LANDING

The game begins with a short cinematic showing scores of Global Defense Force (GDF) Destroyer-class starships approaching planet Stroggos— the homeworld of the Strogg, an advanced, warlike alien race bent on intergalactic conquest. Word has spread that a lone GDF marine has somehow managed to breach the Strogg's core defenses and defeat the Makron—the supreme leader of the Strogg race. That nameless marine's incredible efforts have turned the tide of a war, which many on earth had deemed utterly hopeless. Now, the GDF is sparing no cost in capitalizing on this fortunate turn of events and crushing the vile Strogg once and for all. The fate of humanity hinges on their success.

Rhino Squad—the GDF's most brazen and talented squadron of marines—awaits deployment in an GDF dropship aboard the destroyer USS *Patton*. Corporal Mathew Kane—the newest member of Rhino Squad and an infamously cold-blooded soldier whose name is known to all in the GDF— makes no effort at small talk as his team straps themselves in and prepares for launch.

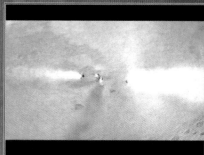

Though the Makron has been elimi-nated, the Strogg are still showing strong signs of resistance. Hundreds of Strogg air defense cannons stationed about the planet's surface fire at the incoming GDF destroyers and dropships, killing thousands of marines before they even enter the atmosphere. A tracking missile eventually strikes Rhino Squad's dropship, causing all systems to fail. Without guidance or propulsion systems, the crew is at the mercy of Stroggos's gravity. The ride into enemy territory is a rough one, and Corporal Kane soon loses consciousness.

Kane awakens in the wreckage of his squad's downed dropship, finding himself in the midst of an intense battle between Strogg and man. As he struggles to come to his senses, the dazed corporal watches helplessly as several of his comrades are shot and killed right before his eyes. Kane's vertigo ultimately subsides, and he finally manages to find his feet. He wastes no time freeing his standard-issue blaster from its holster...

OBJECTIVE: REGROUP WITH RHINO SQUAD

WALKTHROUGH:
PART 1

AIR DEFENSE BUNKER

AIR DEFENSE TRENCHES

HANGAR PERIMETER

INTERIOR HANGAR

MCC LANDING SITE

OPERATION: ADVANTAGE

CANYON

PERIMETER DEFENSE STATION

AQUEDUCTS

AQUEDUCTS ANNEX

+ MEDIC   Ⓐ CONNECTION

1 WAYPOINT

NOTE

To speak to a character, approach him; when your reticule changes to show his name, rank, and GDF squadron affiliation, press Ⓑ to speak with him. Speak to a character several times to get additional information.

WAYPOINT #1

Your dropship has crash-landed right outside a Strogg air defense bunker. Approach Sergeant Morris (Rhino Squad), who's frantically trying to contact HQ on his laptop. Morris tells you to regroup with the rest of Rhino Squad, who have taken cover inside the nearby Strogg bunker.

Medic Anderson (Rhino Squad) is also outside the bunker, attempting to heal a fallen marine. Talk to him and he gives you a shot to heal you. He says to speak with an GDF medic whenever you're injured and they'll heal you. Enter the nearby bunker afterward.

Sergeant Miller

CHAPTER 1 WELCOME TO QUAKE 4

CHAPTER 2 BASIC TRAINING

CHAPTER 3 WEAPONS AND ITEMS

CHAPTER 4 VEHICLES

CHAPTER 5 CHARACTERS

CHAPTER 6 ENEMIES

CHAPTER 7 WALKTHROUGH

CHAPTER 8 MULTIPLAYER

CHAPTER 9 GAMERSCORE ACHIEVEMENTS

AMMUNITION

HEALTH

WEAPON

EXPLOSIVE BARREL

=denotes item below or behind an object

ENEMY SPAWN

1 WAYPOINT

A CONNECTION

Tip

Press ⓨ to turn on your blaster's flashlight and improve visibility in dark areas.

WAYPOINT #3

Collect two small health packs as you make your way to this room. Grab a machine gun off a fallen marine as you enter the room. Use the machine gun to defeat the Strogg marine that attacks you right after you acquire the weapon. Nab the two clips in the room, reload, then kill the next two Strogg marines that attack from the room's far end.

WAYPOINT #2

Private Webb (Badger Squad) joins you as you enter the bunker; he helps you battle a group of Strogg marines you encounter at this area. Stay close to Webb and help him defeat the Strogg marines, but keep your distance from the explosive barrels in the room—stray bullets can easily ignite them. When the area is clear, Webb tells you to move onward and find the rest of your squad.

WAYPOINT #4

Private First Class Kovitch (Badger Squad) kills a fearsome Strogg grunt with his shotgun. He then joins you as you travel to this area, where another grunt attacks you. Help Kovitch defeat the grunt and then proceed onward.

OBJECTIVE: RETRIEVE MEDIC

WAYPOINT #5

Badger Squad has secured this room, but at the cost of one of their men being gravely wounded. After spotting you, Sergeant Miller (Badger Squad) orders you to retrieve Medic Anderson so he can heal the fallen marine. Collect the nearby clips and then backtrack out of the room.

WALKTHROUGH:
PART 1

AIR DEFENSE BUNKER

AIR DEFENSE TRENCHES

HANGAR PERIMETER

INTERIOR HANGAR

MCC LANDING SITE

OPERATION: ADVANTAGE

CANYON

PERIMETER DEFENSE STATION

AQUEDUCTS

AQUEDUCTS ANNEX

Sergeant Miller

Medic Anderson

AMMUNITION	**EXPLOSIVE BARREL**
ARMOR	**ENEMY SPAWN**
HEALTH	**1** WAYPOINT
MEDIC	**A** CONNECTION
WEAPON	

= denotes item below or behind an object

WAYPOINT #6

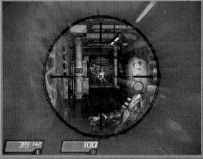

You're attacked by a grunt and a group of Strogg marines as you backtrack through this area. Keep your distance, strafe to dodge their fire, and use your machine gun's scope (press LT) to score headshots on the Strogg marines. If any of them close in, forget the scope and continue to strafe as you fire away.

WAYPOINT #7

Corporal Pierce (Kodiak Squad) is impaled by a Strogg berserker as you backtrack through this area. The berserker then charges at you. Open fire as you backpedal to keep away from the berserker—as you've just seen, they're lethal at close range. Proceed through the door from which the berserker entered.

OBJECTIVE: ESCORT ANDERSON

WAYPOINT #8

Medic Anderson comes under attack by three Strogg marines as you enter this room. Help Anderson defeat the Strogg marines and then approach him to complete the "Retrieve Medic" objective. You must now escort

Anderson back to Sergeant Miller and the wounded Badger Squad marine. Keep your machine gun at the ready—you encounter a grunt, a few more berserkers, and a couple of Strogg marines on the way there.

> **TIP**
>
> Speak to Anderson if you're injured, and he quickly heals you to full health.

> **TIP**
>
> A Strogg grunt pops out of the floor as you return to the wounded marine. After you destroy it, you can drop through the floor to grab a small armor vest and some clips.

AMMUNITION	WEAPON
ARMOR	EXPLOSIVE BARREL
HEALTH	ENEMY SPAWN
MEDIC	1 WAYPOINT

=denotes item below or behind an object

WAYPOINT #9

Medic Anderson rushes to heal the wounded Badger Squad marine when you return to this area. This completes the "Escort Anderson" objective. Afterward, Sergeant Miller says you're free to continue your search for your fellow Rhino Squad members. Proceed through the door he unlocks to reach the next waypoint.

WAYPOINT #10

Corporal Cortez (Rhino Squad) finishes off a few Strogg as you enter this area. He then greets you and says he must stay and guard this area but that you must proceed through the door to the left. Enter the door, face the control panel inside, and press Ⓑ to exit the level.

AIR DEFENSE TRENCHES

OVERVIEW

You've survived the crash-landing onto planet Stroggos and have helped your fellow GDF marines secure the air defense bunker. Now it's time to find the rest of your squad members. Air Defense Trenches is a hot combat zone full of Strogg, and it's far from being fully secured. Fortunately, you have only a short trek through this dangerous area. Stay alert as you navigate the trenches—shoot first, ask questions later.

ENEMIES ENCOUNTERED
- Grunt
- Berserkers
- Strogg marines

WEAPONS ACQUIRED
- Machine gun

UPGRADES ACQUIRED
- None

AMMUNITION ACQUIRED
- Clips

ITEMS ACQUIRED
- Armor shards
- Armor vest, small
- Health pack, large
- Health pack, small

OBJECTIVE: REGROUP WITH RHINO SQUAD

START

AMMUNITION

ARMOR

WEAPON

ENEMY SPAWN

1 WAYPOINT

A CONNECTION

=denotes item below or behind an object

WAYPOINT #1

Take the elevator up to this first room. Nab the small armor vest, then defeat the grunt that attacks you as you cross the room.

AIR DEFENSE BUNKER

AIR DEFENSE TRENCHES

HANGAR PERIMETER

INTERIOR HANGAR

MCC LANDING SITE

OPERATION: ADVANTAGE

CANYON

PERIMETER DEFENSE STATION

AQUEDUCTS

AQUEDUCTS ANNEX

WAYPOINT #2

AMMUNITION

HEALTH

ENEMY SPAWN

1 WAYPOINT

A CONNECTION

=denotes item below or behind an object

You encounter no further Strogg resistance on your path to the trenches. Collect numerous pick-ups on your way to this waypoint, where a large wave of Strogg marines is swarming Private First Class Damato (Kodiak Squad). Help Damato secure the area before you move on; use the rock formations as cover when you need to reload.

OBJECTIVE: DESTROY STROGG AIRCRAFT HANGARS

Chapter 1 WELCOME TO QUAKE 4

Chapter 2 BASIC TRAINING

Chapter 3 WEAPONS AND ITEMS

Chapter 4 VEHICLES

Chapter 5 CHARACTERS

Chapter 6 ENEMIES

Chapter 7 WALKTHROUGH

Chapter 8 MULTIPLAYER

Chapter 9 GAMERSCORE ACHIEVEMENTS

AMMUNITION		ENEMY SPAWN	
HEALTH		1 WAYPOINT	
EXPLOSIVE BARREL		A CONNECTION	

=denotes item below or behind an object

WAYPOINT #3

You finally regroup with your fellow squad members at this location. Speak to Sergeant Bidwell (Rhino Squad) to complete the "Regroup with Rhino Squad" objective. Bidwell greets you and then receives a transmission from Lieutenant Voss, the leader of Rhino Squad, ordering you to infiltrate and destroy the Strogg aircraft hangars. Nab the nearby clips and then proceed through the trenches.

WAYPOINT #4

You encounter heavy resistance a short distance past Sergeant Bidwell—a berserker ambushes you, and several Strogg marines open fire from farther down the trench. Fortunately, Sergeant Morris has been assigned to escort you to the hangars, and he's a great shot with his machine gun. Kill the Berserker quickly and then use the nearby crates as cover as you return fire at the distant Strogg marines.

TIP

Though it takes a bit of getting used to, the machine gun's scope is very handy. It improves the weapon's accuracy against distant enemies, letting you conserve ammunition and score headshots.

WAYPOINT #5

Two more Strogg marines attack as you proceed toward the hangars. Cut them down quickly, then pass through the door beyond. Face the control panel inside the door; press Ⓑ to activate it and exit the level.

HANGAR PERIMETER

OVERVIEW

You've made your run through the volatile air defense trenches and have arrived at the perimeter of the Strogg's aircraft hangars. You must now navigate the perimeter in order to reach the interior of the complex and destroy the Strogg aircraft hangars. Sergeant Morris still has your back, which is a good thing—the hangar perimeter is full of Strogg, and they aren't happy to see you. Enemies grossly outnumber you in many battles here, so use objects in the environment as cover to help you overcome the odds.

ENEMIES ENCOUNTERED
- Grunt
- Berserkers
- Strogg gunners
- Strogg marines

WEAPONS ACQUIRED
- Shotgun
- Machine gun

UPGRADES ACQUIRED
- None

AMMUNITION ACQUIRED
- Clips
- Shells

ITEMS ACQUIRED
- Armor shards
- Armor vest, small
- Health packs, small

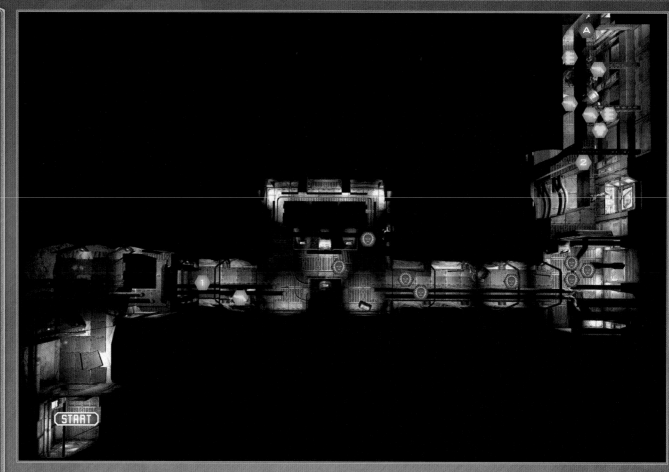

START

🔋 AMMUNITION	💀 ENEMY SPAWN
🛡 ARMOR	1 WAYPOINT
🔫 WEAPON	Ⓐ CONNECTION

WAYPOINT #1

After a short journey through some tunnels, you encounter a new enemy at this waypoint—a powerful Strogg gunner. He's not alone, either. Several distant Strogg marines open fire at you as well.

Backpedal through the doorway and use your machine gun's scope to score headshots on the gunner. Whenever the gunner opens fire or you need to reload, strafe to the left and take cover behind the wall near the doorway. You can make short work of these enemies with Morris backing you up.

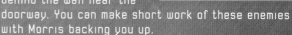

CAUTION

Strogg gunners also fire red grenades. If you see them launch one, back up to avoid its splash damage.

More Strogg marines and a berserker attack you as you proceed down the tunnel directly ahead. Strafe to dodge the Strogg marines' fire as you pepper the advancing berserker. Pick off the Strogg marines after you drop the berserker, then move on.

WAYPOINT #2

You meet up with three members of Viper Squad a short distance ahead—Corporal Mahler, Technician Li, and Medic Hayes. Their mission is the same as yours—to destroy the Strogg aircraft hangars. They gladly join you, and Corporal Mahler hands you a shotgun, saying you'll be needing it real soon. Sergeant Morris agrees to stay behind and watch

your backs. Grab the nearby pick-ups, then lead Viper Squad through the door ahead.

TIP

If you're low on health or armor, speak to Medic Hayes or Technician Li. Medics heal you, and Technicians repair your armor.

NOTE

Check the "Weapons and Items" portion of this guide for complete details on the shotgun.

WAYPOINT #3

A Strogg gunner attacks from the distant walkway at the far side of this large room. Pick him off from range and dodge the nails he fires. After you drop the gunner, six Strogg marines attack

from the room's far end—snipe them from range and then follow Viper Squad through the door beyond.

▤	AMMUNITION	1	WAYPOINT
✚	HEALTH	△	CONNECTION
☻	ENEMY SPAWN		

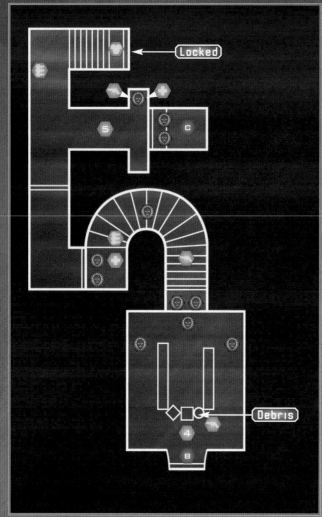

Locked

5   c

Debris

4

B

	AMMUNITION		ENEMY SPAWN
ARMOR		**1**	WAYPOINT
HEALTH		**A**	CONNECTION
WEAPON			

solid line = wall/object on upper floor
dotted line = wall/object on lower floor
small, thin rectangle = door

WAYPOINT #4

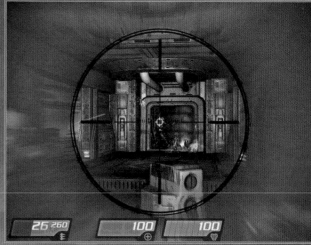

26 260   100   100

You encounter several more Strogg marines in this next room. Use your machine gun to help Viper Squad defeat them. Switch to your shotgun before you proceed—you'll soon need it.

WAYPOINT #5

7 36   100   100

You encounter a berserker and two Strogg solders on your route to this elevator, but they don't pose much of a challenge with Viper Squad behind you. A grunt also ambushes you just before you reach the elevator. Finally, two Strogg marines guard the elevator itself. Defeat them with your shotgun, and collect the various pick-ups from the surrounding corridors before you board the elevator.

TIP

If you have your shotgun out (or any other weapon besides the blaster), you can press **Y** *to switch to your machine gun.*

☀ ENEMY SPAWN	Ⓐ CONNECTION
① WAYPOINT	

WAYPOINT #6

A lot of Strogg ambush you in this large chamber. Use your machine gun's scope to kill the gunner on the high footbridge, then open fire on the Strogg marines across the room. Many more Strogg marines jump down from the room's upper balcony as you move across—switch to your shotgun and quickly defeat them with close-range blasts.

OBJECTIVE: CIRCUMVENT GLASS

The path toward the hangars is sealed off by shatterproof glass. Corporal Mahler orders you to scout ahead and find a way to open the path, saying he and the rest of Viper Squad will remain in the chamber to guard it. A final berserker then jumps out of the door opposite Corporal Mahler—unleash your shotgun on it, then reload and switch back to your machine gun.

TIP

Speak to Medic Hayes and Technician Li to heal up and recover your armor before you leave.

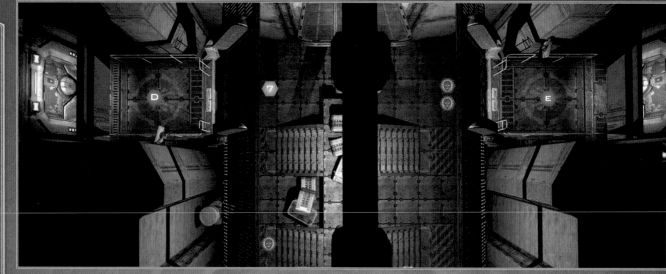

⬡ ENEMY SPAWN ⬡ A CONNECTION

① WAYPOINT

WAYPOINT #7

Three Strogg marines ambush you in this area. Keep moving to dodge their attacks as you defeat them. Proceed through the door across the room, and climb up the ladder.

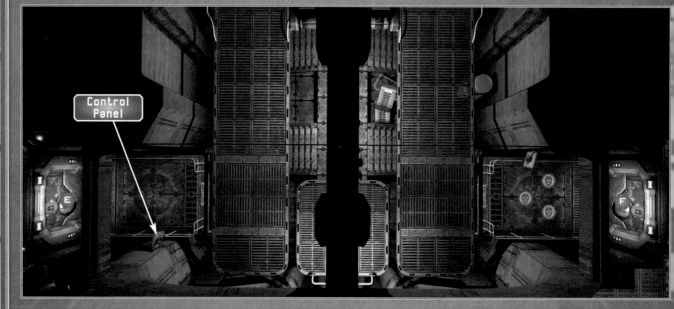

Control Panel

⬡ ENEMY SPAWN ⬡ A CONNECTION

Activate the control panel on the room's second floor to create a walkway and reach the door beyond. A berserker and two Strogg marines attack as you cross the walkway—defeat them and then proceed through the door.

Control Panels

▣ **AMMUNITION**	① **WAYPOINT**	
▽ **ARMOR**	◬ **CONNECTION**	
◇ **WEAPON**		

WAYPOINT #8

You arrive at the second floor of the chamber where Viper Squad awaits. Activate the nearby control panel to lower a Strogg aircraft's massive booster, which comes to a rest on a docking station directly in front of the shatterproof glass. Cross the footbridge and use the lift to join Viper Squad on the ground floor.

Tip

Drop off the footbridge and land on the empty booster docking station next to the aircraft booster you've just lowered to quickly reach the ground floor without using the lift.

Move to the control panel behind the booster you lowered and activate it. An intense stream of fire shoots from the booster and quickly melts the shatterproof glass. This completes the "Circumvent Glass" objective. Lead Viper Squad through the new pathway you've created.

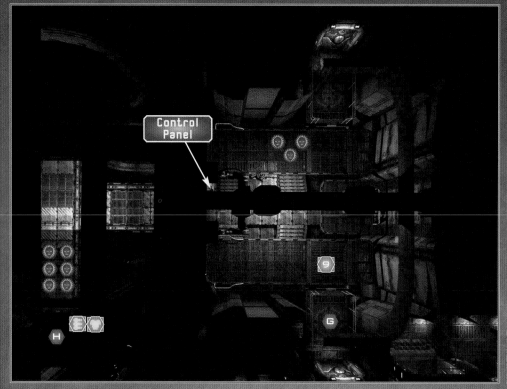

Control Panel

AMMUNITION

HEALTH

ARMOR

ENEMY SPAWN

1 WAYPOINT

A CONNECTION

=denotes item below or behind an object

Waypoint #9

40 ²²⁷   100   100

Defeat the berserker and pair of Strogg marines that attack from the upper walkways at this room's far side. Activate the control panel in the room's center

to extend a footbridge across the chasm beyond. Several more Strogg marines attack from the chasm's opposite end while the walkway extends—kill them all from range, then cross the bridge and pass through the door beyond.

Tip

Descend the ladder to the right of the door to claim some hidden pick-ups.

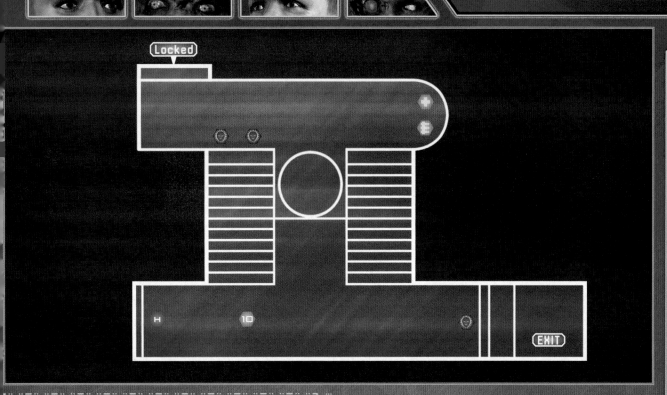

Locked

EXIT

WALKTHROUGH:
PART 1

AIR
DEFENSE
BUNKER

AIR
DEFENSE
TRENCHES

HANGAR PERIMETER

INTERIOR
HANGAR

MCC
LANDING
SITE

OPERATION:
ADVANTAGE

CANYON

PERIMETER
DEFENSE
STATION

AQUEDUCTS

AQUEDUCTS
ANNEX

solid line = wall/object on upper floor
dotted line = wall/object on lower floor
small, thin rectangle = door

WAYPOINT #10

You enter onto the second floor of this final chamber. Strogg marines quickly open fire from the ground floor to the left—defeat them before crossing any farther into the room. A gunner then enters through the far door ahead and attacks. Dodge his nails and drop him fast. Collect the items from the chamber's lower portion, then proceed through the door, step onto the elevator, and activate its control panel to exit the level.

INTERIOR HANGAR

OVERVIEW

Battle continues to heat up as you near your objective of destroying the Strogg aircraft hangars. Now that you've penetrated the hangar perimeter, you're in position to destroy the Strogg's aircraft hangars and strike a blow that'll greatly help the GDF ground troops in securing the trenches surrounding the air defense cannon. You need the help of Corporal Rhodes, Rhino Squad's demolition expert, in order to get the job done—make sure you both survive long enough to complete the mission.

ENEMIES ENCOUNTERED
    Strogg grunt
    Strogg gunners
    Strogg marines
WEAPONS ACQUIRED
    Shotguns
    Machine gun
UPGRADES ACQUIRED
    None
AMMUNITION ACQUIRED
    Clips
    Shells
ITEMS ACQUIRED
    Armor vest, small
    Health packs, large
    Health packs, small

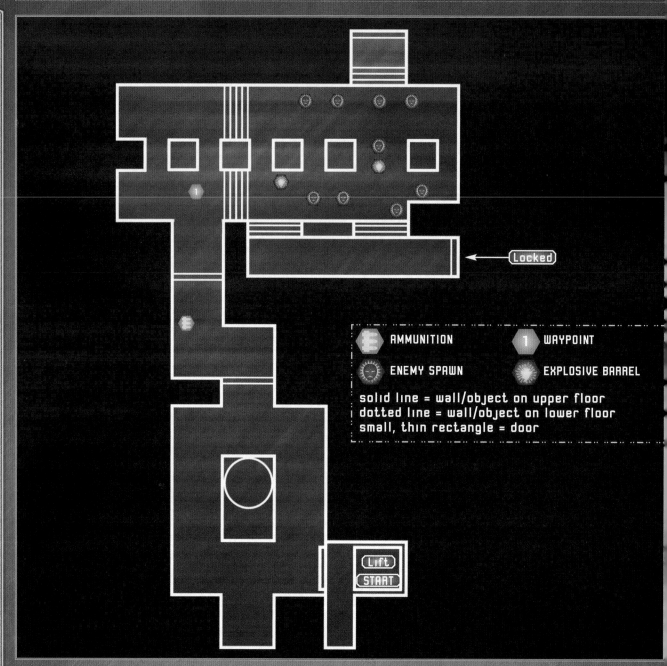

Locked

E AMMUNITION **1** WAYPOINT

ENEMY SPAWN EXPLOSIVE BARREL

solid line = wall/object on upper floor
dotted line = wall/object on lower floor
small, thin rectangle = door

Lift
START

WAYPOINT #1

The lights shut off just before you enter this tight, cluttered room—keep close to Viper Squad as you head in. Several Strogg marines emerge from the room's

far end, accompanied by a grunt. To make matters worse, a few gun turrets drop from the ceiling and begin to blaze away. Strafe about to dodge incoming fire as you combat these threats, and use your machine gun's flashlight to see in the darkness.

CAUTION

There are several explosive barrels in the room. Use them to your advantage but don't wander near them.

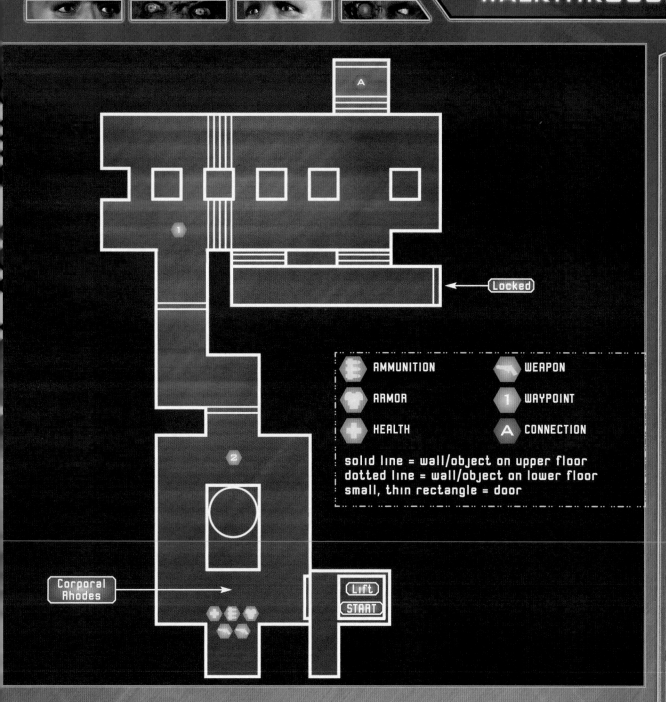

Locked

AMMUNITION

WEAPON

ARMOR

1 WAYPOINT

HEALTH

A CONNECTION

solid line = wall/object on upper floor
dotted line = wall/object on lower floor
small, thin rectangle = door

Corporal
Rhodes

Lift
START

WALKTHROUGH:
PART 1

AIR
DEFENSE
BUNKER

AIR
DEFENSE
TRENCHES

HANGAR
PERIMETER

INTERIOR HANGAR

MCC
LANDING
SITE

OPERATION:
ADVANTAGE

CANYON

PERIMETER
DEFENSE
STATION

AQUEDUCTS

AQUEDUCTS
ANNEX

OBJECTIVE: MEET RHODES

Securing the room at
Waypoint #1 completes the
"Clear Area of Enemies"
objective. Sergeant Morris
then radios in and orders
you to meet Rhino Squad's
demolition expert, Corporal
Rhodes, at the elevator you
took to reach this level.
Backtrack to the elevator to speak with Rhodes and
complete the "Meet Rhodes" objective.

OBJECTIVE: PROTECT RHODES

Viper Squad is ordered to
return to the hangar
perimeter to prevent the
Strogg from recapturing it.
Your new assignment is to
protect Corporal Rhodes as
the two of you head to the
hangars. Collect the pick-
ups near the elevator, then
lead Rhodes as you retrace your steps through
Waypoint #1.

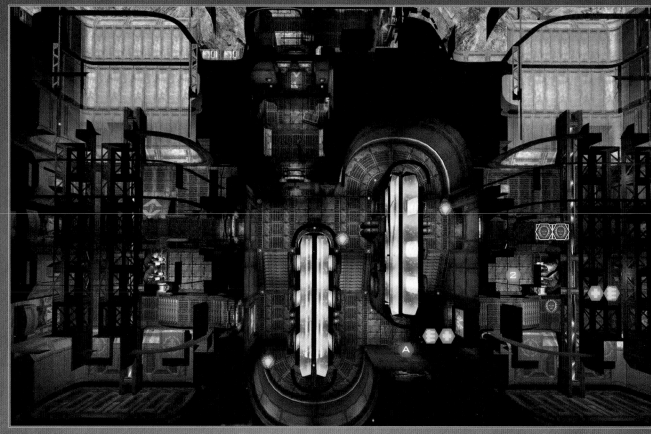

QUAKE 4

CHAPTER 1 WELCOME TO QUAKE 4

CHAPTER 2 BASIC TRAINING

CHAPTER 3 WEAPONS AND ITEMS

CHAPTER 4 VEHICLES

CHAPTER 5 CHARACTERS

CHAPTER 6 ENEMIES

CHAPTER 7 WALKTHROUGH

CHAPTER 8 MULTIPLAYER

CHAPTER 9 GAMERSCORE ACHIEVEMENTS

 AMMUNITION

 EXPLOSIVE BARREL

HEALTH

1 WAYPOINT

 ENEMY SPAWN

A CONNECTION

 =denotes item below or behind an object

WAYPOINT #2

The first bomb site is weakly defended by three Strogg marines. Clip them all from range with your machine gun. Rhodes then places the first charge at the room's bomb site.

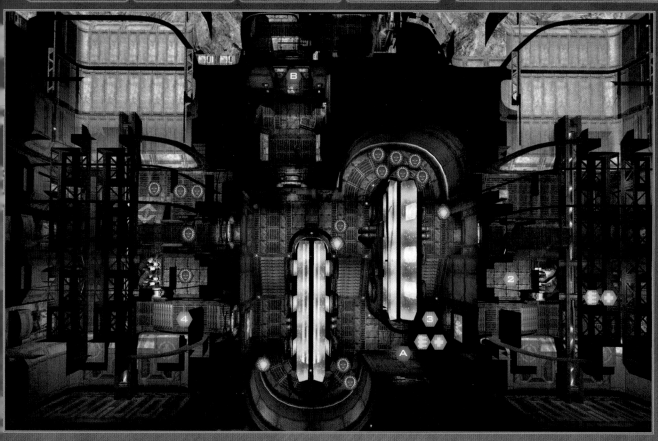

WALKTHROUGH: PART 1

AIR DEFENSE BUNKER

AIR DEFENSE TRENCHES

HANGAR PERIMETER

INTERIOR HANGAR

MCC LANDING SITE

OPERATION: ADVANTAGE

CANYON

PERIMETER DEFENSE STATION

AQUEDUCTS

AQUEDUCTS ANNEX

Legend

AMMUNITION		EXPLOSIVE BARREL	
HEALTH		1	WAYPOINT
ENEMY SPAWN		A	CONNECTION

  = denotes item below or behind an object

Waypoint #3

The curved corridors you passed through on your way to Waypoint #2 were empty before, but now they're full of Strogg marines and a couple of gunners. Use your machine gun to kill

most of the Strogg marines and the first gunner from a distance, then switch to your shotgun and move up the stairs to secure the rest of the room.

CAUTION

There are more exploding barrels in this room. Keep your distance and use them to your advantage.

Waypoint #4

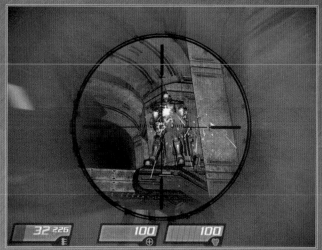

The second and final bomb site is better defended than the first by several Strogg marines. A gunner is also stationed at the footbridge above the room's center. Kill the gunner first or he rains grenades down on you. Then wipe out the Strogg marines so Rhodes can place the last charge. This completes the "Protect Rhodes" objective.

MCC LANDING SITE

OVERVIEW

Having destroyed the Strogg's ability to deploy hornets and dropships near the air defense cannon that your own dropship crashed next to, it's now only a matter of time before the GDF ground troops can secure the surrounding trenches. You've been ordered to regroup with your squad leader, Lieutenant Voss, at the MCC (Mobile Command Center) landing site, where you receive further instructions. Looks like you're starting to impress your squadmates, Corporal.

ENEMIES ENCOUNTERED
Grunts
Berserkers
Gunners
Strogg marines

WEAPONS ACQUIRED
Grenade launcher
Machine gun
Shotgun

UPGRADES ACQUIRED
None

AMMUNITION ACQUIRED
Clips

ITEMS ACQUIRED
Armor vest, small
Health packs, large
Health packs, small

1 WAYPOINT   A CONNECTION

solid line = wall/object on upper floor
dotted line = wall/object on lower floor
small, thin rectangle = door

OBJECTIVE: REGROUP WITH VOSS

WAYPOINT #5

Rhodes advises that you move to a safe location to detonate the bombs. Follow him to this room and then watch the fireworks through the window. This completes the "Destroy Strogg Aircraft Hangars" objective. Sergeant Morris then radios in, ordering you to regroup with Lieutenant Voss, the leader of Rhino Squad. Corporal Rhodes is ordered to remain at the hangar to keep it secure. Move to the large elevator in this room and activate its control panel to exit the level.

OBJECTIVE: REGROUP WITH VOSS

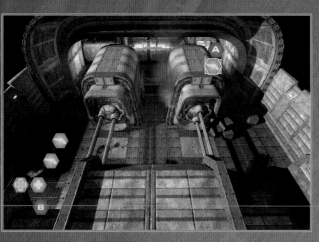

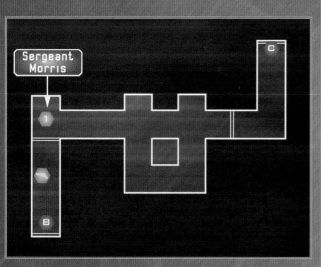

Sergeant Morris

AMMUNITION	**WEAPON**
HEALTH	**1 WAYPOINT**
MEDIC	**A CONNECTION**
TECHNICIAN	

= denotes item below or behind an object

solid line = wall/object on upper floor
dotted line = wall/object on lower floor
small, thin rectangle = door

WAYPOINT #1

You must backtrack through the hangar perimeter and into the air defense trenches in order to reach Lieutenant Voss and the rest of Rhino Squad. You meet up with Sergeant Morris here, right where you left him in the hangar perimeter. The entire area is now crawling with GDF marines, who are studying the new Strogg technology and aircraft you've helped them capture. Follow Morris out of the hangar perimeter.

WALKTHROUGH:
PART 1

AIR DEFENSE BUNKER

AIR DEFENSE TRENCHES

HANGAR PERIMETER

INTERIOR HANGAR

MCC LANDING SITE

OPERATION: ADVANTAGE

CANYON

PERIMETER DEFENSE STATION

AQUEDUCTS

AQUEDUCTS ANNEX

OBJECTIVE: CAPTURE THE AIR DEFENSE CANNON

Lieutenant Voss

Symbol	Legend		
AMMUNITION		ENEMY SPAWN	
ARMOR		1 WAYPOINT	
HEALTH		A CONNECTION	
WEAPON			

WAYPOINT #2

Lieutenant Voss and Lance Corporal Sledge await you and Sergeant Morris just outside the hangar perimeter. Voss greets you and hands you a new weapon—the mighty grenade launcher. He then gives you new orders: The four of you must navigate the trenches ahead to capture the nearby Strogg air defense cannon so the destroyer USS *Hannibal* can land safely.

NOTE

Check the "Weapons and Items" section of this guide for complete details on the grenade launcher.

It's a pitched battle through the trenches as you make your way to a bunker that leads to the air defense cannon. Strogg marines jump into the trenches from all sides in an attempt to stop you, but they're simply no match for four well-armed Rhino Squad members. Cut each one down in turn.

WAYPOINT #3

The bunker door is sealed and can't be opened by force. Lieutenant Voss orders you to find a way to open the door while the rest of the squad takes up a defensive position. Collect pick-ups from the stacked crates near the door, equip your shotgun, and then jump up the crates to reach the top of the trenches.

A grunt emerges from a hole in the ground the moment you reach the top of the trenches. Blast it with your shotgun to quickly kill it; then enter the bunker by dropping through the hole the grunt crawled out of. Use the nearby control panel to open the bunker door and let your squadmates in.

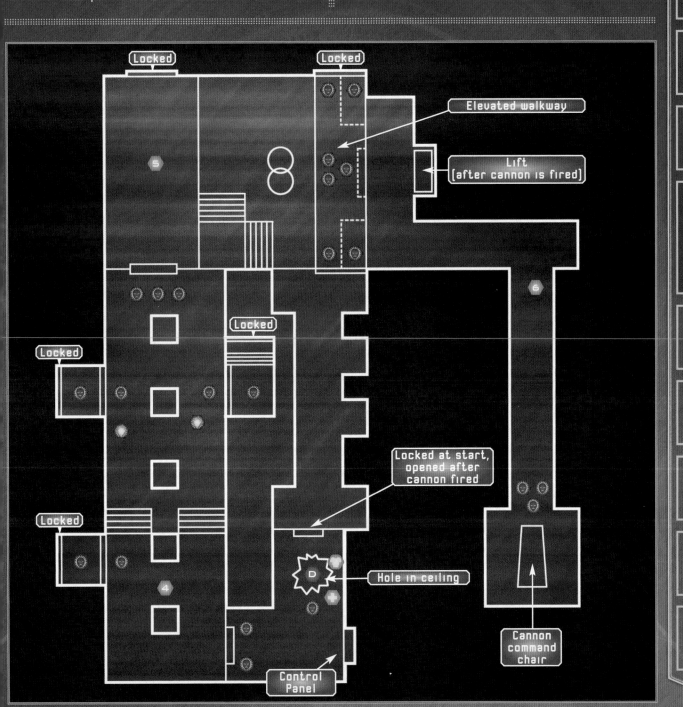

Locked

Locked

Elevated walkway

Lift [after cannon is fired]

Locked

Locked

Locked at start, opened after cannon fired

Locked

Hole in ceiling

Cannon command chair

Control Panel

WALKTHROUGH: PART 1

AIR DEFENSE BUNKER

AIR DEFENSE TRENCHES

HANGAR PERIMETER

INTERIOR HANGAR

MCC LANDING SITE

OPERATION: ADVANTAGE

CANYON

PERIMETER DEFENSE STATION

AQUEDUCTS

AQUEDUCTS ANNEX

ARMOR

  HEALTH

ENEMY SPAWN

EXPLOSIVE BARREL

1 WAYPOINT

A CONNECTION

solid line = wall/object on upper floor
dotted line = wall/object on lower floor
small, thin rectangle = door

A Strogg marine drops through the hole to attack, but it doesn't stand a chance against the three of you. A few more Strogg marines enter from the door to the left—kill them and then follow Voss and Sledge through the door.

WAYPOINT #4

The long room beyond the bunker entrance is teeming with Strogg marines. They pour out from the doors at

either side of the room and from the room's far end. Help your squadmates kill them all, then follow your team through the far door.

WAYPOINT #5

Combat erupts again in this next wide room. Numerous Strogg marines pour from the first- and second-floor doors on the room's opposite side, accompanied by a gunner. Remain on the balcony and lend a hand to

your squadmates by sniping the Strogg with your machine gun. When the room is clear, jump over the railing and proceed through the lower door.

WAYPOINT #6

The Strogg put up a final resistance here, at the air defense cannon control room. A few Strogg marines and a gunner engage you, but they're no match for your team. Kill them all

from a safe distance, and then approach the air defense cannon's command chair to complete the "Capture the Air Defense Cannon" objective.

OBJECTIVE: FIRE AWAY

With the cannon secured, Lieutenant Voss orders you to use it to blast a hole through the sealed security gate that's blocking your path to the MCC landing site. Approach the cannon's command chair and press ❽ to enter it.

Aim the air defense cannon at the distant security gate and then fire away. The powerful cannon destroys the gate (along with some Strogg), creating a way forward. This completes the "Fire Away" objective.

Chapter navigation: CHAPTER 1 WELCOME TO QUAKE 4 · CHAPTER 2 BASIC TRAINING · CHAPTER 3 WEAPONS AND ITEMS · CHAPTER 4 VEHICLES · CHAPTER 5 CHARACTERS · CHAPTER 6 ENEMIES · CHAPTER 7 WALKTHROUGH · CHAPTER 8 MULTIPLAYER · CHAPTER 9 GAMERSCORE ACHIEVEMENTS

OBJECTIVE: LOCATE THE MCC LANDING ZONE

WALKTHROUGH:
PART 1

AIR DEFENSE BUNKER

AIR DEFENSE TRENCHES

HANGAR PERIMETER

INTERIOR HANGAR

MCC LANDING SITE

OPERATION: ADVANTAGE

CANYON

PERIMETER DEFENSE STATION

AQUEDUCTS

AQUEDUCTS ANNEX

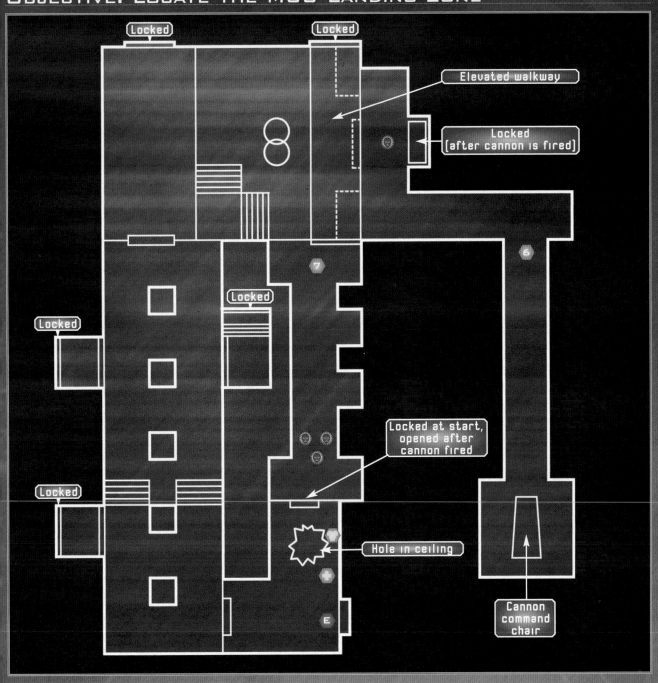

Locked

Locked

Elevated walkway

Locked
(after cannon is fired)

6

7

Locked

Locked

Locked

Locked at start, opened after cannon fired

Hole in ceiling

Cannon command chair

E

ARMOR

HEALTH

ENEMY SPAWN

1 WAYPOINT

A CONNECTION

solid line = wall/object on upper floor
dotted line = wall/object on lower floor
small, thin rectangle = door

Press Ⓑ to exit the air defense cannon's control seat. Lieutenant Voss then orders you to travel to the MCC landing site and help secure the area so the USS *Hannibal* can safely land there. Backtrack down the hallway, kill the lone Strogg marine that pops out to attack you, then use the nearby lift to reach the bunker's second floor.

WAYPOINT #7

You're attacked by a berserker, several Strogg marines, and a gunner in this corridor. Kill them all and then proceed down the hall. Activate the control panel to open the far door and exit the bunker.

![ammo]	AMMUNITION
![armor]	ARMOR
![health]	HEALTH
1	WAYPOINT
A	CONNECTION

WAYPOINT #8

The trenches are now secure. Collect pick-ups as you exit the bunker, then head up the ramp toward the security gate, which you recently destroyed. Private Law (Raven Squad) greets you near the ruined security gate and says they're just about

to blow the air defense cannon. Turn around and admire the view, then follow Private Law through the smoldering security gate.

CAUTION

There's fire in the security gate—don't touch it or you'll suffer damage.

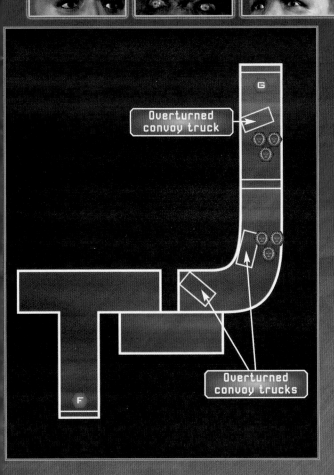

ENEMY SPAWN   **A** **CONNECTION**

solid line = wall/object on upper floor
small, thin rectangle = door

Overturned
convoy truck

Overturned
convoy trucks

You encounter a handful of Strogg marines and a grunt in the security tunnels beyond the ruined gate. Cut them all down as you and Private Law head to the LZ.

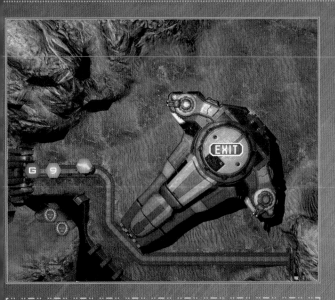

ENEMY SPAWN   **A** **CONNECTION**

1 **WAYPOINT**   **WEAPON**

OBJECTIVE: BOARD THE *HANNIBAL*

WAYPOINT #9

A distant Strogg fortification to the right features a few gun turrets that fire at you as you exit the security gate tunnels and move to the LZ. Run to take cover behind the crates ahead and then wait for the USS *Hannibal* starship

to fly overhead and obliterate them with a few cannon blasts as it prepares to land at the LZ.

When the massive USS *Hannibal* lands, approach it and run underneath it. A large elevator soon lowers to the ground, and several GDF marines hop off to secure the area. Walk onto the elevator to board the *Hannibal* and exit the level.

OPERATION: ADVANTAGE

CHAPTER 1
WELCOME TO
QUAKE 4

CHAPTER 2
BASIC TRAINING

CHAPTER 3
WEAPONS AND
ITEMS

CHAPTER 4
VEHICLES

CHAPTER 5
CHARACTERS

CHAPTER 6
ENEMIES

CHAPTER 7
WALKTHROUGH

CHAPTER 8
MULTIPLAYER

CHAPTER 9
GAMERSCORE
ACHIEVEMENTS

Sergeant
Swekel
(extended
clip mod)

START

1 WAYPOINT

OVERVIEW

Welcome aboard the USS *Hannibal*, Corporal Kane. She's
not the newest ship in the GDF fleet, but there's plenty
for you to see and do here. Spend some time wandering
about the *Hannibal* and speaking to your fellow
marines—some of them have interesting bits of gossip
to share.

ENEMIES ENCOUNTERED
None
WEAPONS ACQUIRED
None
UPGRADES ACQUIRED
Extended clip mod (machine gun)
AMMUNITION ACQUIRED
None
ITEMS ACQUIRED
None

OBJECTIVE: REPORT TO BRIEFING

Your first objective is to report to Rhino Squad's
briefing room, but there's no rush—explore the *Hannibal*
and speak to everyone you see.

WAYPOINT #1

Before you may proceed,
you must enter the decon-
tamination chamber here
and wait for the medic to
fill the chamber with
chemicals that kill any
alien bacteria you might
have carried with you onto
the ship.

WAYPOINT #2

Your tour of the *Hannibal*
takes you through Drop Pod
Control. This is a busy place,
and none of the marines
here have time to chat.

WAYPOINT #3

The mess hall is located here. Private Babcock (Wolf Squad) gives you confirmation that the Makron has indeed been killed by a lone GDF marine. Staff Sergeant Nomo and Corporal Spence (both of Badger Squad) seem to have heard of you—as well they should!

WAYPOINT #4

Several medics are hard at work as you pass through the halls near the medical bay. They're conducting experiments on Strogg they've captured; you overhear some interesting remarks if you stick around.

WAYPOINT #5

This is Rhino Squad's briefing room. Arriving here completes the "Report to Briefing" objective. During the briefing, you're told that all of the Strogg forces are linked by a device called the "Nexus"—a massive central intelligence system that allows Strogg leaders to instantly communicate with their troops. Your squad's mission is to escort a convoy of EMP (electromagnetic pulse) bombs into the Nexus Hub, where they will be detonated to disable the Nexus. This should create mass confusion amongst the Strogg and make them vulnerable.

OBJECTIVE: GEAR UP

You receive a new objective after the briefing: find the armory and restock your supply of weapons. Be sure to speak with each member of Rhino Squad before you leave the briefing room—they have interesting things to tell you.

WAYPOINT #6

This is the armory. Technician Lee (Wolf Squad) tells a funny story about your fellow squadmates Sergeant Bidwell and Technician Strauss. Listen to the tale and then head to the armory's northeast corner to gear up.

Sergeant Swekel (Raven Squad) stands at the armory's northeast corner. Approach him and he hands you the extended clip mod for your machine gun. This modification increases your machine gun's clip size to double capacity, giving you 80 rounds per clip.

After obtaining the shotgun and the clip extension mod from the armory, proceed toward the elevator you used to enter the *Hannibal*. (Look at the map to see that you're right near it.) Speak to Corporals Rhodes and Cortez if you like, then step onto the elevator to exit the level.

CANYON

OVERVIEW

It seems that defeating the Makron isn't the solution to eradicating the Strogg—a new Makron simply rises in the former one's place. You must instead destroy (or disable) the Nexus—a massive central intelligence system that allows the Strogg to communicate with one another instantaneously. Your new mission is to escort an GDF convoy of EMP bombs to the Nexus Hub, where the bombs will be detonated near the Tetranode—a giant device that transmits communication signals from the Nexus to the Strogg. The Strogg should be fairly easy to decimate without the aid of their mass communication system.

ENEMIES ENCOUNTERED
Berserkers
Grunts
Gun turrets
Drop turrets
Missile turrets
Strogg marines

WEAPONS ACQUIRED
None

UPGRADES ACQUIRED
None

AMMUNITION ACQUIRED
None

ITEMS ACQUIRED
None

OBJECTIVE: LOCATE RIDE TO DEATH CONVOY

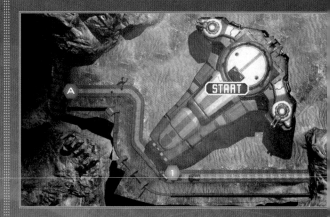

A	CONNECTION	**1**	WAYPOINT

WAYPOINT #1

After exiting the USS *Hannibal*, run toward the collection of GDF convoy trucks, which is located here. Jump onto the back of the leading convoy truck to join Corporal Spencer and Corporal Hawkins (both of Viper Squad), who await you. This completes the "Locate Ride to Death Convoy" objective. The convoy rolls out after you do so.

	ENEMY SPAWN	**1**	WAYPOINT
A	CONNECTION		

WAYPOINT #2

You aren't directly engaged by any Strogg forces until you enter this tunnel. Several Strogg marines emerge from either side of the tunnel, and the convoy stops until you defeat them all and the GDF marines you saved get on the back of the truck.

OBJECTIVE: LOCATE BIDWELL

Seargeant Bidwell

	ENEMY SPAWN	1	WAYPOINT
A	CONNECTION		WEAPON

WAYPOINT #3

The convoy comes to a stop here. Corporal Hawkins informs you that Sergeant Bidwell (Rhino Squad) is waiting for you farther ahead. Walk off the back of the convoy truck and then head through the side corridor to the left.

OBJECTIVE: PROTECT THE CONVOY

WAYPOINT #4

Sergeant Bidwell awaits you here, next to another GDF convoy truck. Approach him to complete the "Locate Bidwell" objective. Bidwell then orders you to protect the next convoy from Strogg attackers. Climb onto the back of the nearby convoy truck, then man the heavy machine gun that's mounted to the truck's roof.

NOTE

Check the "Vehicles" section of this guide for complete details on the convoy truck.

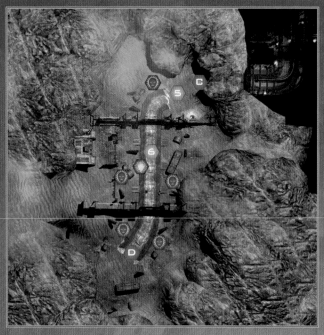

ENEMY SPAWN	1 WAYPOINT
EXPLOSIVE BARREL	A CONNECTION

WAYPOINT #5

A Strogg dropship flies overhead and deploys a drop turret as you pass through this area. Fire at the drop turret as it falls from the sky to quickly destroy it.

NOTE

Refer to the "Vehicles" section of this guide to learn all about drop turrets.

WAYPOINT #6

Things are relatively easy until you reach this area, where Corporal Rhodes must disarm several land mines on the ground ahead of you. He then detonates the mines after you move to a safe distance to

prevent the swarming Strogg infantry from chasing after the convoy.

Scores of Strogg berserkers and grunts attack from both sides of the road as Rhodes tries to complete his task. Kill them all quickly to prevent them from killing Rhodes, paying special attention to the ones that go after him. Passing this challenging area completes the "Protect the Convoy" objective.

OBJECTIVE: CLEAR AREA OF TURRETS

ENEMY SPAWN	1 WAYPOINT
A CONNECTION	

Lieutenant Voss (Rhino Squad) orders your convoy truck to move ahead so you can clear the entire area surrounding the nearby Perimeter Defense Station of gun and missile turrets. This allows the convoy to proceed unharmed.

WAYPOINT #7

The first two gun turrets are on your left, and a Strogg dropship deploys a drop turret to your right a short distance ahead. A missile turret also hangs from the curved post that extends from the corner of the Perimeter Defense Station. Destroy the missile turret first, then go after the others.

CAUTION

The missile turrets positioned on the Perimeter Defense Station's curved posts fire heavy tracking missiles at you. You can try to shoot down the missiles they fire, but it's tough to hit them. Quickly destroy the missile turrets instead.

WAYPOINT #8

Your path forward is blocked by debris here. Your driver backs up to turn around and head counterclockwise around the station. Blast the missile turret that hangs from the curved post past the debris as you back up.

TIP

Aim to fire at the tops of each gun and missile turret to ensure hits and destroy them quickly.

WAYPOINT #9

There are two more gun turrets to your right here, and there's a missile turret on the arched post at the corner of the central building. Dropships deploy more drop turrets as you pass by here as well. Destroy all of these targets as you roll around the structure, taking out the missile turret first. Fire at the missile turret on the building's northwest corner.

WAYPOINT #10

After destroying the drop turret that's deployed near this force field, you get a chance to catch your breath a bit—your convoy truck stops behind some cover while Lieutenant Voss transmits communications. You soon continue moving counterclockwise around the structure again. Destroy the missile turrets at the building's north and southwest corners, if you haven't already. Then go after the drop turrets that fall from the sky.

WAYPOINT #11

This is the end of the line—you've come full circle and are back at the impenetrable wall of debris again. Destroy the two gun turrets on the outside wall and the drop turret that falls and lands near the debris. Finish off any other turrets you may have missed as you ride back toward the station's entrance.

OBJECTIVE: LOCATE VOSS

WAYPOINT #12

Destroying every turret in the area completes the "Clear Area of Turrets" objective. Climb off the convoy truck when it stops near the station's entrance, then enter the facility. Move toward the large red exit door inside, then activate the nearby control panel to exit the level.

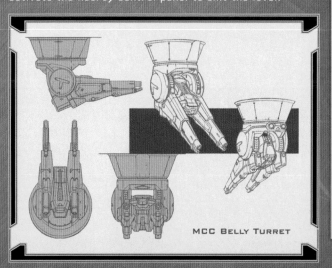

MCC Belly Turret

PERIMETER DEFENSE STATION

OVERVIEW

The Perimeter Defense Station is the first complex you must secure on your way to the Tetranode, which is located deep within the Nexus Hub. Stay sharp as you navigate this facility—the Strogg are aware of your plans to disrupt their mass communication system and will make every effort to stop this from happening. Your first task is to locate Lieutenant Voss, who provides further instructions.

ENEMIES ENCOUNTERED
- Gladiator
- Grunts
- Gunners
- Strogg marines

WEAPONS ACQUIRED
- Nailgun

UPGRADES ACQUIRED
- None

AMMUNITION ACQUIRED
- Clips
- Shells
- Nails

ITEMS ACQUIRED
- Armor shards
- Armor vest, small
- Health pack, large
- Health pack, small

OBJECTIVE: LOCATE VOSS

AMMUNITION

HEALTH

TECHNICIAN

1 WAYPOINT

A CONNECTION

Corporal Shilder (nailgun)

START

WAYPOINT #1

Corporal Schilder (Raven Squad) hands you a nailgun when you approach him in this first room. Collect the pick-ups in the room and speak to Technician Newquist (Raven Squad), who's standing nearby to repair your armor. Then take the elevator down to the floor below.

NOTE

Check the "Weapons and Items" section of this guide for complete details on the nailgun.

OBJECTIVE: RETRIEVE ENGINEER

WALKTHROUGH:
PART 1

AIR DEFENSE BUNKER

AIR DEFENSE TRENCHES

HANGAR PERIMETER

INTERIOR HANGAR

MCC LANDING SITE

OPERATION: ADVANTAGE

CANYON

PERIMETER DEFENSE STATION

AQUEDUCTS

AQUEDUCTS ANNEX

Lieutenant Voss

Legend:

- AMMUNITION
- ARMOR
- HEALTH
- MEDIC
- WEAPON
- ENEMY SPAWN
- 1 WAYPOINT
- A CONNECTION

⬡ =denotes item below or behind an object

WAYPOINT #2

Lieutenant Voss (Rhino Squad) awaits you in this control room. Approach him to complete the "Locate Voss" objective. Voss then orders you to head down to

the complex's basement and retrieve an engineer, who can cut through a door that's sealed off nearby.

WAYPOINT #3

You meet up with Private Rodriguez (Badger Squad) and Private First Class Singer (Raven Squad) just before entering this room. Multiple Strogg marines attack from the room's upper

walkways. Back up your fellow marines and then call the elevator (located in the room) by using the control panel in the room's northwest corner. Step onto the elevator, wait for your buddies to join you, and then activate the elevator's control panel to ride down to the basement.

WAYPOINT #4

Your teammates take up defensive positions in this room's lower center portion. Move to the control panel on the upper walkway; activate it to open the massive door ahead. A grunt and two Strogg marines rush at you from the door after you open it—help your teammates defeat them and then proceed ahead.

- ARMOR
- WAYPOINT
- 1 CONNECTION
- A

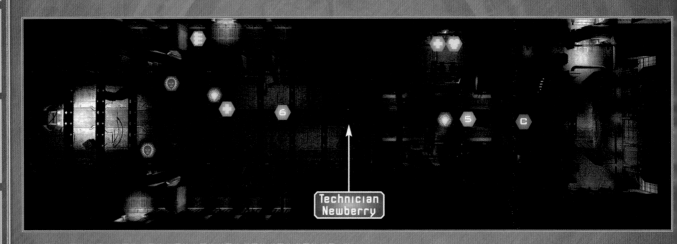

Technician Newberry

- AMMUNITION
- ARMOR
- HEALTH
- ENEMY SPAWN
- 1 WAYPOINT
- A CONNECTION

into the long, wide tunnel. Marines crash in on a convoy truck—help them defeat the waves of Strogg marines that attack from the tunnel's side alcoves.

OBJECTIVE: ESCORT NEWBERRY

WAYPOINT #6

Defeat all of the Strogg that attack the convoy truck, and then scout the area for pick-ups. When you're finished, approach Technician Newberry (Viper Squad) to complete the "Retrieve Engineer" objective. Your new

orders are to escort Newberry back up to the first floor, where he can open a sealed door. Retrace your steps to the elevator you used to reach the basement; use it to return to the first floor.

WAYPOINT #5

You encounter another sealed door in the next chamber. Collect the pick-ups on the elevated platform; then activate the nearby control panel to open the door ahead. Hurry

Please refer to Map on pg. 82]

WAYPOINT #7

You get a few
scares in these
corridors—the
Strogg are trying
to get at you, but
they can't
penetrate the
complex's sealed
windows and
doors. Continue to
Waypoint #8.

OBJECTIVE: SHUT DOWN THE DEFENSE GRID

WAYPOINT #8

You encounter Private First Class Pupino (Cobra Squad)
in this corridor. He gives
you a new objective: find a
way into the Perimeter
Control Room and activate
the control panel within to
shut down the laser defense
grid. This allows the EMP
bomb convoy to proceed
toward the Nexus Hub.

WAYPOINT #9

The door at this room's
south end is the one
Technician Newberry must
cut through. This
completes the "Escort
Newberry" objective. As
Newberry goes about his
task, collect the pick-ups
to the door's right and
then equip your shotgun. Once the door is open, follow
Newberry and Private First Class Jones (Warthog Squad)
into the following room.

After entering the door, a grunt ambushes PFC Jones
and quickly kills him. Blast the grunt and then use the

nearby control
panel to call the
room's lift. Use
the lift to reach
the floor above,
then cross the
walkways and
corridors until
you reach the
next waypoint.

WAYPOINT #10

A portion of the walkway's railing is broken in this
area—this allows you to drop down into the room below.
Activate the control panel in the room to gain access to

another control
panel located in
the same room.
Activate the
second control
panel to shut
down the laser
defense grid and
complete the "Shut
Down the Defense
Grid" objective.

Turn around—
through the
room's shatter-
proof window, you
witness a grunt
kill a hapless
marine. The grunt
then circles
around to enter
the room you're in
through its only
door. Switch to your shotgun as you wait for the grunt
to arrive, then kill it.

OBJECTIVE: REGROUP WITH RHINO SQUAD

Sergeant Bidwell radios in after you kill the grunt. He
orders you to find a way out of the complex and
regroup with your squad. Proceed through the door that
the grunt used to enter the room and head to the next
waypoint.

TIP

On the way to Waypoint #11, head through the first
door on your left to acquire some clips and shells.

WAYPOINT #11

You get your first glimpse
of a Strogg gladiator as
you cross the corridors
and walkways here. You
can't hurt him, so don't
waste your ammo.
Continue along toward
the lift ahead; ride it
down to the first floor.

WALKTHROUGH: PART 1

AIR DEFENSE BUNKER

AIR DEFENSE TRENCHES

HANGAR PERIMETER

INTERIOR HANGAR

MCC LANDING SITE

OPERATION: ADVANTAGE

CANYON

PERIMETER DEFENSE STATION

AQUEDUCTS

AQUEDUCTS ANNEX

	AMMUNITION	**1**	WAYPOINT
	HEALTH	**A**	CONNECTION

Waypoint #13

The elevator brings you back up to the station's entrance. Nab the pick-ups in this room, if you didn't before; then exit the facility through the same door you used to enter.

	AMMUNITION	**1**	WAYPOINT
	WEAPON	**A**	CONNECTION
	ENEMY SPAWN		

Waypoint #12

You now backtrack through the areas of the station's first floor that you previously visited, but they're no longer secure—the Strogg have overrun the marines and killed them all. You're attacked by a fearsome Strogg gladiator in these corridors. Switch to your nailgun and pepper him from range. Strafe back and forth constantly to avoid his railgun fire. After defeating the gladiator, proceed to the southeast elevator and use it to return to the facility's entrance chamber.

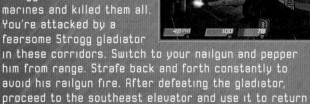

NOTE

Refer to the "Enemies" section of this guide for complete details on the gladiator.

AQUEDUCTS

OVERVIEW

You've shut down the defense grid, and the EMP bomb convoy has taken off toward the Nexus Hub. You're now playing catch-up and must use an GDF hover tank to tear through the Aqueducts as you venture to regroup with your squad. The Aqueducts are heavily defended by Strogg vehicular forces and ground troops, but using the hover tank makes matters much easier for you.

CHAPTER 1 WELCOME TO QUAKE 4

CHAPTER 2 BASIC TRAINING

CHAPTER 3 WEAPONS AND ITEMS

CHAPTER 4 VEHICLES

CHAPTER 5 CHARACTERS

CHAPTER 6 ENEMIES

CHAPTER 7 WALKTHROUGH

CHAPTER 8 MULTIPLAYER

CHAPTER 9 GAMERSCORE ACHIEVEMENTS

ENEMIES ENCOUNTERED
- Hornets
- Gunner
- Gun turrets
- Drop turrets
- Roller creatures
- Heavy tanks
- Strogg marines

WEAPONS ACQUIRED
- None

UPGRADES ACQUIRED
- Firepower mod (nailgun)

AMMUNITION ACQUIRED
- None

ITEMS ACQUIRED
- None

OBJECTIVE: REGROUP WITH RHINO SQUAD

Technician Holtz (Raven Squad) approaches you at the start of the level and installs an upgrade to your nailgun—the firepower mod. Your nailgun now features an enhanced rate of fire and can hold two clips, giving you twice the amount of nails. Speak to Holtz after you receive the firepower mod upgrade if you need to recover armor. Medic Morte (Raven Squad) is also standing nearby; speak to him if you need healing.

When you're ready to go, head through the large orange door and approach the GDF hover tank beyond. Press Ⓑ to enter the hover tank, then roll outside toward Waypoint #1.

NOTE
Please refer to the "Vehicles" section of this guide for complete information on the GDF hover tank.

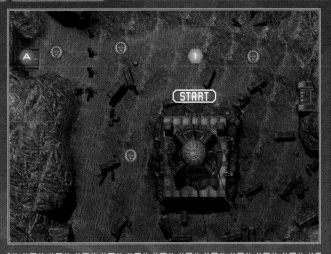

- ⊙ ENEMY SPAWN   Ⓐ CONNECTION
- ① WAYPOINT

WAYPOINT #1
Two Strogg hornets attack you from either side the moment you roll out of the compound. Dodge their tracking missiles and use the hover tank's cannon to bring them both down. Familiarize yourself with the hover tank's unique controls as you do so.

NOTE
Refer to the "Vehicles" section of this guide for complete details on hornets.

There are two other hornets in the area—defeat them both as you continue to gain a feel for the hover tank. Proceed through the large gate to the northwest when you're ready.

NO TIME TO DIE
You'll probably want to defeat each enemy you encounter as you roll through the Aqueducts and Aqueducts Annex levels in your hover tank. But you don't have to! If you are having too much trouble with these areas, simply speed through each zone, stopping only to destroy enemies that block your path. After all, discretion is the better part of valor…

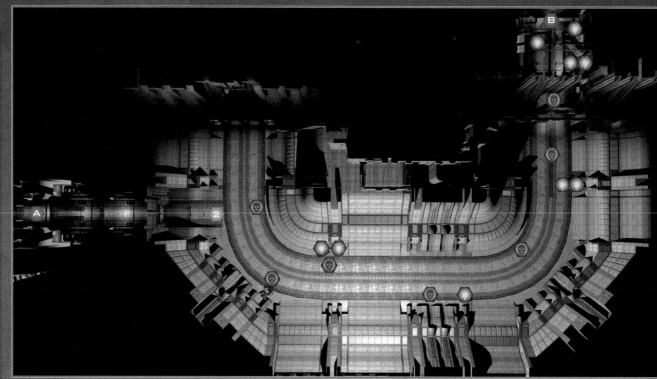

 ENEMY SPAWN

 EXPLOSIVE BARREL

 WAYPOINT

 CONNECTION

WAYPOINT #2

Strogg dropships deploy multiple drop turrets as you roll through this area. Quickly blast each one with the hover tank's cannon.

TIP

Whenever you sustain damage, wait a few seconds and let the hover tank's shields recharge.

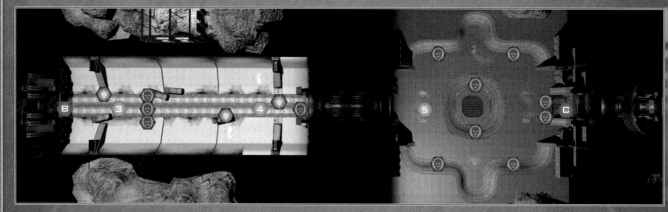

 ENEMY SPAWN

 EXPLOSIVE BARREL

 WAYPOINT

 CONNECTION

WAYPOINT #3

Three hornets lie in wait ahead here. Destroy them as you roll forward. Keep an eye to the sky, and avoid the bombs dropped by the Strogg dropships that fly past as you combat the hornets.

WAYPOINT #4

A Strogg heavy tank engages you as you approach this path's opposite end. Dodge the heavy tracking missiles it fires and pummel it with the hover tank's cannon; then proceed through the large door beyond.

NOTE

Check the "Enemies" section of this guide to learn all about heavy tanks.

WAYPOINT #5

Two hornets fly in from your left as you enter this wide area. They each deploy a Strogg roller creature before they attack. Dodge all hostile fire and destroy the roller creatures; then down the hornets.

Several more roller creatures shoot into the area from the pipes to the north and south. Blast each one with your hover tank's cannon when they become stationary.

NOTE

Refer to the "Vehicles" section of this guide for complete details on roller creatures.

Finally, two heavy tanks enter the area from the large door at the opposite end of the area. Avoid their heavy tracking missiles as best you can, and decimate each one in turn.

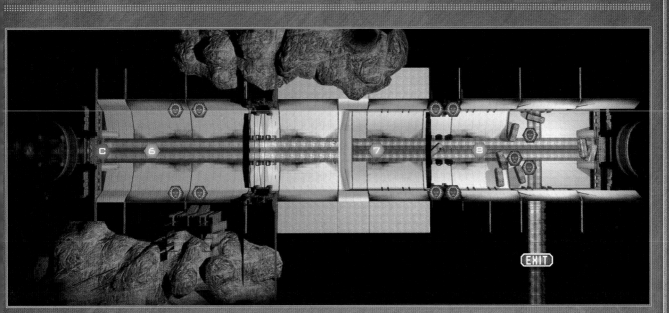

EXIT

Legend

- ⬡ ENEMY SPAWN
- 1 WAYPOINT
- A CONNECTION

WAYPOINT #6

Multiple roller creatures roll down from the banks to your left and right as you enter this long stretch. Blow each one to bits as you strafe to dodge their fire. Roll onward after defeating them all and drop off the edge ahead to land on a lower portion of the path.

WALKTHROUGH: PART 1

AIR DEFENSE BUNKER

AIR DEFENSE TRENCHES

HANGAR PERIMETER

INTERIOR HANGAR

MCC LANDING SITE

OPERATION: ADVANTAGE

CANYON

PERIMETER DEFENSE STATION

AQUEDUCTS

AQUEDUCTS ANNEX

CHAPTER 1
WELCOME TO
QUAKE 4

CHAPTER 2
BASIC TRAINING

CHAPTER 3
WEAPONS AND
ITEMS

CHAPTER 4
VEHICLES

CHAPTER 5
CHARACTERS

CHAPTER 6
ENEMIES

CHAPTER 7
WALKTHROUGH

CHAPTER 8
MULTIPLAYER

CHAPTER 9
GAMERSCORE
ACHIEVEMENTS

WAYPOINT #7

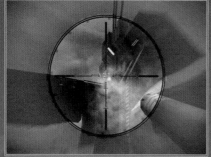

There are four gun turrets affixed to the outside walls high above this portion of the path. The hover tank's cannon can't aim upward very high, so you must fire at them from range to destroy them. Use the cannon's scope to improve accuracy and confirm their destruction before you move on.

WAYPOINT #8

A dropship deploys a host of Strogg marines here, who take cover behind the large train cars. There's a gunner among these troops as well. Kill them all quickly and then proceed down the south tunnel to exit the level.

AQUEDUCTS ANNEX

OVERVIEW

Your race to join up with your squadmates continues through Aqueducts Annex. You encounter much tougher opposition in this level, due in large part to the formidable Strogg harvesters you face. React quickly to enemy ambushes and keep your wits about you at all times.

ENEMIES ENCOUNTERED
- Hornets
- Gunners
- Drop turrets
- Strogg marines
- Harvesters

WEAPONS ACQUIRED
- None

UPGRADES ACQUIRED
- None

AMMUNITION ACQUIRED
- None

ITEMS ACQUIRED
- None

OBJECTIVE: REGROUP WITH RHINO SQUAD

☀	ENEMY SPAWN
1	WAYPOINT
A	CONNECTION

WAYPOINT #1

You witness a giant Strogg harvester rip apart two GDF hover tanks as you enter this area. The harvester then turns its attention to you.

NOTE

Refer to the "Vehicles" section of this guide for complete details on harvesters.

Fire your hover tank's cannon at the harvester's legs to destroy it—you must knock out two legs in order to drop the harvester. Keep your distance from the harvester as you combat it; dodge the mega tracking missiles it fires or shoot them down with your hover tank's heavy machine gun. Be careful not to fall into the large pit that the harvester crawls out of—doing so means instant death. Proceed through the north door after you've killed the harvester.

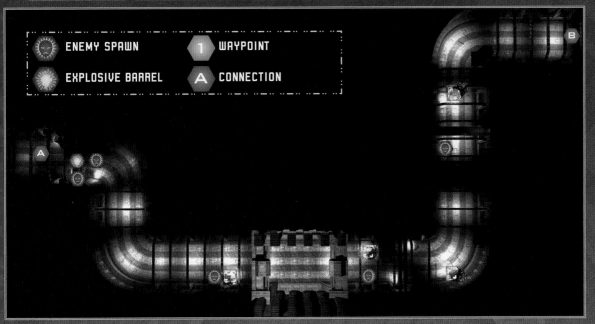

ENEMY SPAWN

EXPLOSIVE BARREL

1 WAYPOINT

A CONNECTION

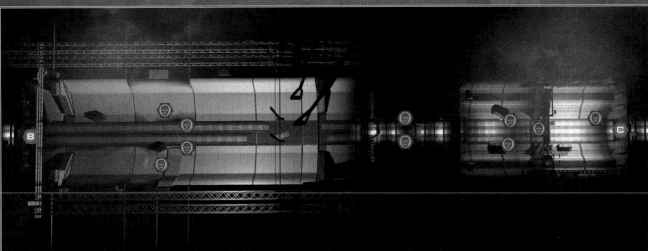

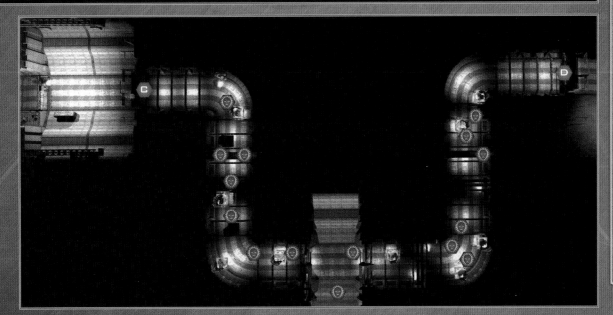

AIR DEFENSE BUNKER

AIR DEFENSE TRENCHES

HANGAR PERIMETER

INTERIOR HANGAR

MCC LANDING SITE

OPERATION: ADVANTAGE

CANYON

PERIMETER DEFENSE STATION

AQUEDUCTS

AQUEDUCTS ANNEX

TERRIBLE TWOSOME

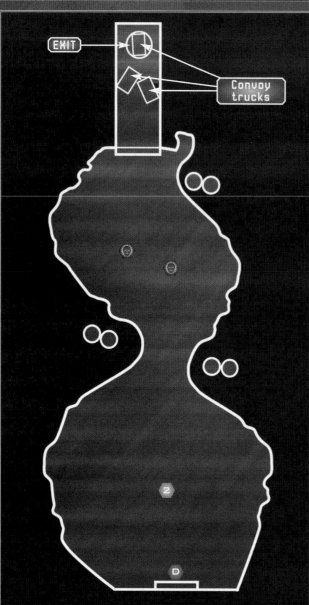

EXIT

Convoy
trucks

 ENEMY SPAWN   ▲ CONNECTION

 WAYPOINT

solid line = wall/object on upper floor
dotted line = wall/object on lower floor
small, thin rectangle = door

WAYPOINT #2

You encounter little resistance after defeating the harvester at the level's beginning. Here, however, you're faced with *two* harvesters at once. Don't rush into the fray—keep your distance and target the legs of the nearest harvester with your hover tank's cannon (use the cannon's scope to improve accuracy). Destroy one harvester, then the other.

[Vehicle Locked]

If you keep your distance, the harvesters can only attack you with their slow-moving mega tracking missiles. Let the missiles come to you as you continue to blast at the harvesters' legs. When the missiles begin to arch downward toward you, switch to your hover tank's heavy machine gun and fire to destroy them. Back up and strafe as necessary to keep the missiles at bay—they inflict massive splash damage when they explode.

NEXUS HUB TUNNELS

The fight becomes much easier after you drop the first harvester. Keep backing up to maintain distance from the second harvester as it advances; continue firing at its legs and missiles as you do so.

TIP

If the harvester's missiles are giving you too much trouble, try destroying the large barrel-shaped missile launchers on their backs.

TIP

Stuck at this harvester fight? No problem—speed past them both and enter the large door beyond to avoid the fight entirely.

After defeating both harvesters, drive into the large door beyond them—Sergeant Morris and Technician Strauss await you inside. This completes the "Regroup with Rhino Squad" objective. Press Ⓑ to exit the hover tank and then run toward your squadmates to exit the level.

OVERVIEW

The Nexus Hub Tunnels lead directly toward the Tetranode, which your squad has been ordered to destroy. However, the EMP bomb convoy cannot proceed through the tunnels until your squad opens the security gates and eliminates the Strogg's defenses. Work with your squadmates to help Technician Strauss reach the control terminals he needs to access in order to allow the convoy to proceed. Expect to encounter extreme resistance from the Strogg through this area—you're getting dangerously close to their central intelligence and communication systems.

ENEMIES ENCOUNTERED
- Berserkers
- Sentries
- Gladiators
- Grunts
- Gunners
- Strogg marines

WEAPONS ACQUIRED
- Hyperblaster

UPGRADES ACQUIRED
- None

AMMUNITION ACQUIRED
- Batteries
- Clips
- Grenades
- Nails
- Shells

ITEMS ACQUIRED
- Armor shards
- Armor vest, small
- Health pack, large
- Health pack, small

WALKTHROUGH: PART 2

NEXUS HUB TUNNELS

NEXUS HUB

STROGG MEDICAL FACILITIES

CONSTRUCTION ZONE

DISPERSAL FACILITY

RECOMPOSITION CENTER

PURIFICATION CENTER

WASTE PROCESSING FACILITY

OPERATION: LAST HOPE

DATA STORAGE TERMINAL

OBJECTIVE: DESTROY THE TETRANODE

AMMUNITION		ENEMY SPAWN
ARMOR		WAYPOINT
HEALTH		CONNECTION

WAYPOINT #1

Collect the many pick-ups in this first area after you complete the long ride down the elevator with Morris and Strauss—you're going to need them. Approach Lieutenant Voss afterward, listen to his instructions, and then follow your squadmates into the next room.

OBJECTIVE: PROTECT STRAUSS

WAYPOINT #2

Strauss hacks into a computer terminal in this area. He then turns on the lights and unlocks the nearby tunnel's sealed security gates so the EMP bomb convoy can proceed through the tunnel to reach the Tetranode. Strauss then informs Voss that the tunnel's temperature is supercool—it would be hazardous for the convoy to proceed until he finds the

tunnel's temperature controls and makes the environment less hostile. Voss agrees and orders you to protect Strauss as he moves to locate the tunnel's temperature controls.

Tip

Strauss may not be the best company, but he is able to restore your armor. Take full advantage.

Waypoint #3

You're ambushed by a gladiator and a few Strogg marines in this chamber— the gladiator enters using the chamber's central elevator. Use your nailgun to make short work of the gladiator, then switch to your machine gun and finish off the Strogg marines. Make sure Strauss survives the assault.

	AMMUNITION		ENEMY SPAWN	A	CONNECTION
	HEALTH	1	WAYPOINT		

Waypoint #4

The temperature controls Strauss seeks are located here. There are pick-ups nearby as well. Guard Strauss from the numerous sentries that attack as he hacks into the temperature controls. This completes the "Protect Strauss" objective.

Note

Check the "Enemies" section of this guide to learn all about sentries.

OBJECTIVE: RETURN TO RHINO SQUAD

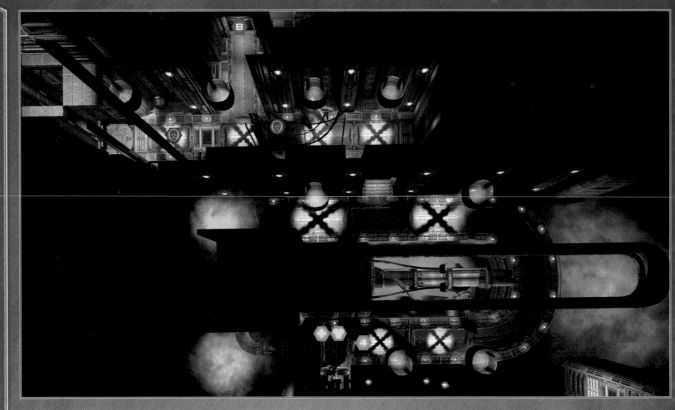

 AMMUNITION
 ARMOR
HEALTH

 ENEMY SPAWN
 WAYPOINT
 CONNECTION

Strauss must remain at the temperature controls in order to maintain them. Lieutenant Voss orders you back to his position. Retrace your steps back to Voss.

WAYPOINT #5

You regroup with Voss and Morris here; they are combating several Strogg marines and a grunt. Help your squadmates kill these enemies, and then proceed through the door ahead. This completes the "Regroup with Rhino Squad" objective.

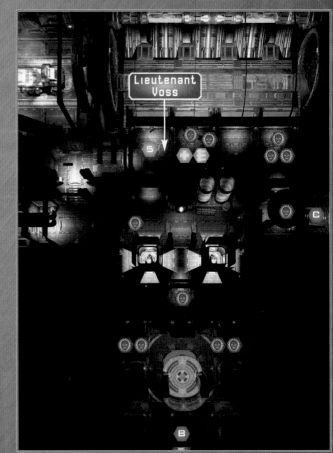

Lieutenant Voss

WALKTHROUGH:
PART 2

NEXUS HUB TUNNELS

NEXUS HUB

STROGG MEDICAL FACILITIES

CONSTRUCTION ZONE

DISPERSAL FACILITY

RECOMPOSITION CENTER

PUTRIFICATION CENTER

WASTE PROCESSING FACILITY

OPERATION: LAST HOPE

DATA STORAGE TERMINAL

▪ AMMUNITION		◆ ENEMY SPAWN	
♥ ARMOR		**1** WAYPOINT	
✚ HEALTH		Ⓐ CONNECTION	

OBJECTIVE: DEACTIVATE THE FORCE FIELD

WAYPOINT #7

A giant force field blocks the way forward here. Lieutenant Voss orders you to explore the area beyond the nearby door and find a way to deactivate the force field. Collect the nearby pick-ups and then proceed through the door.

WAYPOINT #6

Two berserkers rush you on your way to this waypoint—quickly kill them both. Multiple Strogg marines and a gladiator attack you here. Pick off the Strogg marines on the elevated footbridge, then

lob a few grenades at the ground troops. Immediately equip your nailgun and lay into the gladiator to drop him quickly. Switch to your machine gun and finish off any Strogg marines that remain.

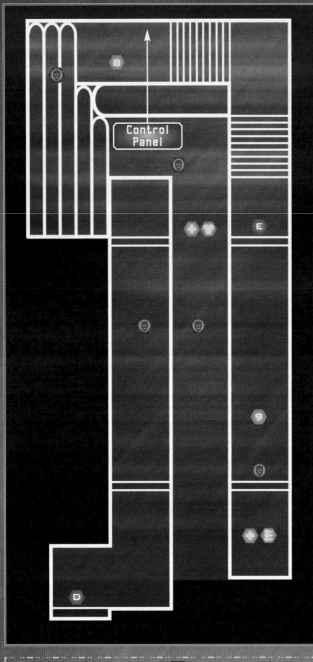

Control
Panel

Legend

 AMMUNITION

ARMOR

HEALTH

 ENEMY SPAWN

1 **WAYPOINT**

A **CONNECTION**

solid line = wall/object on upper floor
dotted line = wall/object on lower floor
small, thin rectangle = door

OBJECTIVE: RETURN TO THE CONVOY

WAYPOINT #8

This room houses the control panel that shuts off the force field. Defeat the sentries you encounter on your way here and then activate the control panel to complete the "Deactivate the Force Field" objective. Voss then radios in and orders you to return to the squad.

Right after you activate the control panel, two Strogg marines enter the room from a higher door—kill them both and then head through the door they emerged from.

WAYPOINT #9

Blast the berserker that charges you as you cross this elevated walkway to reach the far room, where several pick-ups are located. Grab the pick-ups and then back out of the room. Drop down off the upper walkway and land on the thick pipes below. Collect the pick-ups that

are hidden on the pipes and then cross the pipes to reach the lower walkway. Backtrack to your squadmates afterward; they await you beyond the now-deacti-vated force field.

To Crawlspace

| 1 WAYPOINT | A CONNECTION |

WAYPOINT #10

Meeting up with your squad here completes the "Return to the Convoy" objective. Rhino Squad is just about to set off their EMP bomb when a giant Strogg harvester storms in. Don't waste your ammo on the harvester—you can't kill it. The harvester destroys the EMP bomb and kills Sergeant Bidwell before it leaves.

Strauss radios in, saying he believes he knows another way to shut down the Tetranode. Voss orders you to meet

Strauss and help him carry out the mission. You must navigate a series of crawlspaces in order to reach Strauss. Voss stomps a hole in the floor to reveal an entrance to the first crawlspace. Drop into the hole to proceed.

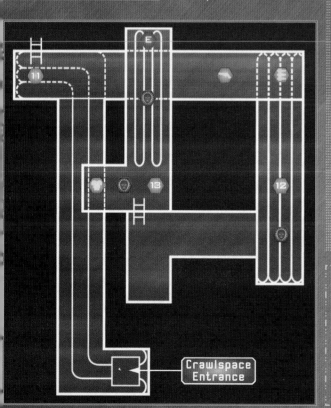

Crawlspace Entrance

WAYPOINT #11

Navigate the first crawlspace until you reach the ladder here. Climb up the ladder, then crouch and crawl to your right to enter the upper crawlspace.

You acquire the hyperblaster as you cross the upper crawlspace, but there's no time to play with it now—a battle is occurring above you, and the crawlspace's glass ceiling won't protect you from harm. Hurry across and drop off the edge ahead before you take too much damage. Proceed through the lower crawlspace ahead.

NOTE

Refer to the "Weapons and Items" section of this guide to learn all about the hyperblaster.

WAYPOINT #12

Defeat the sentry that attacks you at the end of the lower crawlspace. Then perform a jump-crouch maneuver [⬛+Ⓐ, L1] to enter the opening to your right; this leads into yet another crawlspace. You

reach a ladder a short distance ahead—climb up the ladder to proceed.

WAYPOINT #13

Defeat the pair of sentries that attack you after you climb the ladder. Collect the nearby armor shards and then run across the thick pipes that lead toward the next room. There are several pick-ups in the room beyond

the pipes—grab all the ones you need and then head to the next waypoint.

🟦 AMMUNITION		⬡ ENEMY SPAWN	
🛡 ARMOR		1 WAYPOINT	
🔫 WEAPON		A CONNECTION	

solid line = wall/object on upper floor
dotted line = wall/object on lower floor
small, thin rectangle = door

QUAKE 4

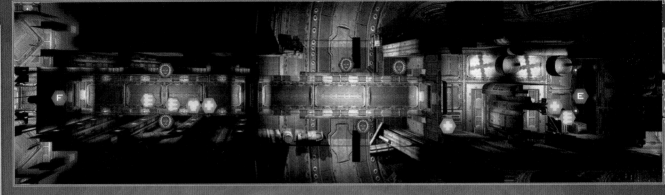

CHAPTER 1
WELCOME TO QUAKE 4

CHAPTER 2
BASIC TRAINING

CHAPTER 3
WEAPONS AND ITEMS

CHAPTER 4
VEHICLES

CHAPTER 5
CHARACTERS

CHAPTER 6
ENEMIES

CHAPTER 7
WALKTHROUGH

CHAPTER 8
MULTIPLAYER

CHAPTER 9
GAMERSCORE ACHIEVEMENTS

NEXUS HUB

OVERVIEW

To say things haven't gone as planed would be the understatement of the century. The EMP bomb has been destroyed, along with most of the transport convoy. Rhino Squad's own Sergeant Bidwell is among the dead. Things are looking grim, indeed.

As a last resort, you've been ordered to meet up with Strauss at the Nexus Hub. Strauss has come up with a contingency plan, but if this mission fails, the war against the Strogg may well become a lost cause.

ENEMIES ENCOUNTERED
- Berserkers
- Sentries
- Gladiators
- Grunts
- Gunners
- Makron
- Nexus protector
- Strogg marines

WEAPONS ACQUIRED
- None

UPGRADES ACQUIRED
- None

AMMUNITION ACQUIRED
- Batteries
- Clips
- Grenades
- Nails
- Shells

ITEMS ACQUIRED
- Armor shards
- Armor vest, small
- Health pack, large
- Health pack, small

 AMMUNITION   ENEMY SPAWN

ARMOR   **1** WAYPOINT

HEALTH   **A** CONNECTION

=denotes item below or behind an object

WAYPOINT #14

Defeat the enemies that attack you in this giant chamber as you move up the steps to reach the overhead walkway. Use the walkway's elevator to exit the level.

OBJECTIVE: DESTROY THE TETRANODE WITH STRAUSS

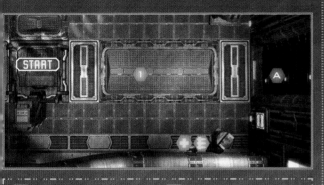

▣ AMMUNITION	⬡ 1 WAYPOINT
✚ HEALTH	Ⓐ CONNECTION

WAYPOINT #1

Strauss radios in as you ride the elevator into this first room of the Nexus Hub. He asks you to hurry and meet him, saying he's in great danger. Grab the pick-ups in the corner of the room, and then use the east elevator to proceed.

OBJECTIVE: ACTIVATE THE POWER PLANT

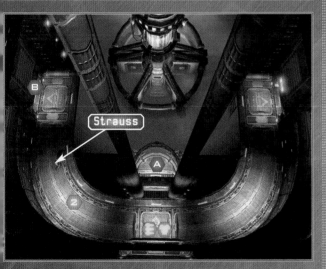

▣ AMMUNITION	⬡ 1 WAYPOINT
⬖ ARMOR	Ⓐ CONNECTION

WAYPOINT #2

The elevator brings you to this wide chamber, where you meet up with Strauss. This completes the "Destroy the Tetranode with Strauss" objective. Strauss points toward the giant device in the chamber's center and informs you that it is the Tetranode—the object you must destroy to cripple the Strogg's communication system. Strauss then tells you he must find and activate the facility's power plant. Protect Strauss and ensure he survives the journey. Lead him through the chamber's west door.

TIP

Climb down the utility ladder near the chamber's locked east door to locate a secret cache of pick-ups beneath the central elevator.

WALKTHROUGH: PART 2

NEXUS HUB TUNNELS
NEXUS HUB
STROGG MEDICAL FACILITIES
CONSTRUCTION ZONE
DISPERSAL FACILITY
RECOMPOSITION CENTER
PUTRIFICATION CENTER
WASTE PROCESSING FACILITY
OPERATION: LAST HOPE
DATA STORAGE TERMINAL

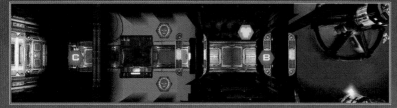

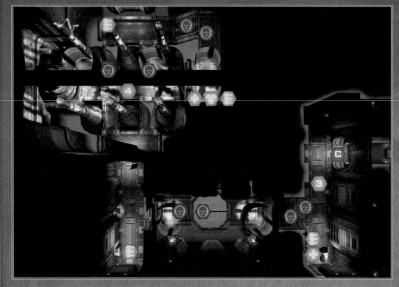

WAYPOINT #3

Two sentries attack you on your way to these corridors, and the battle really heats up here. Two grunts and several Strogg marines come at you in waves—kill them all quickly and don't let the grunts come near Strauss. After the fight, collect the pick-ups in these corridors and speak with Strauss to recover your armor.

WAYPOINT #4

This large chamber is full of Strogg. Defeat the two sentries hovering in the room's center; then move to kill the Strogg marines and gunner on the east balcony. Strauss then rushes to a control panel on the east balcony and activates the facility's power plant, hoping to cause the Tetranode to overheat and self-destruct. This completes the "Activate the Power Plant" objective.

AMMUNITION		ENEMY SPAWN
ARMOR		WAYPOINT
HEALTH		CONNECTION

OBJECTIVE: FIND THE EMERGENCY SHUTOFF CONTROLS

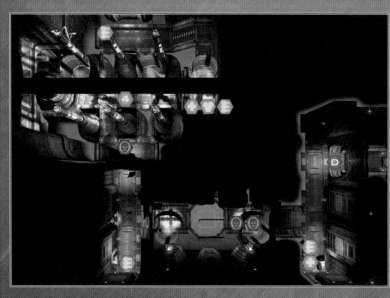

Next, Strauss informs you that he must locate the facility's emergency shutoff controls—he needs to hack them to prevent the emergency shutoff system from stopping the Tetranode from overheating. A gladiator then stomps into the chamber from the same door you entered from. Defeat the gladiator, collect the many nearby pick-ups, and then backtrack toward the Tetranode chamber.

Legend

- 🔋 **AMMUNITION**
- 🛡️ **ARMOR**
- ✚ **HEALTH**
- ☀️ **ENEMY SPAWN**
- **1** **WAYPOINT**
- **A** **CONNECTION**

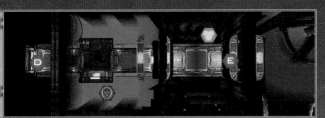

WALKTHROUGH:
PART 2

NEXUS HUB TUNNELS

NEXUS HUB

STROGG MEDICAL FACILITIES

CONSTRUCTION ZONE

DISPERSAL FACILITY

RECOMPOSITION CENTER

PURIFICATION CENTER

WASTE PROCESSING FACILITY

OPERATION: LAST HOPE

DATA STORAGE TERMINAL

WAYPOINT #5

Your backtracking voyage is largely uneventful—you face only a few enemies on your way to this waypoint. Enter the now-unlocked east door in the Tetranode chamber to reach these corridors, where you face a tough fight against a Strogg marine, a grunt, and a gunner. The gunner is on an elevated ledge and can't attack you if you don't rush in, so keep your distance and defeat the other two enemies first. Then move to eliminate the gunner.

WAYPOINT #6

You're ambushed by a grunt shortly after you enter this chamber, and there's a Strogg marine farther ahead. You see a gladiator in the distance as well, but he must walk around to the north stairs before he can enter the chamber and attack you. Defeat the grunt and the Strogg marine, then open fire on the gladiator as it approaches from the north stairs. Equip your shotgun and proceed up the stairs after you destroy the gladiator.

WAYPOINT #7

A grunt jumps at you as you move through this corridor—kill it quickly with the shotgun. Another grunt and a Strogg marine ambush you as you round the following corner, and a distant Strogg marine opens fire from the hall's far end. Kill the grunt first and then defeat the two Strogg marines. Next, use the lift ahead to reach the floor above.

Objective: Shut Down the Coolant Pumps

AMMUNITION		**ENEMY SPAWN**	
ARMOR		1 **WAYPOINT**	
HEALTH		A **CONNECTION**	

Waypoint #8

Strauss runs to the emergency shutoff controls in this large room and disables them. This completes the "Find the Emergency Shutoff Controls" objective. He then tells you to locate and deactivate the coolant pumps, which will cause the Tetranode to quickly overheat. Move to the stockpile of pick-ups to the east, gear up, then turn around and head through the far west door.

Coolant Pump controls

The Makron

Waypoint #9

No enemies attack you on your trip to this large chamber, where the coolant pump controls are located. Equip your hyperblaster, then activate the control panel in the chamber's

center to shut down the coolant pump system. This completes the "Shut Down the Coolant Pumps" objective.

You've done your part to destroy the Tetranode and render the Nexus useless to the Strogg, but you're not out of danger yet—two Strogg cyberspiders (the Nexus protectors) enter the chamber and attack you at once.

Open fire on one of the cyberspiders with your hyperblaster as you backpedal to avoid their initial flamethrower assault. Strafe to dodge the rockets they fire next, and jump to reduce the amount of splash damage you suffer from near misses. Keep firing until you slay one cyberspider and then unleash your hyperblaster on the other.

Note

Refer to the "Enemies" section of this guide for complete details on cyberspiders.

The Makron's Revenge

With little warning, the Makron—the supreme leader of the Strogg—tears through the massive door at the chamber's far end and attacks. Lay into him with your hyperblaster, and strafe constantly to avoid his volleys of heavy blaster shots. The Makron eventually fires several red-colored grenades into the air, which land around the chamber and then detonate—stay clear of the grenades to reduce the amount of splash damage you suffer.

If you survive the Makron's grenade attack, he becomes tired of toying with you and unleashes his dark matter gun on you. There's no way to avoid this devastating attack, and you're not meant to...the Makron wins this fight.

CHAPTER 1 WELCOME TO QUAKE 4
CHAPTER 2 BASIC TRAINING
CHAPTER 3 WEAPONS AND ITEMS
CHAPTER 4 VEHICLES
CHAPTER 5 CHARACTERS
CHAPTER 6 ENEMIES
CHAPTER 7 WALKTHROUGH
CHAPTER 8 MULTIPLAYER
CHAPTER 9 GAMERSCORE ACHIEVEMENTS

STROGG MEDICAL FACILITIES

OVERVIEW

The Makron did not kill you, though he easily could have. Instead, you awaken in the Strogg's Medical Facilities—but you're not here to be nursed. You are "Stroggified" instead; many of your appendages are severed and replaced with mechanical ones. You are now a cybernetic organism, and you would have been forced to join the Strogg race if it weren't for a timely rescue by your fellow Rhino Squad marines. Now you must fight your way out of the facility.

ENEMIES ENCOUNTERED
- Berserkers
- Gladiator
- Gunners
- Strogg marines
- Strogg scientist
- Strogg tactical
- Tele dropper

WEAPONS ACQUIRED
- Blaster
- Grenade launchers
- Hyperblaster
- Nailgun
- Rocket launcher
- Shotgun

UPGRADES ACQUIRED
- None

AMMUNITION ACQUIRED
- Clips
- Grenades
- Nails
- Shells

ITEMS ACQUIRED
- Armor shards
- Armor vest, large
- Armor vest, small
- Health pack, large
- Health pack, small

OBJECTIVE: FOLLOW ANDERSON

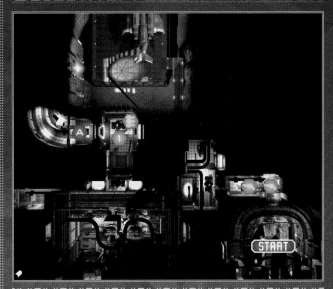

E AMMUNITION		**1** WAYPOINT	
WEAPON		**A** CONNECTION	

Rhino Squad has saved you from complete Stroggification at the very last second, but most of the damage has been done—you're now a horrific hybrid of Strogg and man. Follow Medic Anderson, who has been ordered to escort you to safety. You have no weapons at the start of this level, so grab all the ones you see as you follow Anderson to the first waypoint.

OBJECTIVE: REGROUP WITH RHINO SQUAD

WAYPOINT #1

Follow Anderson to this waypoint, collecting a blaster, a shotgun, and a grenade launcher on your way. Here, you witness the Strogg shoot down the GDF dropship *Falcon 5*—your ride to safety has been destroyed. This completes  the "Follow Anderson" objective. Lieutenant Voss then radios in, ordering you and Anderson to regroup. Follow Anderson to the next waypoint.

WAYPOINT #2

A Strogg scientist kills Anderson in this room. After the cutscene, defeat the three scientists that attack you. Collect Anderson's machine gun afterward.

NOTE

Refer to the "Enemies" section of this guide for complete details on scientists.

Now that you are part Strogg, you can use any Strogg Health Station you see. After killing the scientists, approach the one in this room and activate its control panel to heal up. (You have a maximum of 125 health and armor now that you're part Strogg.) Activate the nearby control panel afterward to open the room's doors and then proceed to the next waypoint.

Legend

AMMUNITION	ENEMY SPAWN
HEALTH	1 WAYPOINT
WEAPON	A CONNECTION

Control Panel

Control Panel

WAYPOINT #3

	AMMUNITION		ENEMY SPAWN
	ARMOR	1	WAYPOINT
	HEALTH	A	CONNECTION
	WEAPON		

Collect the nailgun and nails in this corridor, then defeat the enemies that ambush you. Take the conveyer belt ahead to reach the next waypoint.

WAYPOINT #4

Defeat the Strogg marines in this room, then use the nearby control panel to call an elevator. Use the elevator to reach a higher floor.

WAYPOINT #5

Defeat the two Strogg marines and the berserker that attack you in this room. Collect the rocket launcher from the nearby corpse and nab the other pick-ups in the area before moving on.

WALKTHROUGH: PART 2

NEXUS HUB TUNNELS

NEXUS HUB

STROGG MEDICAL FACILITIES

CONSTRUCTION ZONE

DISPERSAL FACILITY

RECOMPOSITION CENTER

PUTRIFICATION CENTER

WASTE PROCESSING FACILITY

OPERATION: LAST HOPE

DATA STORAGE TERMINAL

CHAPTER 1 WELCOME TO QUAKE 4
CHAPTER 2 BASIC TRAINING
CHAPTER 3 WEAPONS AND ITEMS
CHAPTER 4 VEHICLES
CHAPTER 5 CHARACTERS
CHAPTER 6 ENEMIES
CHAPTER 7 WALKTHROUGH
CHAPTER 8 MULTIPLAYER
CHAPTER 9 GAMERSCORE ACHIEVEMENTS

WAYPOINT #6

At this waypoint, a gladiator and a few Strogg marines round the bend ahead and attack. Kill the gladiator first and then go after the Strogg marines. Collect the nearby health packs and proceed to the next waypoint.

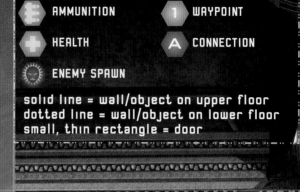

AMMUNITION		1	WAYPOINT
HEALTH		A	CONNECTION
ENEMY SPAWN			

solid line = wall/object on upper floor
dotted line = wall/object on lower floor
small, thin rectangle = door

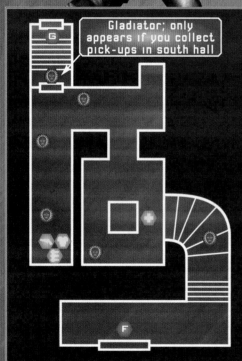

Gladiator; only appears if you collect pick-ups in south hall

WAYPOINT #7

After battling your way past a host of enemies, you finally encounter Lieutenant Voss here. However, you are separated from him by a door that won't open. Voss tells you to find another way around.

WAYPOINT #8

After talking to Voss, backtrack down the stairs and move to this waypoint. Kill the berserker that rushes through a door that was previously locked, then enter the door and use the lift beyond to proceed.

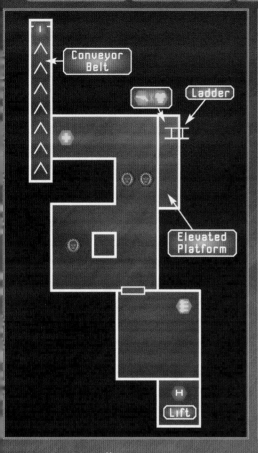

WALKTHROUGH:
PART 2

NEXUS HUB TUNNELS

NEXUS HUB

STROGG MEDICAL FACILITIES

CONSTRUCTION ZONE

DISPERSAL FACILITY

RECOMPOSITION CENTER

PURIFICATION CENTER

WASTE PROCESSING FACILITY

OPERATION: LAST HOPE

DATA STORAGE TERMINAL

Waypoint #9

Use a conveyer belt to reach this odd chamber. Then use one of the rotating platforms in this chamber to reach the south passage and proceed.

🔋 AMMUNITION		⬡ ENEMY SPAWN	
🛡 ARMOR		1 WAYPOINT	
➕ HEALTH		A CONNECTION	
🔫 WEAPON			

solid line = wall/object on upper floor
dotted line = wall/object on lower floor
small, thin rectangle = door

Waypoint #10

You finally meet up with Voss in this room. This completes the "Regroup with Rhino Squad" objective. The reunion is cut short when a Strogg tactical smashes out of his cryotube, grabs Voss, and then escapes through a hole in the floor. You can't follow after Voss, so kill the berserker that rushes in to attack and then continue onward.

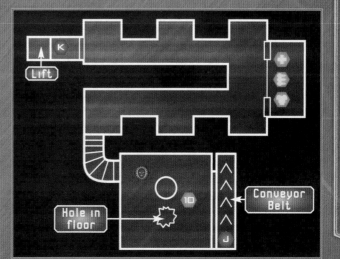

OBJECTIVE: REGROUP

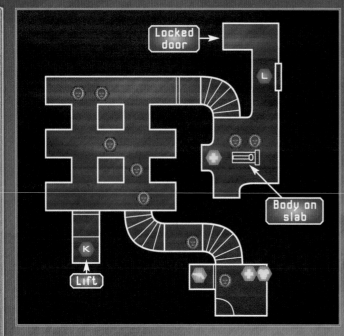

Locked door

L

Body on slab

K

Lift

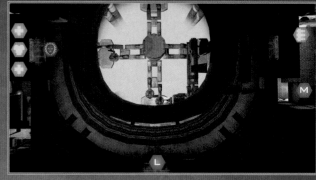

L

N

M

HQ soon radios in and orders you to regroup with the remaining marines at the complex's waste facility. Use the nearby lift to reach a higher floor.

WAYPOINT #11

You acquire the hyper-blaster as you enter this dark crawlspace. You also catch your first glimpse of a frightening Strogg tele-dropper. Collect pick-ups in the crawlspace before you leave—a tough fight is ahead.

125   125

NOTE

Check the "Enemies" section of this guide to learn all about tele droppers.

▤ AMMUNITION		✹ ENEMY SPAWN	
✊ ARMOR		1 WAYPOINT	
✚ HEALTH		A CONNECTION	
🔫 WEAPON			

⬡ =denotes item below or behind an object

solid line = wall/object on upper floor
dotted line = wall/object on lower floor
small, thin rectangle = door

CHAPTER 1 WELCOME TO QUAKE 4
CHAPTER 2 BASIC TRAINING
CHAPTER 3 WEAPONS AND ITEMS
CHAPTER 4 VEHICLES
CHAPTER 5 CHARACTERS
CHAPTER 6 ENEMIES
CHAPTER 7 WALKTHROUGH
CHAPTER 8 MULTIPLAYER
CHAPTER 9 GAMERSCORE ACHIEVEMENTS

O

11

N

ENEMY SPAWN

1 WAYPOINT

A CONNECTION

WALKTHROUGH:
PART 2

NEXUS HUB
TUNNELS

NEXUS HUB

STROGG
MEDICAL
FACILITIES

CONSTRUCTION ZONE

DISPERSAL
FACILITY

RECOMPOSITION
CENTER

PUTRIFICATION
CENTER

WASTE
PROCESSING
FACILITY

OPERATION:
LAST HOPE

DATA
STORAGE
TERMINAL

WAYPOINT #12

Equip your grenade launcher as you exit the crawl-space and enter this wide chamber. A trapdoor in the middle of chamber's floor opens to reveal a tele dropper. Keep your distance and fire multiple grenades at the tele dropper to quickly kill it—the splash damage from your grenades kills the enemies that the tele dropper attempts to spawn. Proceed to the level's exit point afterward.

CONSTRUCTION ZONE

OVERVIEW

Exiting the Strogg Medical Facility was no easy task, but you've done it. The cost was high, however—many of your squadmates have been killed... or worse. The Construction Zone is a huge area, and you must cover a lot of ground in order to reach the next facility. Fortunately, you have the aid of an GDF walker to help you complete the journey.

ENEMIES ENCOUNTERED

- Hornets
- Gladiators
- Gunners
- Heavy tanks
- Drop turrets
- Roller creatures
- Strogg marines
- Harvester

WEAPONS ACQUIRED

- Hyperblaster
- Machine gun
- Shotgun

UPGRADES ACQUIRED

- None

AMMUNITION ACQUIRED

- Grenades

ITEMS ACQUIRED

- Armor vest, small
- Health pack, large
- Health pack, small

CHAPTER 1
WELCOME TO
QUAKE 4

CHAPTER 2
BASIC TRAINING

CHAPTER 3
WEAPONS AND
ITEMS

CHAPTER 4
VEHICLES

CHAPTER 5
CHARACTERS

CHAPTER 6
ENEMIES

CHAPTER 7
WALKTHROUGH

CHAPTER 8
MULTIPLAYER

CHAPTER 9
GAMERSCORE
ACHIEVEMENTS

OBJECTIVE: LOCATE THE DISPERSAL FACILITY

- **AMMUNITION**
- **ARMOR**
- **HEALTH**
- **ENEMY SPAWN**
- **WEAPON**
- **1 WAYPOINT**
- **A CONNECTION**

Collect the many pick-ups near the starting point and then enter the nearby GDF walker. Familiarize yourself with the walker's controls and features as you pick off the distant gunner on your way to the first waypoint.

NOTE

Refer to the "Vehicles" section of this guide for complete details on the GDF walker.

WAYPOINT #1

Two hornets enter from the right and deploy roller creatures before engaging you. Use the walker's heavy machine gun to destroy these threats.

TIP

The walker's shields aren't nearly as sturdy as the hover tank's. Be sure to let them recharge after each skirmish.

WAYPOINT #2

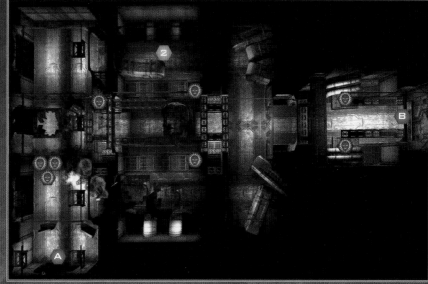

Kill the Strogg marines and gunner on your way to this location. Here, two gladiators emerge from nearby lifts and attack. Kill each one in turn using the walker's heavy machine gun, and strafe to dodge their devastating railgun attacks. Then proceed to the next waypoint, killing the pair of gunners that ambush you as you go.

WALKTHROUGH:
PART 2

NEXUS HUB TUNNELS

NEXUS HUB

STROGG MEDICAL FACILITIES

CONSTRUCTION ZONE

DISPERSAL FACILITY

RECOMPOSITION CENTER

PUTRIFICATION CENTER

WASTE PROCESSING FACILITY

OPERATION: LAST HOPE

DATA STORAGE TERMINAL

| ENEMY SPAWN | 1 WAYPOINT | A CONNECTION |

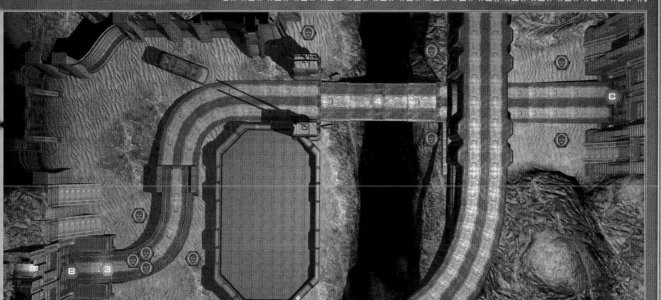

WAYPOINT #3

Kill the trio of Strogg marines you encounter here. Two drop turrets fall in to attack a short distance ahead. Fire at one as it falls, destroying it before its shields come up when it lands. Then blast the other.

WAYPOINT #4

You're ambushed by two heavy tanks as you cross this bridge. Defeat each heavy tank in turn as you shoot down their heavy tracking missiles, and strafe to dodge their nailgun fire.

TIP

Drop turrets make an earsplitting sound as they drop from the sky—look up when you hear that sound and start shooting.

Waypoint #5

Kill the Strogg marines and gunner that attack you as you approach this waypoint. You intercept a Strogg communication that tells you an aerial strike is en route. Move forward until you see a Strogg dropship fly overhead and then immediately backpedal. Wait for the subsequent wave of dropships to deploy all of their bombs before you proceed.

Waypoint #6

The Dispersal Facility isn't far from here, and the Strogg put up a strong defense. You face multiple Strogg marines and a couple of hornets that deploy roller creatures. You also encounter some drop turrets and a couple of heavy tanks. Allow your walker's shields to recharge after each wave of enemies you defeat, and keep moving to avoid their attacks.

⬡ ENEMY SPAWN   1 WAYPOINT   A CONNECTION

Waypoint #7

ENEMY SPAWN

1 WAYPOINT

A CONNECTION

A formidable harvester engages you as you near this waypoint. Keep away from the harvester throughout the fight and fire at its legs with your walker's weaponry. You can strafe to dodge the harvester's nailgun fire, but your walker can't outmaneuver its mega tracking missiles. Use your walker's heavy machine gun to shoot the hostile missiles from the sky whenever they draw near. Then continue to pound away at the harvester's legs until you defeat it. The pipes over the lower area can be used as cover from the harvester's tracking missiles, but they will be destroyed if they take too much damage. The lower area is a great place to maneuver around the harvester and hide while regenerating armor and shields, but once the pipes are destroyed, the harvester can follow you in, effectively blocking your escape.

DISPERSAL FACILITY

OVERVIEW

You've battled your way into the Dispersal Facility, which is the first of three complexes you must traverse in order to reach the Waste Processing Facility, where all surviving GDF marines have been ordered to regroup. This level has a few tricky areas—right at the start, you must combat a hoard of Strogg tacticals backed by a gladiator. Keep your eyes peeled for pick-ups as you navigate the facility and proceed with caution.

ENEMIES ENCOUNTERED
- Gladiators
- Grunts
- Gunners
- Tacticals
- Strogg marines
- Harvester

WEAPONS ACQUIRED
- Hyperblasters
- Machine guns
- Railguns
- Shotguns

UPGRADES ACQUIRED
- None

AMMUNITION ACQUIRED
- Batteries
- Clips
- Grenades
- Nails
- Shells

ITEMS ACQUIRED
- Armor shards
- Armor vest, large
- Armor vest, small
- Health pack, large
- Health pack, small

Press **B** to exit your walker after you destroy the harvester. Run to the level's exit door and activate the nearby control panel to enter the Strogg's Dispersal Facility. This completes the "Locate the Dispersal Facility" objective.

WALKTHROUGH: PART 2

NEXUS HUB TUNNELS

NEXUS HUB

STROGG MEDICAL FACILITIES

CONSTRUCTION ZONE

DISPERSAL FACILITY

RECOMPOSITION CENTER

PUTRIFICATION CENTER

WASTE PROCESSING FACILITY

OPERATION: LAST HOPE

DATA STORAGE TERMINAL

OBJECTIVE: REGROUP

You're ambushed by several Strogg tacticals as soon as you enter the Dispersal Facility. One of these enemies is armed with a railgun, so be on your guard and use objects in the environment as cover. A gladiator eventually makes his way into the fight from the area's far side. Defeat all of these enemies and collect the weaponry they drop to bolster your ammo cache and acquire the awesome railgun.

TIP

Scour this first area thoroughly to find multiple health packs and armor vests.

NOTE

Refer to the "Enemies" section of this guide for complete details on tacticals. Check the "Weapons and Items" section to learn all about the railgun.

WAYPOINT #1

Use a lift to reach this elevated catwalk. A mammoth harvester fires its twin nailguns at you as you run along the rail. Fire a rocket or two at the harvester to distract it while you run past. Crouch to pass under the wreckage at the rail's far end and proceed.

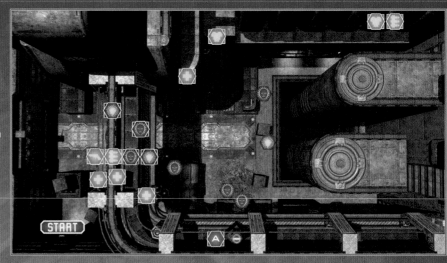

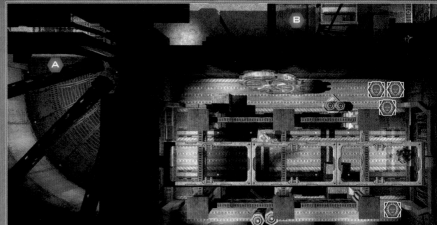

AMMUNITION	✚ HEALTH	✦ EXPLOSIVE BARREL	1 WAYPOINT
ARMOR	⬟ WEAPON	✸ ENEMY SPAWN	A CONNECTION

⬡ =denotes item below or behind an object

Waypoint #2

You encounter nothing stronger than a few grunts and gunners on your way to this waypoint. At the waypoint, however, a gladiator engages you, along with a few Strogg marines. The confines of this area make it tough to battle the gladiator, so don't hold back—unleash your rocket launcher on him to drop him quickly, and keep your distance to avoid splash damage.

AMMUNITION

HEALTH

WEAPON

EXPLOSIVE BARREL

ENEMY SPAWN

1 WAYPOINT

A CONNECTION

AMMUNITION	HEALTH	EXPLOSIVE BARREL	1 WAYPOINT
ARMOR	WEAPON	ENEMY SPAWN	A CONNECTION

= denotes item below or behind an object

solid line = wall/object on upper floor
dotted line = wall/object on lower floor
small, thin rectangle = door

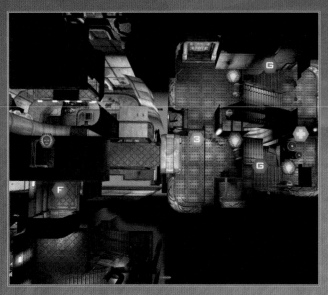

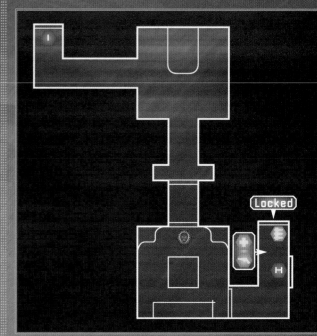

WAYPOINT #3

This waypoint marks the top of a long double-flight of stairs with five separate landings. Here you face multiple tacticals and a gunner; watch out for the numerous explosive barrels as well. Proceed with caution and listen for the sounds of the tacticals' chatter to help identify their locations. Try to use the explosive barrels to your advantage—you can push most of them downstairs and then fire at them to weaken or kill enemies below.

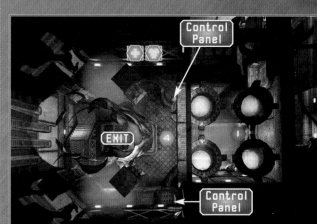

WAYPOINT #4

You must activate two separate control panels in this room in order to cause the giant, pulsating heart in the room's center to "malfunction." Two Strogg repair bots then float out of a passage that opens up below the heart. Drop into the passage and crawl into the tunnel to exit the level.

CHAPTER 1 WELCOME TO QUAKE 4
CHAPTER 2 BASIC TRAINING
CHAPTER 3 WEAPONS AND ITEMS
CHAPTER 4 VEHICLES
CHAPTER 5 CHARACTERS
CHAPTER 6 ENEMIES
CHAPTER 7 WALKTHROUGH
CHAPTER 8 MULTIPLAYER
CHAPTER 9 GAMERSCORE ACHIEVEMENTS

RECOMPOSITION CENTER

OVERVIEW

The Recomposition Center is a tough area full of Strogg. You face many difficult combat scenarios in the outdoor areas here, where tacticals open fire at you from nearly all directions. Use the explosive barrels in the environment to your advantage as you combat these enemies, and scour each area for pick-ups. Exercise sound combat tactics, and, if necessary, use heavier weaponry like the nailgun, railgun, and lightning gun.

ENEMIES ENCOUNTERED
- Gladiator
- Grunts
- Gunners
- Light tank
- Strogg marines
- Tacticals
- Tele dropper

WEAPONS ACQUIRED
- Lightning gun
- Machine guns
- Railguns
- Shotguns

UPGRADES ACQUIRED
- Nail seeker mod (nailgun)

AMMUNITION ACQUIRED
- Batteries
- Clips
- Grenades
- Lightning coils
- Nails
- Shells

ITEMS ACQUIRED
- Armor shards
- Armor vest, large
- Armor vest, small
- Health pack, large
- Health pack, small

OBJECTIVE: LOCATE EXIT

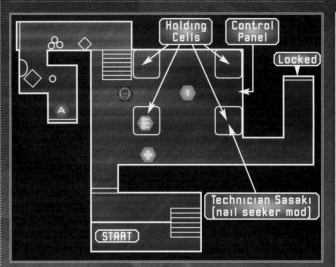

AMMUNITION
HEALTH
ENEMY SPAWN
1 WAYPOINT
A CONNECTION

solid line = wall/object on upper floor
dotted line = wall/object on lower floor
small, thin rectangle = door

WAYPOINT #1

Defeat the gunner in this room and then activate the nearby control panel to free Technician Sasaki (Kodiak Squad) from his holding cell. Sasaki thanks you and upgrades your nailgun with the nail seeker

mod—you may now zoom in on enemies with a scope by pressing LT. Enemies you view in this fashion are targeted by circular reticles. Nails you fire at targeted enemies track the enemy's location—very handy for picking off distant or quick-moving foes.

You must now help Sasaki find a way out of the facility. Proceed to the next waypoint.

TIP

Open the other holding cells in this room to reveal some goodies.

OBJECTIVE: ACTIVATE BARREL PROCESS

CHAPTER 1
WELCOME TO
QUAKE 4

CHAPTER 2
BASIC TRAINING

CHAPTER 3
WEAPONS AND
ITEMS

CHAPTER 4
VEHICLES

CHAPTER 5
CHARACTERS

CHAPTER 6
ENEMIES

CHAPTER 7
WALKTHROUGH

CHAPTER 8
MULTIPLAYER

CHAPTER 9
GAMERSCORE
ACHIEVEMENTS

Broken

AMMUNITION   **ENEMY SPAWN**

HEALTH   **1 WAYPOINT**

WEAPON   **A CONNECTION**

solid line = wall/object on upper floor
dotted line = wall/object on lower floor
small, thin rectangle = door

WAYPOINT #2

Sasaki approaches a control panel in this room. He notices a path above that seems to be a route out of the facility, but it's too high to reach—you must climb the stacks of barrels in the room. Sasaki then tells you to move ahead and find a way to activate the barrel-processing assembly line so he can stack the barrels and create an escape route.

WAYPOINT #3

An GDF marine is being used as a test subject for a powerful Strogg weapon in this chamber—the lightning gun. Deactivate the controls behind the gun to obtain it. The marine dies from the torture, but you now have a powerful new weapon.

NOTE

Check the "Weapon and Items" section of this guide for complete details on the lightning gun.

OBJECTIVE: ACTIVATE PROCESS

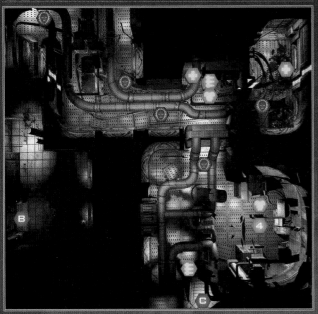

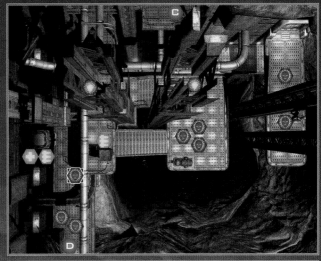

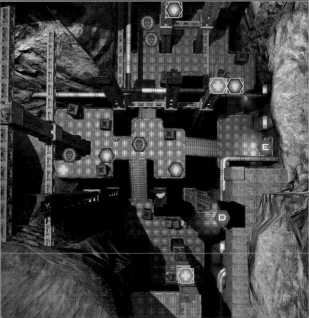

WALKTHROUGH: PART 2

- NEXUS HUB TUNNELS
- NEXUS HUB
- STROGG MEDICAL FACILITIES
- CONSTRUCTION ZONE
- DISPERSAL FACILITY
- RECOMPOSITION CENTER
- PUTRIFICATION CENTER
- WASTE PROCESSING FACILITY
- OPERATION: LAST HOPE
- DATA STORAGE TERMINAL

Legend

⬡ AMMUNITION		⬡ ENEMY SPAWN	
⬡ ARMOR		1 WAYPOINT	
⬡ HEALTH		A CONNECTION	
⬡ EXPLOSIVE BARREL			

⬡ =denotes item below or behind an object

WAYPOINT #4

Activate the control panel in this room to activate the barrel-processing assembly line. This completes the "Activate Barrel Process" objective. Sasaki radios in and says you must next activate the barrel sterilization process in order to get the barrels moving on the assembly line. Proceed through the nearby door toward the sterilization controls.

WAYPOINT #5

You face a tough fight against multiple Strogg tacticals and a gladiator in this wide area of stairs and walkways. Use the many explosive barrels in the environment to help you weaken and kill these enemies. Use the lightning gun or rocket launcher against the gladiator to quickly defeat him.

OBJECTIVE: ACTIVATE PROCESS

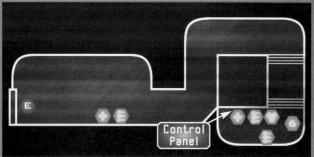

Legend:
- AMMUNITION
- ARMOR
- HEALTH
- EXPLOSIVE BARREL
- ENEMY SPAWN
- 1 WAYPOINT
- A CONNECTION
- = denotes item below or behind an object

WAYPOINT #6

Activate the control panel in this chamber to reboot the sterilization system and complete the "Activate Process" objective. Sasaki then radios in and confirms that the barrel assembly line is online and functioning; he tells you to double back to his position so you both can make your escape.

WAYPOINT #7

You encounter a Strogg light tank as you exit the sterilization control room and reenter this area. These guys are tough and like to charge you, so run up the stairs to your right to gain some distance; then equip your nailgun. Strafe to dodge the light tank's ranged attacks as you pepper him with nails, and use your nailgun's new scope and tracking ability to ensure hits are scored.

NOTE

Refer to the "Enemies" section of this guide to learn all about light tanks.

OBJECTIVE: USE BARREL CONTROLS

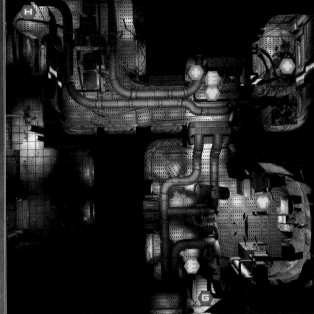

WALKTHROUGH:
PART 2

NEXUS HUB TUNNELS

NEXUS HUB

STROGG MEDICAL FACILITIES

CONSTRUCTION ZONE

DISPERSAL FACILITY

RECOMPOSITION CENTER

PURIFICATION CENTER

WASTE PROCESSING FACILITY

OPERATION: LAST HOPE

DATA STORAGE TERMINAL

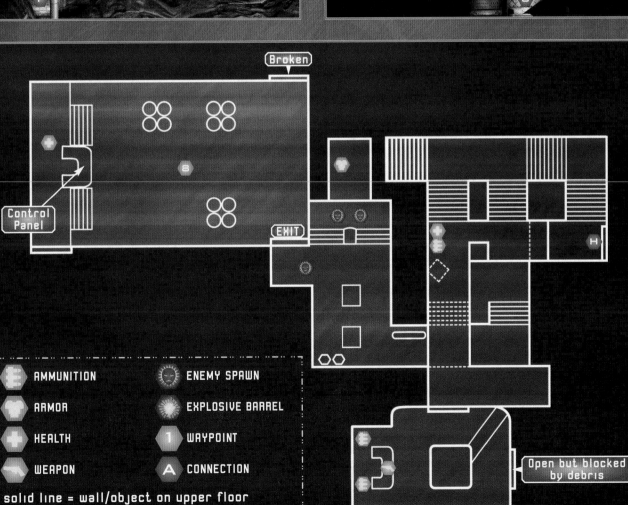

Broken

Control
Panel

EXIT

Open but blocked
by debris

AMMUNITION

ARMOR

HEALTH

WEAPON

ENEMY SPAWN

EXPLOSIVE BARREL

1 WAYPOINT

A CONNECTION

solid line = wall/object on upper floor
dotted line = wall/object on lower floor
small, thin rectangle = door

[Please refer to Maps on pg. 121]

WAYPOINT #8

As you return to the barrel control room, you witness Sasaki's unfortunate end at the claws of a grunt. There's no saving him, and the grunt doesn't come after you, but now you must manipulate the barrel controls yourself in order to escape the compound. Activate the control panel Sasaki was monitoring to lower a steel pallet. The pallet slides to the far end of the room and a stack of barrels is automatically loaded onto it. The pallet then returns, hauling the stack of barrels toward you.

Jump onto the control panel after the barrels arrive and then turn to your right and jump onto the control

deck's higher portion. Then jump onto the stack of barrels and across to the elevated walkway.

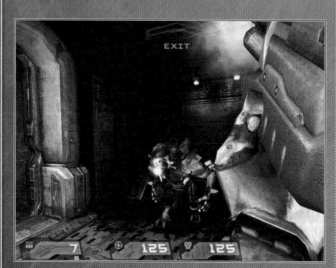

Proceed along the walkway and enter the red door you encounter. Kill the grunt that crawls out of a shaft, then drop into the shaft to exit the level on a conveyer belt.

PUTRIFICATION CENTER

OVERVIEW

Battling your way through the Recomposition Center was no easy feat, and although you face less direct combat at the Putrification Center, things start to become very, very disturbing. As you navigate this frightening facility, you discover that the Strogg are using GDF marines who didn't take to "Stroggification" as sources of energy by pulverizing them and then feeding their grisly remains to a massive, horrific creature you encounter near the level's end. Your ability to avoid environmental hazards is put to the ultimate test here—one false move can mean instant death. Stay sharp.

ENEMIES ENCOUNTERED
- Grunts
- Gunners
- Strogg marines
- Tacticals

WEAPONS ACQUIRED
- Hyperblasters
- Machine guns
- Railguns
- Shotguns

UPGRADES ACQUIRED
- None

AMMUNITION ACQUIRED
- Batteries
- Clips
- Grenades
- Lightning coils
- Nails
- Rockets
- Shells

ITEMS ACQUIRED
- Armor shards
- Armor vest, large
- Armor vest, small
- Health pack, large
- Health pack, small

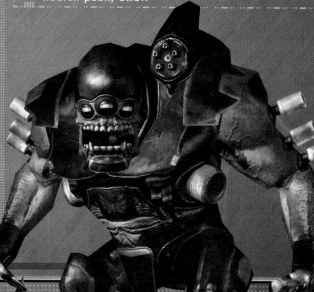

OBJECTIVE: REGROUP

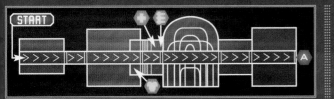

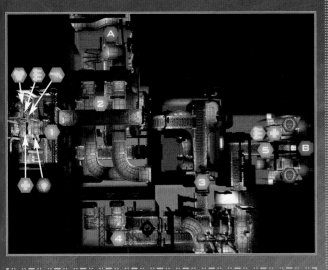

Legend

▤	AMMUNITION	☀	ENEMY SPAWN
▽	ARMOR	✳	EXPLOSIVE BARREL
✚	HEALTH	1	WAYPOINT
▭	WEAPON	A	CONNECTION

solid line = wall/object on upper floor
dotted line = wall/object on lower floor
small, thin rectangle = door

You begin at the start of a long, horrific network of blood-soaked conveyer belts. Avoid the brutal environmental hazards, such as the mechanical buzzsaws, by carefully timing your forward and backpedal movements as you ride along. The conveyer belt maze is actually far less complicated than it appears—unless this walkthrough states otherwise, simply avoid the hazards, ride the belts, and allow yourself to drop down onto the lower belts you encounter in order to progress.

TIP

Keep your eyes peeled for goodies as you ride the belts. Refer to our maps to find their exact locations.

WAYPOINT #1

Step off the conveyer belt here and collect a variety of pick-ups from the left ledge. Return to the conveyer belt afterward to proceed.

WAYPOINT #2

Jump to your right here and land on the belt below. Then turn left and drop onto a lower belt to proceed.

WAYPOINT #3

There are two mechanical stabbers directly ahead of this waypoint, positioned just outside the doors that follow

the pair of flamethrowers. Tap Ⓛ as you approach the second door past the flamethrowers to open it without moving through, watch the stabbers carefully, and then dash forward when the time is right.

WAYPOINT #4

You don't want to fall off this drop in the conveyor belt.

Spy a broken railing to your right and jump through the opening to land safely on the ledge beyond. Turn to your right and then jump onto the nearby conveyer belt that's moving in the opposite direction.

WAYPOINT #5

This is the end of the conveyer belt ride. Two Strogg marines attack your flanks as you approach the edge

ahead. Don't fall off—jump left, right, or straight ahead to land on the surrounding ledge. Quickly defeat the Strogg marines and then take a moment to catch your breath before moving on.

Be very careful when you enter this door—the huge monster in the chamber's center (to your right as you move through this door) throws its hooklike appendage at you with tremendous force when you move through. To progress, you must run to and hide behind each support pillar in front of the monster in turn, stopping to take cover behind each one to avoid the monster's fast, rhythmic attacks. Quickly make your way around to the monster's right side, where you find a control panel.

CAUTION

The monster throws its hook with such force that it destroys each pillar you hide behind. If you must, you can still take cover behind a destroyed pillar by crouching.

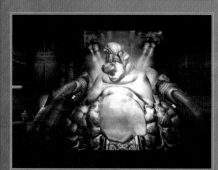

Activate the control panel to release toxins at the monster's head. This infuriates the creature, and it throws its hook through a nearby window, smashing it and creating a way forward. Run and jump through the window quickly—the monster is still alive and tries to attack you as you go.

AMMUNITION

ARMOR

HEALTH

ENEMY SPAWN

EXPLOSIVE BARREL

1 WAYPOINT

A CONNECTION

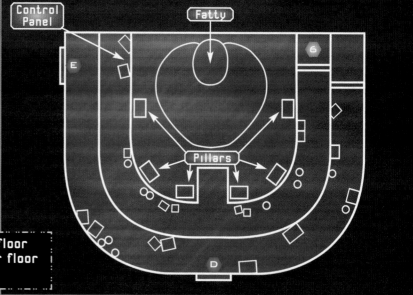

Control Panel

Fatty

E

6

Pillars

D

solid line = wall/object on upper floor
dotted line = wall/object on lower floor
small, thin rectangle = door

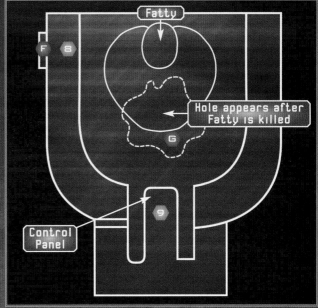

NEXUS HUB TUNNELS

NEXUS HUB

STROGG MEDICAL FACILITIES

CONSTRUCTION ZONE

DISPERSAL FACILITY

RECOMPOSITION CENTER

PUTRIFICATION CENTER

WASTE PROCESSING FACILITY

OPERATION: LAST HOPE

DATA STORAGE TERMINAL

Legend (left box)

- ✚ HEALTH
- ⬡ ARMOR
- **1** WAYPOINT
- **A** CONNECTION
- ⬡ =denotes item below or behind an object

Legend (right box)

- **1** WAYPOINT
- **A** CONNECTION

solid line = wall/object on upper floor
dotted line = wall/object on lower floor
small, thin rectangle = door

Map labels: Fatty — Hole appears after Fatty is killed — Control Panel — F 8 — G — 9

Waypoint #7

After you jump through the shattered glass and enter this chamber's ground floor, head down the short flight of stairs that follow. Crouch and then crawl under the stairs to collect a large armor vest. Then take the lift to reach the chamber's second floor, where a small health pack is located. Head through the east door to enter the hook-monster's chamber on the second-floor balcony.

Waypoint #8

Be very careful when entering the second floor balcony of the hook-monster's chamber—the creature throws its hook at you as soon as you move through the door. Quickly run through the door and hide behind the pillar directly ahead to avoid the monster's first attack. Run to the next pillar ahead to avoid its second attack, and then dart into the south hall to move out of the monster's range.

Waypoint #9

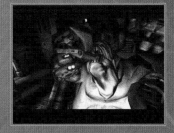

The monster can't harm you once you're in the south hall. At the control panel here, activate the monster's mechanical feeding tube. Force-feed the monster until its guts explode. This kills the horrific creature, whose displaced stomach acids burn a large hole through the floor beneath it. Backtrack to the ground floor of the hook-monster's chamber; drop through the hole to proceed.

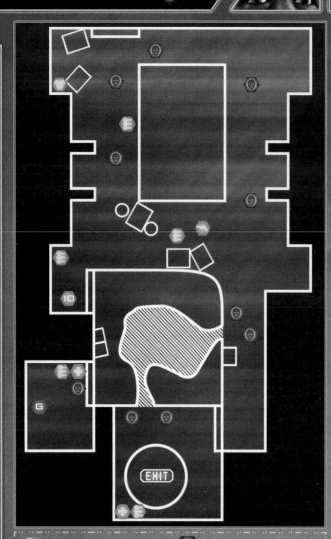

LEGEND

AMMUNITION		**ENEMY SPAWN**	
ARMOR		**WAYPOINT**	1
HEALTH		**CONNECTION**	A
WEAPON			

solid line = wall/object on upper floor
dotted line = wall/object on lower floor
small, thin rectangle = door

Fall so that you land on the next floor below. [Don't fall to the hole's bottom—doing so kills you.] After landing on the floor below, locate a pair of giant intestines that have burst and are flapping about—their acids have burned another hole in the floor. Drop through this second hole to reach a small room below; kill the lone tactical that guards the room. Proceed toward the next waypoint.

WAYPOINT #10

Enter this large room and kill all of the Strogg marines you encounter along with the gunner. Collect the many pick-ups from the room before heading to the nearby exit point. To escape the Putrification Center, jump into the large tunnel that sticks up from the floor.

WASTE PROCESSING FACILITY

OVERVIEW

Getting through the Putrification Center was a frightening, nerve-racking experience, but navigating the Strogg's Waste Processing Facility in your effort to regroup with the surviving GDF marines is downright terrifying. Here, the gruesome remains of failed Stroggification attempts that cannot be used as energy sources are systematically discarded by giant mechanical grinders and processors. You face a highly challenging mix of environmental hazards and tough combat scenarios, and the fate of Lieutenant Voss is at last revealed near the level's end.

ENEMIES ENCOUNTERED

- Berserkers
- Cyber-Voss
- Failed transfer
- Failed transfer torso
- Grunts
- Slimy transfer
- Strogg marines
- Tacticals

WEAPONS ACQUIRED

- Hyperblasters
- Machine guns
- Shotguns

UPGRADES ACQUIRED

- Rocket homing mod [rocket launcher]

AMMUNITION ACQUIRED

- Batteries
- Clips
- Grenades
- Lightning coils
- Nails
- Rockets
- Shells

ITEMS ACQUIRED

- Armor shards
- Armor vest, large
- Armor vest, small
- Health pack, large
- Health pack, small

OBJECTIVE: REGROUP

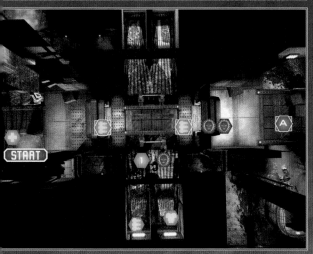

START

AMMUNITION

ARMOR

HEALTH

ENEMY SPAWN

1 WAYPOINT

A CONNECTION

=denotes item below or behind an object

PVT LANIER
Eagle Squad

40 125 125
133

s soon as you exit the starting tunnel, Private Lanier
Eagle Squad) tells you that all GDF squads are moving
o regroup at the Waste Processing Facility's entrance.
e then warns you that this facility has mobile acid
prayers on the ceilings and that their acids can
uickly chew through your armor. Lanier then runs off,
nd, right on cue, an acid sprayer begins slowly moving
oward you. Dash into the tunnel to your right to proceed.

CAUTION

*The acid sprayers also leave a trail of toxic
chemicals. The chemicals dissipate after a few
seconds, but don't touch them.*

WAYPOINT #1

A barrel tips over as you exit the tunnel, and a slimy
transfer crawls
out to attack you.
Drop the slimy
transfer quickly
before it vomits
acid at you, and
then proceed
into the next
tunnel ahead.

37 125 125
133

NOTE

*Refer to the "Enemies" section of this guide for infor-
mation on slimy and failed transfers.*

You encounter another slimy transfer and a failed
transfer shortly after you enter the second tunnel.
Failed transfers carry shotguns, which makes them
dangerous at close range. Kill both enemies, then
continue toward the next waypoint.

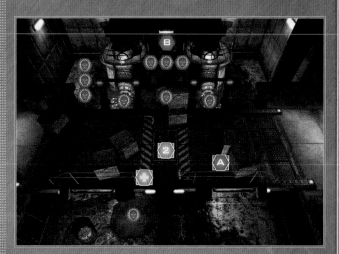

WAYPOINT #2

This blood-spattered chamber features several failed
transfer torsos—some come from the disposal tubes,
while others emerge from the tunnel behind the tubes.
Slimy transfers also pop out of the puddles of murk on
the chamber floor. Kill each of these minor threats and
then head into the tunnel beyond the disposal tubes.

CHAPTER 1
WELCOME TO
QUAKE 4

CHAPTER 2
BASIC TRAINING

CHAPTER 3
WEAPONS AND
ITEMS

CHAPTER 4
VEHICLES

CHAPTER 5
CHARACTERS

CHAPTER 6
ENEMIES

CHAPTER 7
WALKTHROUGH

CHAPTER 8
MULTIPLAYER

CHAPTER 9
GAMERSCORE
ACHIEVEMENTS

WAYPOINT #3

Carefully avoid the mechanical slop-scoopers as you navigate this frightening area. Nothing attacks you at first, so cross to the room's far end; climb the ladder you find there to reach an upper balcony on your way to the next waypoint.

WAYPOINT #4

After climbing the ladder to reach this balcony, waves of tacticals pour out from the balcony's side doors to attack you.
More tacticals emerge from the far balcony's side doors as well. Defeat the tacticals that engage you on this balcony, then use objects as cover while you pick off the tacticals on the opposite balcony. After securing the area, activate the nearby control panel to extend a footbridge so you may reach the opposite balcony and continue onward.

WAYPOINT #5

The steel walkway just ahead of this waypoint crumbles as you cross it. You're subsequently thrust into a fight against multiple slimy transfers that attack from all directions. It's tough to survive this ambush without

suffering any damage, but try to defeat these enemies before they come close enough to spray much acid on you.

WAYPOINT #6

Watch out for the exploding barrel that falls in front of you as you exit the tunnel here. Defeat the slimy and failed transfers that close in to attack after the barrel explodes. Duck into the tunnel to avoid the overhead acid sprayer each time it makes a pass.

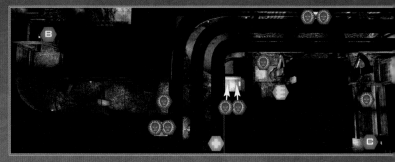

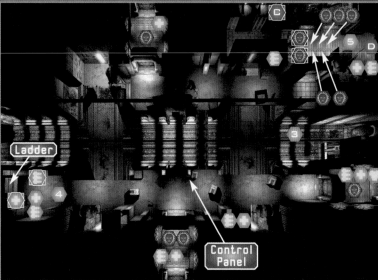

Ladder

Control Panel

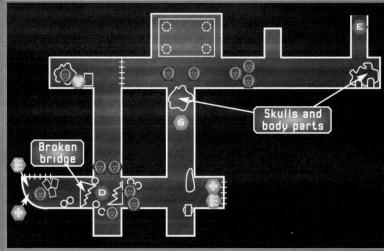

Skulls and body parts

Broken bridge

AMMUNITION	HEALTH	1 WAYPOINT
ARMOR	ENEMY SPAWN	A CONNECTION

⬡ =denotes item below or behind an object

solid line = wall/object on upper floor
dotted line = wall/object on lower floor
small, thin rectangle = door

WAYPOINT #7

You finally meet up with Private Lanier here. He's glad you made it and joins you on your way toward the facility's entrance, where all surviving GDF marines have been instructed to regroup. Lead Lanier to the next waypoint, and help him defeat the tacticals that engage you on your way.

E AMMUNITION   ✷ EXPLOSIVE BARREL   **1** WAYPOINT

▽ ARMOR   ❋ ENEMY SPAWN   **A** CONNECTION

✚ HEALTH

⬡ =denotes item below or behind an object

WALKTHROUGH: PART 2

NEXUS HUB TUNNELS

NEXUS HUB

STROGG MEDICAL FACILITIES

CONSTRUCTION ZONE

DISPERSAL FACILITY

RECOMPOSITION CENTER

PUTRIFICATION CENTER

WASTE PROCESSING FACILITY

OPERATION: LAST HOPE

DATA STORAGE TERMINAL

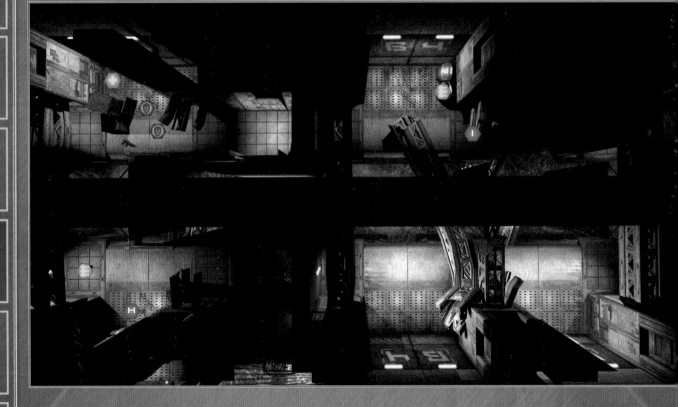

AMMUNITION

ENEMY SPAWN

CONNECTION

HEALTH

WAYPOINT

=denotes item below or behind an object

OBJECTIVE: DEACTIVATE LASER GRID

WAYPOINT #8

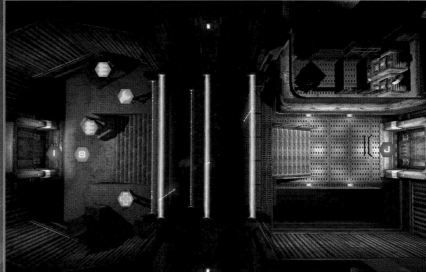

You meet up with the only two other surviving GDF marines here—Technician Ruck and Medic Wong (both of Cobra Squad). They can't pass through the Strogg security laser grid that's directly ahead, but they think you can due to your recent Stroggification experience.

Ruck also installs a new modification to your rocket launcher—the rocket homing mod. Now you can hold ⓛ and use ⓡ to guide rockets you've fired. You can also fire three rockets in quick succession by holding down ⓡⓣ.

Collect the nearby pick-ups and then pass through the laser grid. Equip your rocket launcher before you enter the door beyond—an extremely difficulty fight is almost upon you.

▮ AMMUNITION	🔧 TECHNICIAN
▮ ARMOR	✹ ENEMY SPAWN
✚ HEALTH	1 WAYPOINT
✚ MEDIC	△ CONNECTION

BOSS FIGHT: CYBER-VOSS

WAYPOINT #9

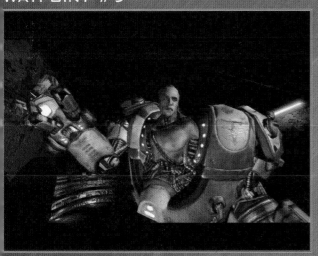

The fate of Lieutenant Voss is finally revealed when you enter this wide chamber—the Strogg have transformed him into a huge, cybernetic monstrosity. Voss implores you to run away, as he's no longer in control of his actions and can't keep himself from attacking you. There's no escape, however—it's time to put Voss's tortured soul to rest.

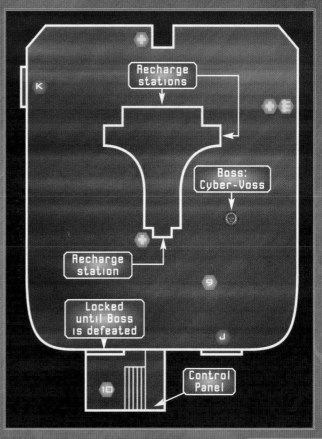

Recharge stations

Boss: Cyber-Voss

Recharge station

Locked until Boss is defeated

Control Panel

WALKTHROUGH: PART 2

NEXUS HUB TUNNELS

NEXUS HUB

STROGG MEDICAL FACILITIES

CONSTRUCTION ZONE

DISPERSAL FACILITY

RECOMPOSITION CENTER

PUTRIFICATION CENTER

WASTE PROCESSING FACILITY

OPERATION: LAST HOPE

DATA STORAGE TERMINAL

[Please refer to Maps on pg. 131 for Waypoint 10]

The moment the fight begins, pound Voss with rockets and constantly circle-strafe around him to avoid his attacks. Voss's ranged weaponry includes volleys of tracking missiles, a powerful lightning gun, and a devastating dark matter gun [see the following list for strategy on avoiding these attacks]. He also executes lethal melee attacks if you move too close, so keep your distance at all times to negate these crushing blows.

Tracking Missiles: Voss's most common attack. Strafe to avoid direct hits. Keep away from walls and jump about to reduce splash damage.

Dark Matter Gun: Voss's second most common attack, which he uses more often as the fight wears on. Strafe to one side to avoid his dark matter projectiles. Keeping your distance gives you more time to dodge this attack.

Lightning Gun: Voss's least common attack. Easily avoided if you keep your distance and circle-strafe throughout the fight.

Voss's Life meter is displayed at your screen's top center—he has both shields and health. You must eliminate his shields [the gray, outside portion of the meter] in order to erode his health [the orange, inner portion of the meter]. The fight ends when you inflict enough damage to empty the health portion of Voss' Life meter.

Once you eliminate Voss's shields, he stops attacking you and moves to a nearby electrified console, which he uses to recharge his shields. Keep hitting him with rockets or other powerful weaponry to chop away at his health, which Voss cannot restore. While Voss recharges his shields, he spawns multiple Strogg marines and grunts to engage you.

Stop attacking Voss and switch to a powerful rapid-fire weapon [such as the hyperblaster or nailgun] each time he spawns his underlings. Stay far away from Voss and let his minions chase after you. Defeat all of Voss's underlings before you resume battling him—his minions will swarm you and make the fight extremely difficult unless you stop to kill them.

Each time Voss uses a shield recharge station, a new section of the arena opens up to reveal another recharge station and a few additional pick-ups for you to grab. There are three recharge stations in total, so Voss recharges his shields three times throughout the fight. Each time he does so, he spawns additional enemies to keep you off his back. Stay far away from Voss and quickly kill these enemies whenever he spawns them. Then continue to pepper Voss with your rocket launcher, grenade launcher, hyperblaster, or nailgun as you jump and circle-strafe to avoid his ranged attacks.

Waypoint #10

The southwest door unlocks after you lay Voss's soul to rest. Enter it and interact with the control panel in the small room beyond to deactivate the security laser grid and allow Cobra Squad to join you. This completes the "Deactivate Laser Grid" objective—proceed to the next waypoint.

CHAPTER 1 WELCOME TO QUAKE 4

CHAPTER 2 BASIC TRAINING

CHAPTER 3 WEAPONS AND ITEMS

CHAPTER 4 VEHICLES

CHAPTER 5 CHARACTERS

CHAPTER 6 ENEMIES

CHAPTER 7 WALKTHROUGH

CHAPTER 8 MULTIPLAYER

CHAPTER 9 GAMERSCORE ACHIEVEMENTS

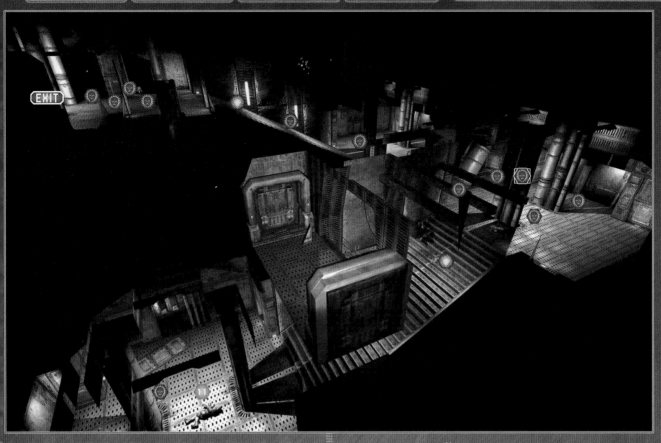

EXIT

WALKTHROUGH:
PART 2

NEXUS HUB
TUNNELS

NEXUS HUB

STROGG
MEDICAL
FACILITIES

CONSTRUCTION
ZONE

DISPERSAL
FACILITY

RECOMPOSITION
CENTER

PUTRIFICATION
CENTER

WASTE PROCESSING
FACILITY

OPERATION:
LAST HOPE

DATA
STORAGE
TERMINAL

☼	ENEMY SPAWN	1	WAYPOINT
✺	EXPLOSIVE BARREL	△	CONNECTION
⬡	=denotes item below or behind an object		

Waypoint #11

Dodge the exploding barrel that comes rolling down the stairs as you enter this stairwell, then help your fellow marines kill the many tacticals on the landing above. A few berserkers drop in to attack when you reach the landing; on the next landing above, there are several more tacticals who roll another exploding barrel at you. Clear the stairwell of foes and proceed through the exit door at the top to escape the ghastly Waste Processing Facility.

OVERVIEW

You've escaped the horrific Waste Processing Facility and have been taken back to the USS *Hannibal* for medical care. Unfortunately, there's nothing the GDF medics can do for you—the Strogg implants are too deeply rooted, and any attempt to remove them would be extremely hazardous to your health. Every dark cloud has a silver lining, however, as you soon discover.

ENEMIES ENCOUNTERED
- None

WEAPONS ACQUIRED
- Shotgun

UPGRADES ACQUIRED
- Clip extension mod (shotgun)

AMMUNITION ACQUIRED
- None

ITEMS ACQUIRED
- None

OBJECTIVE: REPORT TO BRIEFING

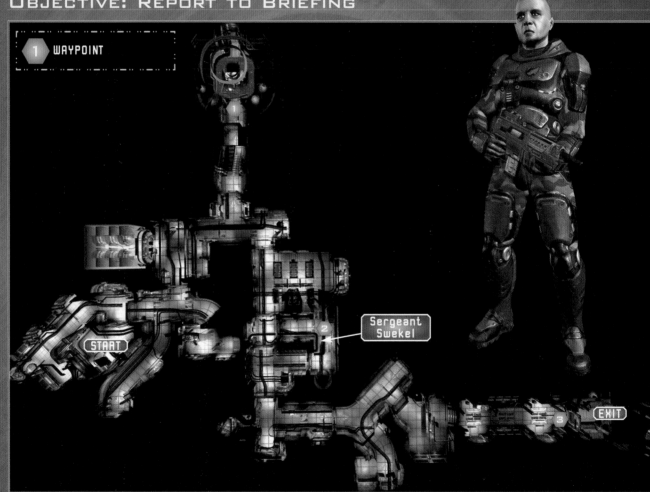

1 WAYPOINT

START

2 Sergeant Swekel

EXIT

After hours of study, the GDF medics regret that they're unable to reverse the effects of your recent Stroggification. They clear you to return to active duty, though. Sledge—who has been promoted to the rank of Sergeant—accompanies you to Rhino Squad's briefing room.

CHAPTER 1 WELCOME TO QUAKE 4

CHAPTER 2 BASIC TRAINING

CHAPTER 3 WEAPONS AND ITEMS

CHAPTER 4 VEHICLES

CHAPTER 5 CHARACTERS

CHAPTER 6 ENEMIES

CHAPTER 7 WALKTHROUGH

CHAPTER 8 MULTIPLAYER

CHAPTER 9 GAMERSCORE ACHIEVEMENTS

WAYPOINT #1

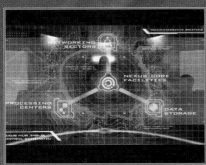

Nearly every GDF marine you encounter on your way to the briefing room located here takes a hostile tone toward your Strogglike appearance, but no one starts a fight thanks to your brooding escort, Sergeant Sledge. Arriving at the briefing room completes the "Report to Briefing" objective.

During the briefing, you learn that your Strogg physiology might be the key to defeating the vile alien race once and for all. The Nexus must still be destroyed in order to cripple the Strogg, but no amount of EMP bombs will get the job done—someone must travel into the Nexus Core and destroy the Nexus by force.

Getting into the Core will be the most difficult task anyone has ever faced. Three security stations must be deactivated in order to access the Core. Your Strogg physiology means you're the only human alive who can do the job.

OBJECTIVE: GEAR UP

WAYPOINT #2

The Strogg initiate an assault on the USS *Hannibal* as the briefing draws to a close. Head to the armory and speak to Sergeant Swekel, who is located here. Swekel hands you a shotgun he has upgraded with the clip extension mod. Your shotgun now features a magazine for fast reloading and holds two extra rounds per clip. This completes the "Gear Up" objective.

OBJECTIVE: REPORT TO DROP POD LAUNCH BAY

WAYPOINT #3

Your final task is to hightail it to the Drop Pod Launch Bay, which is located here. To open the door, activate the control panel near Rhodes and Morris, then enter your drop pod to exit the level.

DATA STORAGE TERMINAL

OVERVIEW

Strogg antiaircraft fire destroys many of the GDF drop pods as they fall toward Stroggos. A wayward drop pod slams into yours and sends you spinning off course. You crash into the Data Storage Terminal, crushing a few Strogg on your way through. Fire and debris abounds in this relatively short level—be sure to avoid environmental hazards as you make your way through.

ENEMIES ENCOUNTERED
Grunts
Gunner
Strogg marines
Tacticals

WEAPONS ACQUIRED
Dark matter gun
Shotguns

UPGRADES ACQUIRED
None

AMMUNITION ACQUIRED
Batteries
Grenades
Lightning coils
Shells

ITEMS ACQUIRED
Armor vest, large
Armor vests, small
Health packs, large
Health packs, small

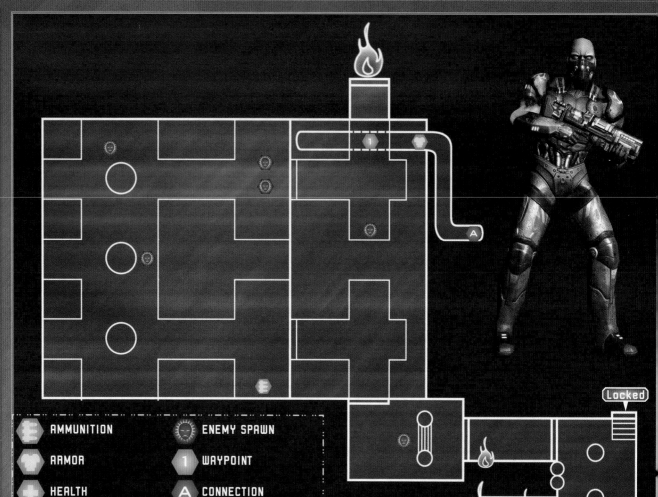

Locked

A

START

AMMUNITION

ARMOR

HEALTH

ENEMY SPAWN

1 WAYPOINT

A CONNECTION

solid line = wall/object on upper floor
dotted line = wall/object on lower floor
small, thin rectangle = door

You survive the crash landing and join up with
Technician Shockley [Viper Squad] after exiting your
ruined drop pod. Lieutenant Hollenbeck [Viper Squad]
then radios in and orders you to regroup with him
farther in the facility. Proceed to the next waypoint.

WAYPOINT #1

Defeat the tacticals that engage you as you head to
this waypoint. Flaming wreckage blocks the north door,
so move beneath the broken pipe that's shooting fire
overhead; then traverse the network of pipes ahead to
reach an opening in the wall. This leads to the next
waypoint. [Shockley cannot follow you.]

OBJECTIVE: REACTIVATE TSDs

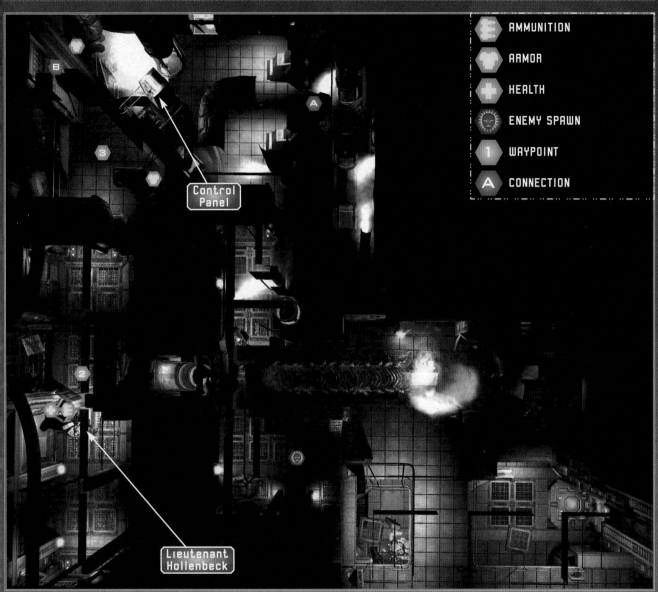

Legend:
- **AMMUNITION**
- **ARMOR**
- **HEALTH**
- **ENEMY SPAWN**
- **1** **WAYPOINT**
- **A** **CONNECTION**

Control Panel

Lieutenant Hollenbeck

WAYPOINT #2

After riding up a lift and navigating through more wreckage, you regroup with Lieutenant Hollenbeck here. He orders you to proceed to the complex's Distribution area and reactivate the Strogg's Torso Storage Devices (TSDs), which supply bioelectric energy to the facility. This will allow you to open the facility's hangar doors and help your fellow marines land safely. Head through the north door to reach the next waypoint.

WAYPOINT #3

Fire on the floor below blocks the way forward. Use the control panel here to have Strogg repair bots fix the  damage and put out the fire. Retrace your steps to the lift you used earlier and return to the lower floor.

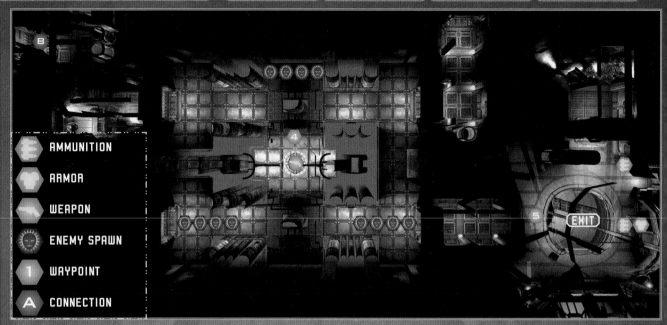

AMMUNITION	
ARMOR	
WEAPON	
ENEMY SPAWN	
1 WAYPOINT	
A CONNECTION	

WAYPOINT #4

Four Strogg repair bots examine a dark matter gun (DMG) in the center of this chamber. Destroy the repair bots to acquire the awesome DMG. Several waves of Strogg marines

swarm into the room from the north, south, and east the moment you acquire the DMG. Run to a corner and then use three to four DMG shots to defeat most of them. Finish off any stragglers with smaller arms.

NOTE

Check the "Weapons and Items" section of this guide to learn all about the dark matter gun.

WAYPOINT #5

Technician Rutger and Private First Class Mills (both of Eagle Squad) join you in this chamber, saying they've been ordered to accompany you down to the facility's Distribution area. Collect the surrounding pick-ups and then use the nearby control panel to call an elevator. Step onto the elevator with your fellow marines; activate its control panel to exit the level.

DATA STORAGE SECURITY

OVERVIEW

Lieutenant Hollenbeck has ordered you to infiltrate the Data Storage compound's Distribution area and reactivate the Torso Storage Devices in order to restore power to the facility. This will allow you to open the facility's hangar doors so that many more squadrons of GDF marines can land safely and help secure the area. The trip through Data Storage Security is a frightening one. Nothing attacks you until you turn on the power—then you face an arduous backtracking journey to reach the exit elevator. Nerves of steel and a quick trigger finger are your two best assets down here.

ENEMIES ENCOUNTERED
- Iron maidens
- Tacticals
- Tele dropper

WEAPONS ACQUIRED
- Machine gun
- Shotguns

UPGRADES ACQUIRED
- Rail penetration mod (railgun)

AMMUNITION ACQUIRED
- Batteries
- Grenades
- Lightning coils
- Rockets
- Slugs

ITEMS ACQUIRED
- Armor shards
- Armor vests, small
- Health packs, small

OBJECTIVE: REACTIVATE TSDs

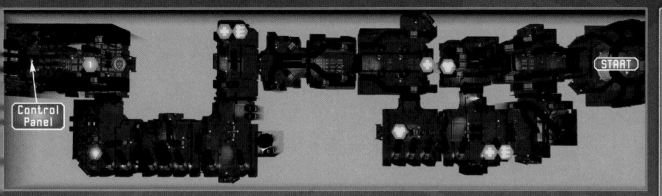

Control Panel

WALKTHROUGH: PART 3

DATA STORAGE SECURITY

DATA STORAGE TERMINAL (REVISITED)

TRAM HUB STATION

TRAM RAIL

DATA PROCESSING TERMINAL

DATA PROCESSING SECURITY

DATA PROCESSING TERMINAL (REVISITED)

DATA NETWORKING TERMINAL

DATA NETWORKING SECURITY

NEXUS CORE

THE NEXUS

AMMUNITION		EXPLOSIVE BARREL
ARMOR		ENEMY SPAWN
HEALTH		1 WAYPOINT

NOTE

Refer to the "Enemies" section of this guide for complete details on iron maidens.

WAYPOINT #1

TECH RUTGER
Eagle Squad

3
17   125   125

As you ride down the elevator, Technician Rutger installs an upgrade to your railgun—the rail penetration mod. Your railgun's slugs are now more powerful and will rip through enemies, hitting ones behind them.

After the elevator stops, Rutger notices an odd object on a nearby wall and says it gives him the creeps. Formidable iron maidens emerge from these objects after you reactivate the TSDs; they harass you as you backtrack toward the elevator. Remember the locations of these objects for future reference.

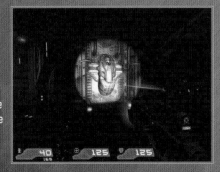

40   125   125

Nothing attacks you until you reach this waypoint, so collect the many pick-ups you see along the way. Here, you encounter your first frightening battle against an iron maiden, which emerges from a sarcophagus-like object on the east wall. Iron maidens usually fire rockets at you, which are quite powerful—use your lightning gun to stun this one and quickly defeat her. Activate the nearby control panel afterward to restore power to the facility and complete the "Reactivate TSDs" objective.

340   107   79

OBJECTIVE: REGROUP

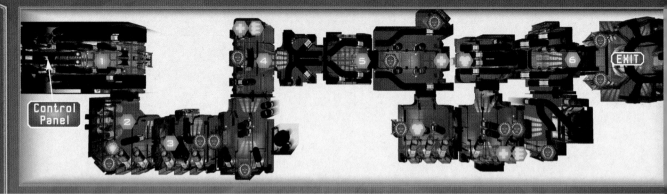

Control Panel

![] AMMUNITION		![] EXPLOSIVE BARREL	
![] ARMOR		![] ENEMY SPAWN	
![] HEALTH		1 WAYPOINT	

Lieutenant Hollenbeck congratulates you on reactivating the TSDs. He then orders you to regroup with him. Backtrack to the elevator you used to reach this area. The trip is a difficult one—you face numerous enemies this time, many of which are iron maidens. Be on your guard and try to ensure that your marine escorts survive (especially Technician Rutger, who can restore your armor).

WAYPOINT #2

An iron maiden emerges from her sarcophagus and attacks you when you backtrack through this room. Fire at the exploding barrel near her sarcophagus to weaken her in the resulting

blast; then quickly finish her off with your lightning gun. Activate the control panel near the east door to open it and proceed.

WAYPOINT #3

The sarcophagus on this room's north wall opens as you enter, but no iron maiden pops out. Instead, two shotgun-wielding tacticals rush in from the far door. Cut them down

quickly and then proceed to the next waypoint.

WAYPOINT #4

You can see a tele dropper in the far west room through the glass doors. The tele dropper runs off  when you approach, and an iron maiden materializes from the sarcophagus behind you. Quickly kill the iron maiden, then equip your grenade launcher and continue onward.

WAYPOINT #5

The tele dropper you saw a moment ago ambushes you when you pass through this door. Back up a bit and lob grenades at the tele dropper to quickly defeat it. Switch to your lightning gun or nailgun and move farther into the room. An iron maiden frees herself from the northeast sarcophagus and attacks. Defeat her and then move on.

WAYPOINT #6

You battle a few more iron maidens and a couple of tacticals on your way to the elevator, but none of these fights are too difficult. Two iron maidens ambush you in the elevator chamber, however—equip your lightning gun or nailgun before you pass through this door to prepare yourself. Quickly defeat both enemies, then use the elevator to exit the level. (Your escorts remain in the elevator chamber to guard it.)

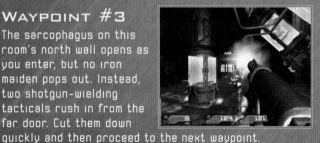

DATA STORAGE TERMINAL (REVISITED)

OVERVIEW

Your second trip through the Data Storage Terminal is far more eventful than the first. Here you face a variety of enemies and a few tough combat scenarios as you attempt to open the facility's hangar doors so the GDF dropship *Falcon I* can land. Unfortunately, opening the hangar doors raises the ire of the network guardian—a massive Strogg creature capable of destroying just about anything.

ENEMIES ENCOUNTERED

- Berserkers
- Grunts
- Gunners
- Light tanks
- Tacticals

WEAPONS ACQUIRED

- Hyperblaster
- Machine guns
- Railgun
- Shotguns

UPGRADES ACQUIRED

- Bounce shot mod (hyperblaster)

AMMUNITION ACQUIRED

- Batteries
- Clips
- Grenades
- Lightning coils
- Nails
- Shells
- Slugs

ITEMS ACQUIRED

- Armor vest, large
- Armor vests, small
- Health packs, large
- Health packs, small

OBJECTIVE: OPEN HANGAR DOORS

Lieutenant Hollenbeck awaits you at the top of the elevator. Meeting him completes the "Regroup" objective from the previous level. He thanks you again for restoring the facility's power and then orders you to find a way to open its hangar doors so that future GDF squadrons can land safely. Collect the nearby pick-ups (which have changed since your last visit), equip your hyperblaster, and proceed to the first waypoint.

AMMUNITION

ARMOR

HEALTH

ENEMY SPAWN

1 WAYPOINT

A CONNECTION

 =denotes item below or behind an object

Lieutenant Hollenbeck

WALKTHROUGH: PART 3

DATA STORAGE SECURITY

DATA STORAGE TERMINAL (REVISITED)

TRAM HUB STATION

TRAM RAIL

DATA PROCESSING TERMINAL

DATA PROCESSING SECURITY

DATA PROCESSING TERMINAL (REVISITED)

DATA NETWORKING TERMINAL

DATA NETWORKING SECURITY

NEXUS CORE

THE NEXUS

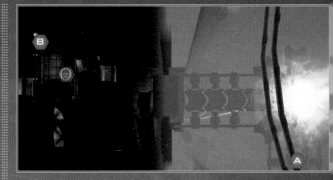

[Please refer to Map on pg. 141]

WAYPOINT #1

Two berserkers rush you when you enter this chamber. Keep your distance and pepper them with your hyper-blaster. Lieutenant Hollenbeck joins in the fight with his machine gun, but he won't follow you any farther into the complex.

WAYPOINT #2

Kill the gunner in this room, then use the lift to reach the floor above.

WAYPOINT #3

Pass through the door ahead of this waypoint. Activate the computer panel that pops out in front of you to raise a bridge across the following chamber. Cross the bridge and head through the door to your left, which is marked "Hangar".

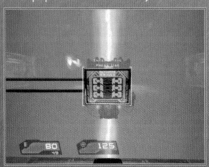

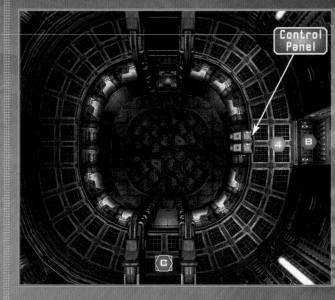

Control Panel

1	WAYPOINT		ENEMY SPAWN
A	CONNECTION		

=denotes item below or behind an object

WAYPOINT #4

Activate the control panel inside the hangar chamber to open the hangar's interior door and lower the large elevator in the chamber's center. Use the small lift to the north to reach the lower floor and then proceed through the south door. Use the lift that follows to reach the next waypoint.

To hangar controls

WALKTHROUGH: PART 3

DATA STORAGE SECURITY

DATA STORAGE TERMINAL (REVISED)

TRAM HUB STATION

TRAM RAIL

DATA PROCESSING TERMINAL

DATA PROCESSING SECURITY

DATA PROCESSING TERMINAL (REVISITED)

DATA NETWORKING TERMINAL

DATA NETWORKING SECURITY

NEXUS CORE

THE NEXUS

1	WAYPOINT	⬡	ENEMY SPAWN
A	CONNECTION	✚	HEALTH
⬡	=denotes item below or behind an object		

After you defeat both enemies, activate the control panel in the room's center to call the lift; use it to reach the cramped hangar door control room. Activate the control panel in this room to open the exterior hangar door, completing the "Open Hangar Doors" objective. Then use the lift to return to the lower floor.

WAYPOINT #5

Two light tanks attack you as you move into this chamber. Use your hyperblaster, nailgun, or rocket launcher to quickly chop them both down. There's plenty of room to move in here and lots of obstacles to hide behind; take advantage of the light tanks' lack of agility and circle-strafe around them to dodge their powerful melee attacks.

Tip

Use the Strogg Health Station behind the room's central lift to heal up after the fight.

OBJECTIVE: FIND RHODES

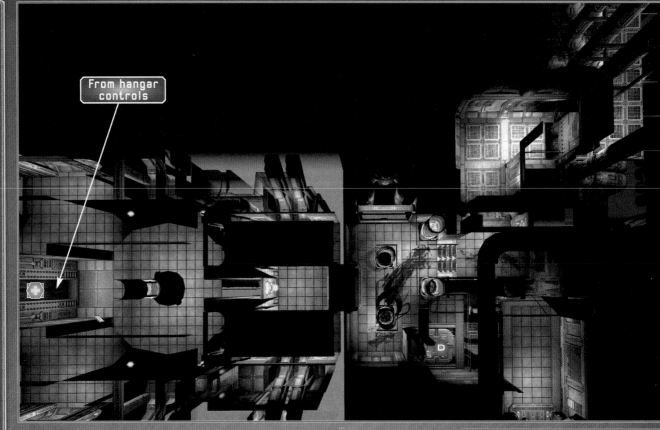

From hangar
controls

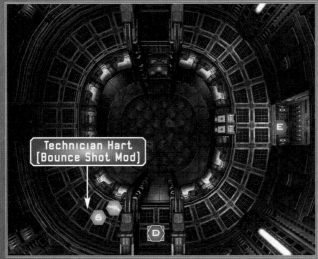

Technician Hart
(Bounce Shot Mod)

Corporal Rhodes radios in after a short time and says you must meet up with him. Backtrack to the hangar chamber, where you witness the enormous network guardian smash through the chamber's floor and zoom off on its jetpack.

WAYPOINT #6

Approach Technician Hart (Badger Squad), who stands here on the hangar chamber's second floor. He hands you a hyperblaster he has upgraded with the bounce shot mod. Now your hyperblaster shots will rebound off walls and objects, allowing you to shoot around corners and such. Continue through the east door.

 1 WAYPOINT   HEALTH

A CONNECTION   WEAPON

 =denotes item below or behind an object

OBJECTIVE: LOCATE SECURITY STATION

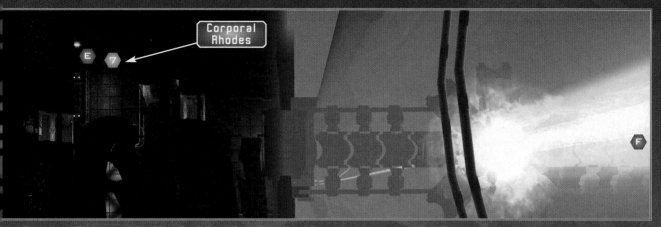

Corporal Rhodes

WALKTHROUGH: PART 3

DATA STORAGE SECURITY

DATA STORAGE TERMINAL (REVISITED)

TRAM HUB STATION

TRAM RAIL

DATA PROCESSING TERMINAL

DATA PROCESSING SECURITY

DATA PROCESSING TERMINAL (REVISITED)

DATA NETWORKING TERMINAL

DATA NETWORKING SECURITY

NEXUS CORE

THE NEXUS

	AMMUNITION		ENEMY SPAWN
	ARMOR	1	WAYPOINT
	HEALTH	A	CONNECTION

solid line = wall/object on upper floor
dotted line = wall/object on lower floor
small, thin rectangle = door

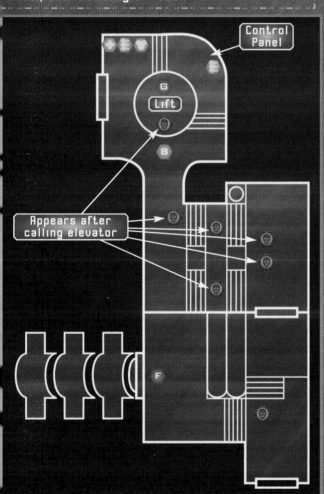

Control Panel

Lift

Appears after calling elevator

WAYPOINT #7

You meet up with Rhodes here. This completes the "Find Rhodes" objective. Strauss then radios in and says you must locate and disable the security station at the top of the Data Storage Terminal. Head east and pass through the door that's marked "Roof—SS".

WAYPOINT #8

Collect the many pick-ups in this chamber, then activate the nearby control panel to call the lift in the room's center. It takes a while for the lift to arrive—numerous tacticals attack from the room's only entrance as you wait. Help Rhodes kill them all, and defeat the grunt that arrives with the elevator. Then use the elevator to reach the next waypoint.

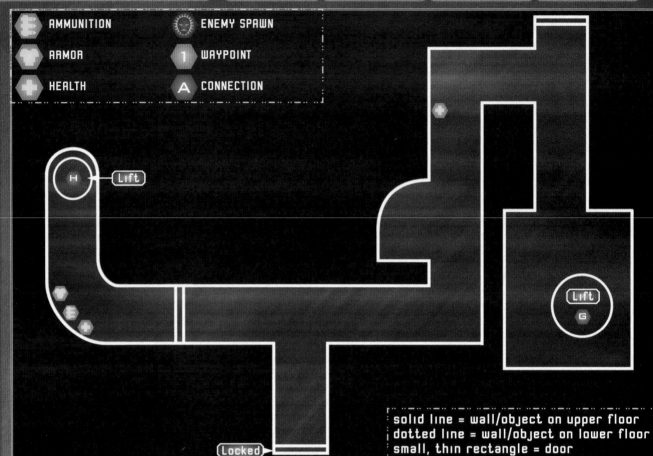

AMMUNITION

ARMOR

HEALTH

ENEMY SPAWN

WAYPOINT

CONNECTION

Lift

Lift

Locked

solid line = wall/object on upper floor
dotted line = wall/object on lower floor
small, thin rectangle = door

CHAPTER 1 WELCOME TO QUAKE 4

CHAPTER 2 BASIC TRAINING

CHAPTER 3 WEAPONS AND ITEMS

CHAPTER 4 VEHICLES

CHAPTER 5 CHARACTERS

CHAPTER 6 ENEMIES

CHAPTER 7 WALKTHROUGH

CHAPTER 8 MULTIPLAYER

CHAPTER 9 GAMERSCORE ACHIEVEMENTS

Control Panel

WAYPOINT #9

You arrive at the top of the Data Storage tower, where a Strogg dropship lands and deploys several tacticals. Quickly defeat them from range with your railgun. One of the tacticals is armed with a railgun as well, so be careful.

OBJECTIVE: RETURN TO TRAM STATION

WAYPOINT #10

Move to this spot after eliminating the tacticals. Activate the nearby control panel to disable the Data Storage tower's security system. This completes the "Locate Security Station" objective. Strauss radios in and congratulates you, then he tells you to backtrack to a now-active elevator and use it to reach a tram station, which will take you to the next tower. Rhodes must remain at the top of the Data Storage tower to guard it. Return to the elevator that brought you to the tower's top; ride it down.

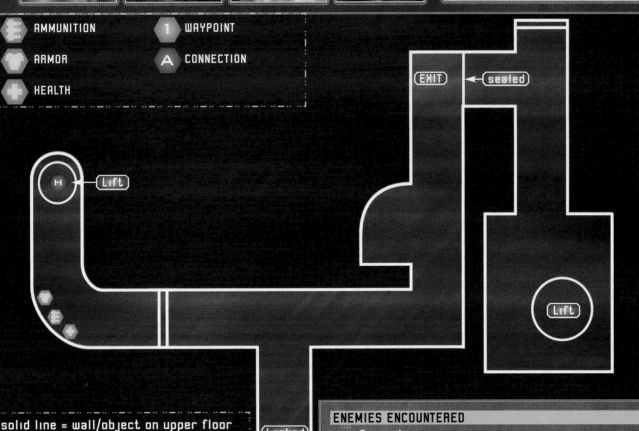

AMMUNITION

ARMOR

HEALTH

1 WAYPOINT

A CONNECTION

EXIT ← sealed

H → Lift

Lift

Locked

solid line = wall/object on upper floor
dotted line = wall/object on lower floor
small, thin rectangle = door

WAYPOINT #11

Backtrack to the now-functional elevator located here and use it to exit the level. This completes the "Return to Tram Station" objective.

TRAM HUB STATION

OVERVIEW

The Tram Hub Station is a long, challenging level full of enemies to kill and puzzles to solve. You must first help the remnants of Scorpion Squad raise a bridge that leads to the tram car area. From there, help Corporal Cortez repair and align the tram car with the proper rail so that you both may travel to the next security tower. You face an onslaught of ambushes and tough combat situations as you go about these tasks. Fortunately, Cortez is Rhino Squad's sharpshooter, and he's absolutely lethal with his machine gun.

ENEMIES ENCOUNTERED

- Berserkers
- Gladiators
- Grunt
- Gunners
- Light tanks
- Strogg marines
- Tacticals
- Tele dropper

WEAPONS ACQUIRED

- Hyperblasters
- Machine guns
- Railgun
- Shotguns

UPGRADES ACQUIRED

- Chain lightning mod (lightning gun)

AMMUNITION ACQUIRED

- Batteries
- Clips
- Grenades
- Lightning coils
- Nails
- Rockets
- Shells
- Slugs

ITEMS ACQUIRED

- Armor shards
- Armor vest, large
- Armor vest, small
- Health packs, large
- Health packs, small

OBJECTIVE: LOCATE TRAM CAR

WAYPOINT #1

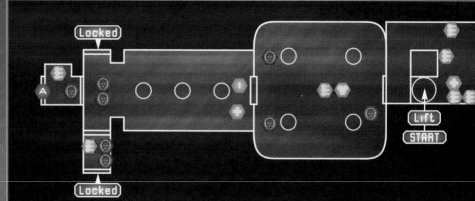

The lights slowly come on as you enter this long room. Two berserkers rush toward you from the room's far end.
Defeat them both and then kill the pair of Strogg marines that attack you. Finally, a light tank emerges from the room's far door. You have lots of room to outmaneuver the light tank. Defeat it and then collect the dark matter cores from the small southwest room before moving on toward the next waypoint.

OBJECTIVE: RAISE THE BRIDGE

WAYPOINT #2

You meet up with Medic Duncanson and Technician Ashworth (both of Scorpion Squad) here. Help them defeat the few tacticals in the area. They inform you that you must raise a bridge in order to reach the tram car. A Strogg dropship then lands and deploys several more tacticals—kill them all.

Approach Ashworth after clearing the area of tacticals. He installs a new upgrade to your lightning gun—the chain lightning mod.
You can now damage multiple enemies at once if they're standing near your target. Scout the area for pick-ups and then follow your new comrades into the next room.

Technician Ashworth (Chain Lightnin Mod)

Deployed by dropship

 AMMUNITION

 ARMOR

 HEALTH

 ENEMY SPAWN

 WAYPOINT

CONNECTION

CHAPTER 1 WELCOME TO QUAKE 4

CHAPTER 2 BASIC TRAINING

CHAPTER 3 WEAPONS AND ITEMS

CHAPTER 4 VEHICLES

CHAPTER 5 CHARACTERS

CHAPTER 6 ENEMIES

CHAPTER 7 WALKTHROUGH

CHAPTER 8 MULTIPLAYER

CHAPTER 9 GAMERSCORE ACHIEVEMENTS

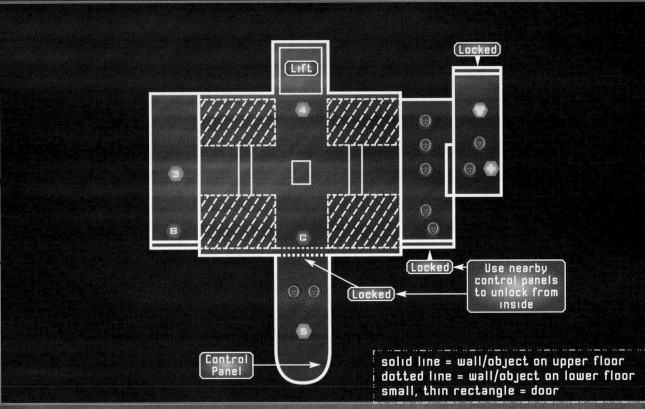

Map labels: Lift · Locked · 4 · 3 · B · C · 5 · Locked · Locked · Use nearby control panels to unlock from inside · Control Panel

solid line = wall/object on upper floor
dotted line = wall/object on lower floor
small, thin rectangle = door

Legend:
- **AMMUNITION**
- **ARMOR**
- **HEALTH**
- **ENEMY SPAWN**
- **1 WAYPOINT**
- **A CONNECTION**

Waypoint #3

Multiple tacticals backed by a gunner attack you from this room's far end. Use your railgun to quickly defeat them all; then equip your hyperblaster and take the nearby lift to the floor above, where the bridge controls are located. (Duncanson and Ashworth remain here to guard your back.)

Waypoint #4

Two berserkers rush at you when you step off the lift. Drop them both with your hyperblaster; circle-strafe to dodge their melee attacks as best you can.

Waypoint #5

The bridge controls are located here—activate the nearby control panel to raise the bridge outside. This completes the "Raise the Bridge" objective. Return to the lift and use it to regroup with Duncanson and Ashworth on the lower floor.

The two inform you that you must now secure the outdoor bridge. Exit through any of the three doors to return to the outdoor area (use the control panels to open the doors.)

QUANE 4

AMMUNITION

ARMOR

HEALTH

ENEMY SPAWN

1 WAYPOINT

A CONNECTION

WAYPOINT #6

A lone Strogg marine attacks from the now-extended bridge, but the real threats here are the gunner and gladiator that enter from the far doors. Starting with the gladiator, nail each one with heavy weaponry until you drop them both; the rocket launcher works well from range. Your comrades must remain at the bridge site to keep it secure—proceed through the far door to reach the next waypoint.

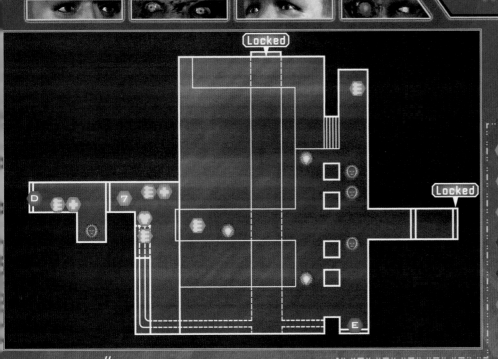

LEGEND

- **AMMUNITION**
- **ARMOR**
- **HEALTH**
- **EXPLOSIVE BARREL**
- **ENEMY SPAWN**
- **1 WAYPOINT**
- **A CONNECTION**

WAYPOINT #7

Take cover and use your railgun to kill the small group of tacticals that attack from this large area's far side. After you defeat them, crawl along the underground pipes and steel beams to reach the area's opposite side.

⬡ =denotes item below or behind an object

solid line = wall/object on upper floor
dotted line = wall/object on lower floor
small, thin rectangle = door

TIP

Don't miss the dark matter cores near the start of the pipes.

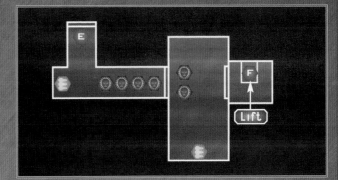

OBJECTIVE: ALIGN TRAM CAR

WAYPOINT #8

You meet up with Corporal Cortez here. He says the tram car must be rotated in order to set it on the correct path toward the next tower. Follow Cortez toward the hub controls.

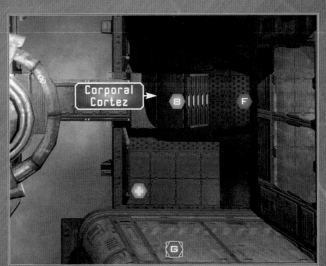

QUAKE 4

AMMUNITION

ARMOR

HEALTH

EXPLOSIVE BARREL

ENEMY SPAWN

1 WAYPOINT

A CONNECTION

=denotes item
below or behind
an object

Control
Panel

WAYPOINT #9

Battle is intense up to this
waypoint—you face multiple
Strogg marines and
tacticals backed by a
gunner in the first room
and a light tank in the
second. You and Cortez
can defeat these enemies
without much trouble.

   Here, you must activate a control panel to raise a
footbridge across the shallow gap ahead. Numerous
Strogg marines and tacticals complicate this task as
they open fire from the area's far end; they are backed
by a mighty gladiator. Launch rockets at the gladiator
while Cortez picks off the weaker enemies. Help Cortez
kill the remaining infantry and then raise the bridge to
cross the gap.

OBJECTIVE:
REPAIR TRAM RAIL

WAYPOINT #10

The alignment controls for
the tram car are located
here. After you enter the
room, activate the control
panel that lowers to
rotate the tram car and
complete the "Align Tram
Car" objective. Cortez
informs you that the tram
rail is damaged, however—you must have some Strogg
repair bots fix the rail. Enter the room to the east,
then climb down the ladder to return to the outdoor
tram car area.

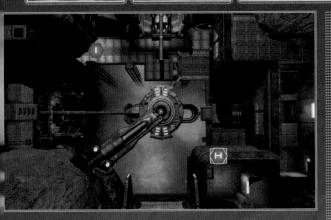

After descending the ladder, use a nearby lift to reach a lower walkway of the outdoor area. Cross the walkway and enter the northwest door to proceed.

AMMUNITION **ENEMY SPAWN**
ARMOR **1 WAYPOINT**
HEALTH **A CONNECTION**

=denotes item below or behind an object

WAYPOINT #11

The lights cut out when you enter this room—equip your shotgun or hyperblaster when the room darkens. Two berserkers then drop through the ceiling to attack you. The north door opens after you defeat the berserkers, and a Strogg marine charges in to attack. Kill him, then equip your grenade launcher and proceed through the north door.

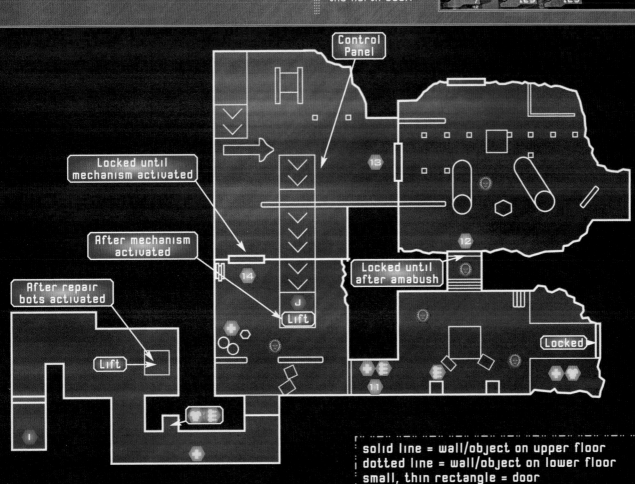

Control Panel

Locked until mechanism activated

After mechanism activated

After repair bots activated

Lift

13

14

Lift

J

Locked until after amabush

12

Locked

11

solid line = wall/object on upper floor
dotted line = wall/object on lower floor
small, thin rectangle = door

[For waypoints 12-14, please refer to Map on pg. 153]

WAYPOINT #12

The tele dropper you've seen running around this area finally attacks when you reach this waypoint. Drill it with grenades until it dies, then head through the west door.

WAYPOINT #13

Use the control panel in this room to activate the room's machinery. Steel pallets are processed and then slapped on a conveyer belt that runs through the room's south wall. Avoid the machinery as you head to the room's south door. Use the nearby control panel to open the door; go through.

WAYPOINT #14

After passing through the door, jump on top of the metal portion of the conveyer belt; wait there with your back to the wall. Jump onto a steel

pallet when it passes by on the conveyer belt. The pallet is eventually lifted upward on the area's central elevator. Ride the pallet up and jump off on the elevated balcony. Enter the north door to collect a large health pack and a large armor vest. Backtrack out and enter the balcony's west door.

WAYPOINT #15

The repair bot controls are located here. Activate the control panel to dispatch a pair of Strogg repair bots, who quickly fix the broken tram rail. This completes the

"Repair Tram Rail" objective. Backtrack out of the room, and use the lift to your right to return to the lower area. Then backtrack to the outdoor area where the tram car is located.

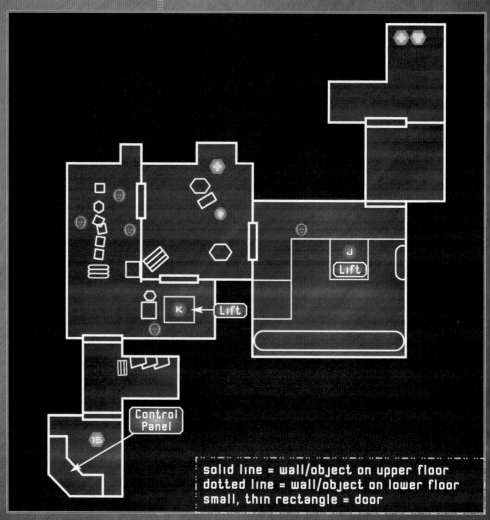

- **AMMUNITION**
- **ARMOR**
- **HEALTH**
- **EXPLOSIVE BARREL**
- **ENEMY SPAWN**
- **1 WAYPOINT**
- **A CONNECTION**

solid line = wall/object on upper floor
dotted line = wall/object on lower floor
small, thin rectangle = door

Control Panel

15

J
Lift

K
Lift

WAYPOINT #16

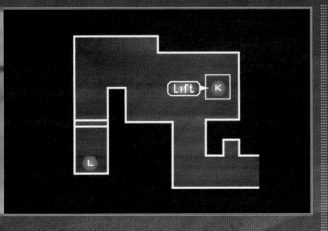

1 WAYPOINT   △ CONNECTION

solid line = wall/object on upper floor
dotted line = wall/object on lower floor
small, thin rectangle = door

Cortez awaits you on the now-functional tram car. Hop on to complete the "Locate Tram Car" objective and exit the level.

TRAM RAIL

OVERVIEW

Tram Rail is one of the shortest levels in the game. You must use your tram car's heavy machine gun to protect your car from a variety of threats as you travel toward the second security tower. Other tram cars that carry tacticals speed after you, and Strogg hornets and dropships also fly overhead to fire missiles and drop bombs. You never leave your tram car during this short level—you simply protect it from enemies until you reach the second tower.

ENEMIES ENCOUNTERED

- Dropships
- Hornets
- Tacticals
- Tram cars

WEAPONS ACQUIRED

- None

UPGRADES ACQUIRED

- None

AMMUNITION ACQUIRED

- None

ITEMS ACQUIRED

- None

OBJECTIVE: PROTECT TRAM CAR

The tram rail features three separate rails. You ride the middle one throughout this level. Your strategy is simple: quickly defeat each enemy tram car and dropship that approaches from behind to attack you.

TIP

Ignore the light hornets that occasionally zip past—their gunfire hardly scratches your tram car, and they're too fast to track.

Dropships are the biggest threat, as their heavy bombs deal severe damage to your car. They must draw very near in order to hit you with their bombs, however, so quickly destroy each one before they come within bombing range. Dropships can't withstand much fire from your tram car's heavy machine gun and are easily destroyed.

Enemy tram cars are your secondary targets. They approach from behind, usually come in pairs, and speed along the rails to your left and right. These enemy cars carry tacticals, and some of them are armed with railguns. Don't try to kill the tacticals, however—fire at

the top portions of their tram cars, which connect the cars to the overhead rails. You can destroy each enemy car in short order in this fashion.

TIP

Cortez yells at you when an enemy tram car is getting too close and warns you which side it's approaching from.

Your heavy machine gun never runs out of ammo, so open fire on each threat the moment you see one approach from behind. If an enemy tram car manages to pull up next to you, quickly destroy it. Otherwise, focus on destroying dropships and fire on tram cars only when no dropships are about. Reaching the end of the rail completes the level and satisfies the "Protect Tram Car" objective.

DATA PROCESSING TERMINAL

OVERVIEW

The tram ride has brought you to the entrance of the second security tower. You must navigate this complex to reach the tower's top and disable its security system. Though you're on your own for the first half of this level, Lance Corporal Sledge joins you shortly after you restore the facility's power. You'll certainly appreciate his help—nearly every room you enter is full of powerful enemies that are backed by tacticals. Be on your guard, save often, and bring out the big guns when necessary.

OBJECTIVE: PROCEED TO THE TOWER ROOFTOP

ENEMIES ENCOUNTERED

- Gladiator
- Gunner
- Iron maidens
- Light tank
- Nexus protectors
- Strogg marines
- Tacticals
- Tele dropper

WEAPONS ACQUIRED

- Machine guns
- Shotguns

UPGRADES ACQUIRED

- None

AMMUNITION ACQUIRED

- Batteries
- Clips
- Grenades
- Lightning coils
- Nails
- Rockets
- Shells
- Slugs

ITEMS ACQUIRED

- Armor shards
- Armor vest, large
- Armor vests, small
- Health packs, large
- Health packs, small

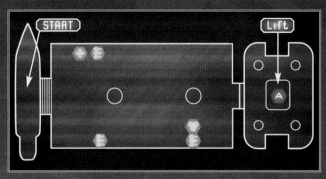

Legend:

AMMUNITION		1	WAYPOINT
ARMOR		A	CONNECTION
HEALTH			

solid line = wall/object on upper floor
dotted line = wall/object on lower floor
small, thin rectangle = door

Lieutenant Morris radios in just as you and Cortez reach the Data Processing Tower. Morris orders you to proceed to the tower's top to disable its security system, and he orders Cortez to move to the Data Networking Tower. Step off the tram car, collect the surrounding pick-ups, and call the elevator in the next room.

OBJECTIVE: RETURN POWER TO THE PROCESSING TOWER

Morris radios in again shortly after you call the elevator. He says the Strogg have shut down the facility's power and orders you to restore it. He then says Lance Corporal Sledge will join you later on but that you're on your own for now. Ride up the elevator after it arrives.

WALKTHROUGH: PART 3

DATA STORAGE SECURITY

DATA STORAGE TERMINAL (REVISITED)

TRAM HUB STATION

TRAM RAIL

DATA PROCESSING TERMINAL

DATA PROCESSING SECURITY

DATA PROCESSING TERMINAL (REVISITED)

DATA NETWORKING TERMINAL

DATA NETWORKING SECURITY

NEXUS CORE

THE NEXUS

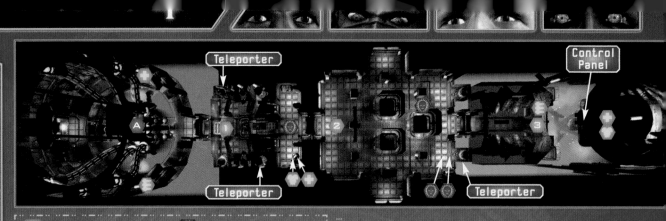

Teleporter

Control Panel

Teleporter

Teleporter

	AMMUNITION		ENEMY SPAWN
	ARMOR	1	WAYPOINT
	HEALTH	A	CONNECTION

WAYPOINT #1

Defeat the gunner at this room's far end, then fire a few charged shots from your blaster to destroy the two teleporters in the room. No enemies appear from the teleporters at this time, but they will on your way back unless you destroy the devices now. Equip your machine gun and then continue through the west door.

WAYPOINT #2

A gladiator guards the far end of this long chamber, and multiple tacticals begin to spawn from the teleporter at the chamber's far end. You don't have time to charge up shots with your blaster, so rush forward and blast your machine gun at

the teleporter to quickly destroy it. Then backpedal and begin to combat your foes.

Start by defeating the tacticals—the gladiator is slow, and you can use the surrounding pillars to stay out of his line of fire as you kill the weaker enemies. Defeat the gladiator after the tacticals and then continue toward the next waypoint.

WAYPOINT #3

Wait for a footbridge to extend in this chamber and then cross it to reach the central control panel. Activate the control panel to restore power to the Data Processing Tower, completing the "Return Power to the Processing Tower" objective. Nab the pick-ups hidden behind the control panel, equip your lightning gun, and backtrack out of the room.

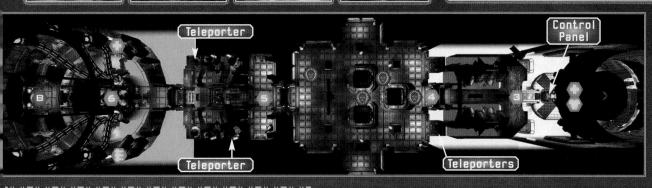

Teleporter

Control Panel

Teleporter

Teleporters

WALKTHROUGH: PART 3

DATA STORAGE SECURITY

DATA STORAGE TERMINAL (REVISITED)

TRAM HUB STATION

TRAM RAIL

DATA PROCESSING TERMINAL

DATA PROCESSING SECURITY

DATA PROCESSING TERMINAL (REVISITED)

DATA NETWORKING TERMINAL

DATA NETWORKING SECURITY

NEXUS CORE

THE NEXUS

▤ AMMUNITION	☀ ENEMY SPAWN
⬡ ARMOR	① WAYPOINT
✚ HEALTH	▲ CONNECTION

WAYPOINT #4

As you backtrack through this long chamber, the first pillar you encounter opens up, revealing a sarcophagus. An iron maiden quickly materializes and then attacks. Kill her with your lightning gun, then continue into the room.

The northernmost pillar opens up as well, and a second iron maiden emerges from its sarcophagus. To make matters worse, a tele dropper rushes toward you and begins to spawn Strogg marines. Quickly defeat the iron maiden with your lightning gun, then use your grenade launcher to kill the tele dropper and its spawn.

Finally, a light tank storms at you from the chamber's far end. Pepper it with your machine gun or hyperblaster as you backpedal and strafe about the room. Use the room's thick pillars as cover and keep your distance at all times. Continue backtracking toward the elevator after you defeat the light tank.

WAYPOINT #5

You would have faced numerous tacticals in this room had you not destroyed its teleporters on your first pass through. There's nothing to combat here now, so continue backtracking toward the elevator you used to reach this area.

OBJECTIVE: ACTIVATE ELEVATOR SYSTEM

WAYPOINT #6

You finally meet up with Sledge here, who uses the central elevator to enter the room. He tells you that you must activate a nearby elevator system in order to reach the tower's top. Use the control panel behind Sledge to raise a footbridge across the gap ahead; then lead your squadmate through the far door.

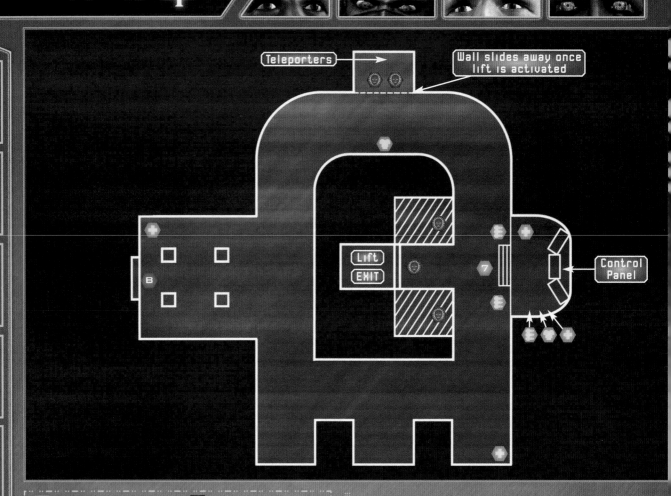

Teleporters

Wall slides away once lift is activated

Lift
EXIT

B

7

Control Panel

CHAPTER 1
WELCOME TO QUAKE 4

CHAPTER 2
BASIC TRAINING

CHAPTER 3
WEAPONS AND ITEMS

CHAPTER 4
VEHICLES

CHAPTER 5
CHARACTERS

CHAPTER 6
ENEMIES

CHAPTER 7
WALKTHROUGH

CHAPTER 8
MULTIPLAYER

CHAPTER 9
GAMERSCORE ACHIEVEMENTS

 AMMUNITION    ENEMY SPAWN

ARMOR   **1** WAYPOINT

HEALTH   **A** CONNECTION

solid line = wall/object on upper floor
dotted line = wall/object on lower floor
small, thin rectangle = door

WAYPOINT #7

Collect the many pick-ups in this room, then activate the control panel in the east alcove to call the elevator you seek. It takes a while for the elevator to arrive; several enemies ambush you in the meantime.

After calling the elevator, immediately equip your machine gun and run north—a portion of the wall has slid away to reveal a teleporter from

which numerous tacticals begin to spawn. Nail the teleporter with machine gun fire, defeat the tacticals with a few more blasts, and turn around.

Three fearsome Nexus protectors crawl out from the pits near the central elevator, one at a time. Keep your distance and use your hyperblaster to help Sledge defeat each one but don't let Sledge do too much of the work, as he can be killed. Whenever a Nexus protector opens fire, strafe around a corner and into a side hall to avoid serious damage. After defeating all three enemies, nab more pick-ups and then use the central elevator to exit the level. This completes the "Activate Elevator System" objective.

DATA PROCESSING SECURITY

OVERVIEW

You've managed to restore power to the Data Processing Tower and have used an express elevator to reach its higher floors. Now you must make your way to the tower's rooftop and disable its security system. This task is complicated by a series of data nodes that are out of alignment—you must correct them in order to unlock certain doors and reach the roof. Naturally, you face powerful Strogg forces as you attempt to reach the tower's security controls—use the environment to your advantage and select your weapons wisely.

ENEMIES ENCOUNTERED

- Berserker
- Gladiators
- Gunners
- Heavy tanks
- Iron maidens
- Light tanks
- Sentries
- Tacticals

WEAPONS ACQUIRED

- Hyperblasters
- Machine guns
- Shotguns

UPGRADES ACQUIRED

- None

AMMUNITION ACQUIRED

- Batteries
- Clips
- Dark matter cores
- Lightning coils
- Nails
- Shells

ITEMS ACQUIRED

- Armor shards
- Armor vests, large
- Armor vests, small
- Health packs, large
- Health packs, small

OBJECTIVE:
REALIGN THE DATA NODES

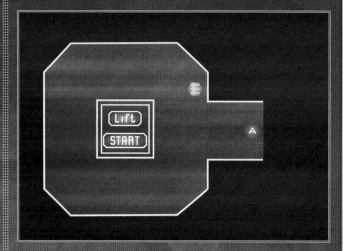

🔋 AMMUNITION		A CONNECTION

solid line = wall/object on upper floor
dotted line = wall/object on lower floor
small, thin rectangle = door

Strauss radios in when the elevator comes to a stop. He says that you must realign the overhead data nodes on this floor in order to proceed to the security tower's rooftop. Proceed to the first waypoint.

TIP

Follow the red data beams emitted by the overhead data nodes and look for areas where the nodes must be realigned.

WALKTHROUGH:
PART 3

DATA STORAGE SECURITY

DATA STORAGE TERMINAL (REVISITED)

TRAM HUB STATION

TRAM RAIL

DATA PROCESSING TERMINAL

DATA PROCESSING SECURITY

DATA PROCESSING TERMINAL (REVISITED)

DATA NETWORKING TERMINAL

DATA NETWORKING SECURITY

NEXUS CORE

THE NEXUS

AMMUNITION

ARMOR

HEALTH

ENEMY SPAWN

WAYPOINT

A CONNECTION

WAYPOINT #2

An iron maiden emerges from the sarcophagus on the wall ahead of this waypoint. Help Sledge kill her, then call the nearby lift. Allow Sledge to board the lift with you, and use it to reach the next waypoint.

WAYPOINT #1

A berserker and a few tacticals attack you as you enter this room. The berserker rushes around to confront you head-on while the tacticals open fire from the north. Defeat all of these enemies and collect the nearby dark matter cores before proceeding.

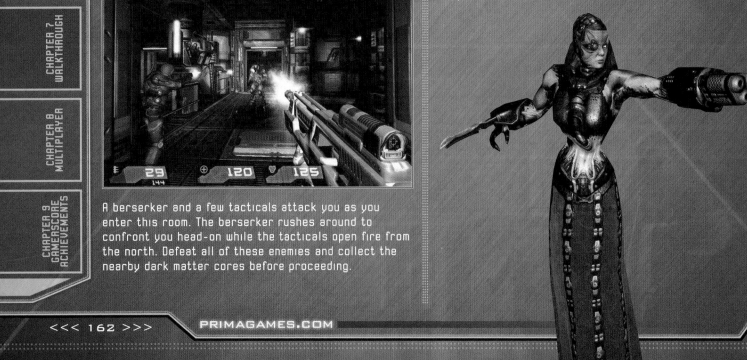

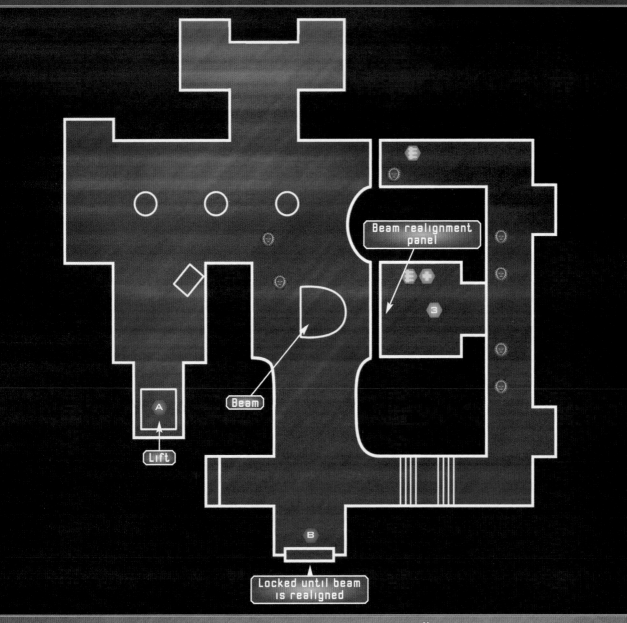

Beam realignment panel

Beam

A

Lift

B

Locked until beam is realigned

AMMUNITION

HEALTH

ENEMY SPAWN

1 WAYPOINT

A CONNECTION

solid line = wall/object on upper floor
dotted line = wall/object on lower floor
small, thin rectangle = door

WAYPOINT #3

As you enter this chamber, defeat the gunner and numerous tacticals that attack you from the chamber's higher portion. The railgun works well here. Proceed to this waypoint after clearing the room. Use the nearby control panel to properly realign the data node on the ceiling so that the data beam is fired toward the sealed south door (as pictured). This opens the south door and lets you continue toward the next waypoint.

solid line = wall/object on upper floor
dotted line = wall/object on lower floor
small, thin rectangle = door

 AMMUNITION

 ARMOR

 HEALTH

 ENEMY SPAWN

1 **WAYPOINT**

A **CONNECTION**

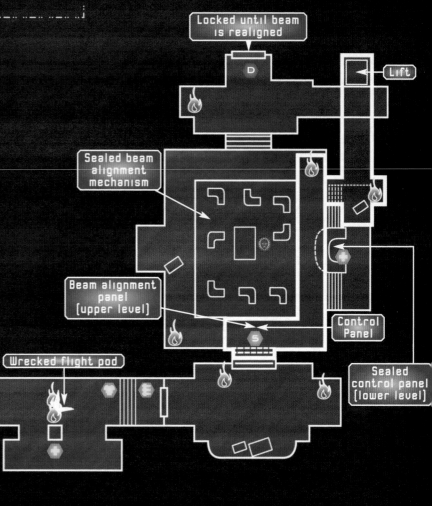

Locked until beam is realigned

Lift

Sealed beam alignment mechanism

Beam alignment panel (upper level)

Control Panel

Sealed control panel (lower level)

Wrecked flight pod

WAYPOINT #4

Equip your lightning gun, then activate the control panel near this waypoint. This opens up this chamber's large central portion, revealing several misaligned data nodes. A sarcophagus rises from the center of

the data node cluster—an iron maiden materializes from it and attacks. Zap her until she drops, then use the north lift to reach the chamber's upper balcony.

WAYPOINT #5

Use the control panel here to realign the data nodes so that the data beam is fired toward the sealed north door (as pictured). This unlocks the door and allows you to proceed.

   Follow these four steps to align the data nodes properly:

1. Rotate the lower-left node twice.
2. Rotate the middle-left node three times.
3. Rotate the middle-right node once.
4. Rotate the top-middle node twice.

CHAPTER 1 WELCOME TO QUAKE 4

CHAPTER 2 BASIC TRAINING

CHAPTER 3 WEAPONS AND ITEMS

CHAPTER 4 VEHICLES

CHAPTER 5 CHARACTERS

CHAPTER 6 ENEMIES

CHAPTER 7 WALKTHROUGH

CHAPTER 8 MULTIPLAYER

CHAPTER 9 GAMERSCORE ACHIEVEMENTS

solid line = wall/object on upper floor
dotted line = wall/object on lower floor
small, thin rectangle = door

- AMMUNITION
- ARMOR
- HEALTH
- ENEMY SPAWN
- 1 WAYPOINT
- A CONNECTION

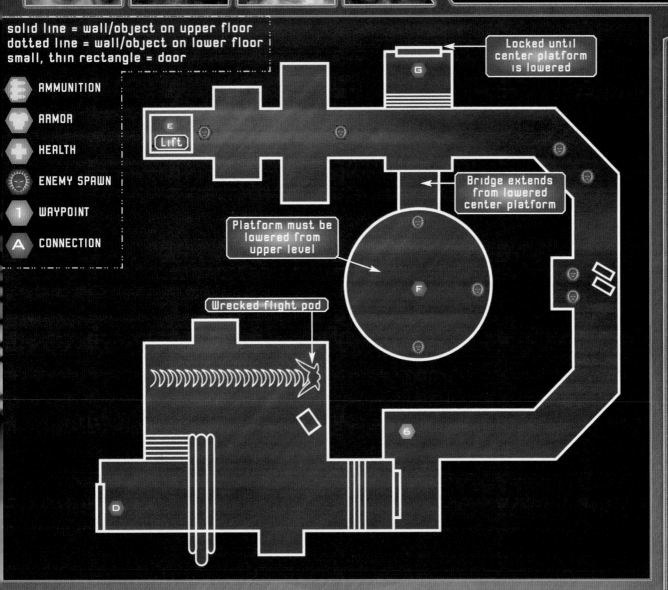

Locked until center platform is lowered

Bridge extends from lowered center platform

Platform must be lowered from upper level

Wrecked flight pod

WAYPOINT #6

This chamber's central platform raises as you enter, which disconnects the data node beam and seals the chamber's north door. You must combat several tacticals as you move along the curved corridor that encircles the central platform; sentries periodically emerge from the central platform as well. Defeat all of these foes and make your way to the north corridor's end.

A light tank rides down the lift at the north corridor's end and attacks you. Backpedal and fire at the light tank until you drop it, then use the lift in which it arrived to reach the floor above. (Sledge remains in the north corridor to guard your back.)

QUAKE 4

- ARMOR
- HEALTH
- ENEMY SPAWN
- 1 WAYPOINT
- A CONNECTION

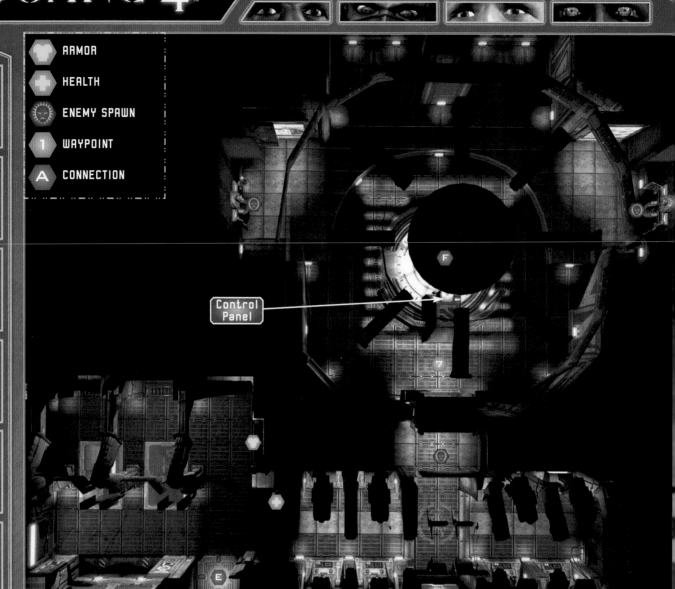

Control Panel

WAYPOINT #7

Defeat the gladiator that attacks you in the hall as you head to this waypoint. Two iron maidens materialize from the east and west sarcophagi as you enter this chamber. Defeat them both in turn and then activate the control panel in the chamber's center. This lowers the central platform—which you're standing on—and reconnects the data beam in the chamber below, completing the "Realign the Data Nodes" objective. Equip your rocket launcher, follow the data beam, and proceed through the now-open north door.

Teleporter

♦ ARMOR

✚ HEALTH

⊚ ENEMY SPAWN

⬡ =denotes item below or behind an object

1 WAYPOINT

A CONNECTION

WAYPOINT #8

From this walkway, fire a rocket at the teleporter in this chamber to destroy it before it spawns any enemies. Switch to your lightning gun and head farther into the chamber. Defeat the two iron maidens that emerge from the north and south sarcophagi. After you kill the iron maidens, a light tank enters the chamber from the east door. Keep your distance and use your machine gun or hyperblaster to quickly cut it down.

WAYPOINT #9

Snag the large health pack and large armor vest hidden under the stairs in this room. There are armor shards and small health packs near the west door as well. Collect these pick-ups and join Sledge on the west elevator.

QUAKE 4

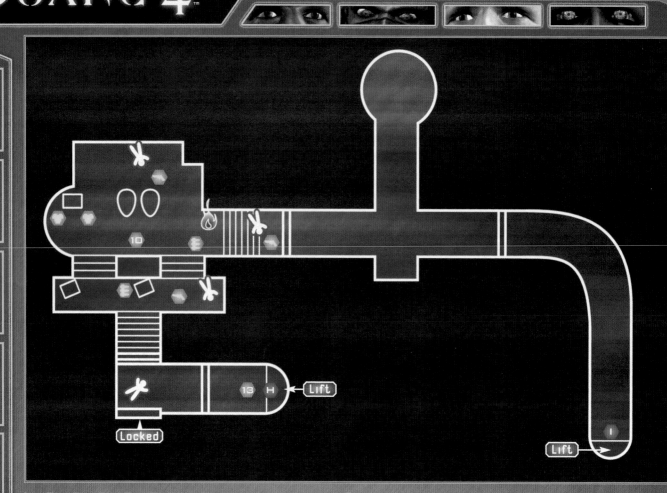

blaster works surprisingly well in this fight—use it exclusively if you've got plenty of ammo. The rocket launcher is another good choice.

E	AMMUNITION	1	WAYPOINT
	ARMOR	A	CONNECTION
	WEAPON		

solid line = wall/object on upper floor
dotted line = wall/object on lower floor
small, thin rectangle = door

WAYPOINT #10

Cougar Squad has been decimated—their gruesome remains lie strewn about this room. Avoid the room's machinery as you collect the multitude of pick-ups here; then proceed through the east door.

[Please refer to Map on pg. 169]

WAYPOINT #11

Two heavy tanks and a gladiator ambush you the moment you step onto the tower's rooftop. You will not get through this fight unscathed. Your hyper-

Start attacking the northernmost heavy tank (on your left as you enter) and then move to defeat the central gladiator and the heavy tank to the south. While you battle your targeted foe, move about the rooftop and use the surrounding walls and objects as cover to shield yourself from enemies you're not currently

Control Panel

12

11

1

⊙ ENEMY SPAWN △ CONNECTION

1 WAYPOINT

fighting. Kill each enemy in turn and then proceed to the next waypoint.

Tip

Fire at the heavy tanks' right arms to increase your odds of destroying their heavy tracking missiles the moment they fire them.

OBJECTIVE: RETURN TO TRAM STATION

WAYPOINT #12

Move to the control panel located here, and activate it to disable the Data Processing Tower's security system. This completes the "Proceed to the Tower Rooftop" objective. Strauss radios in and congratulates you.

He then orders you to return to the tram station so you can travel to the third and final security tower. Sledge must remain here to guard the tower.

WAYPOINT #13
[Please refer to Map on pg. 168]

EXIT

40 260 56 75

Backtrack across the rooftop and use the lift to return to the floor below. Collect pick-ups as you cross the floor and head to this waypoint. Step onto the nearby elevator to travel down toward the tram station and exit the level.

DATA PROCESSING TERMINAL (REVISITED)

OVERVIEW

Your return trip through the Data Processing Terminal is short and sweet. The monstrous network guardian makes another frightening appearance as you ride down the elevator toward the tram station, but you don't battle him quite yet. If you're low on health, grab the two small health packs located near the second elevator after you finish your harrowing ride down the first. Otherwise, there's little to do until you reach the next tower.

ENEMIES ENCOUNTERED
:::: None

WEAPONS ACQUIRED
:::: None

UPGRADES ACQUIRED
:::: None

AMMUNITION ACQUIRED
:::: None

ITEMS ACQUIRED
:::: Health packs, small

OBJECTIVE: RETURN TO TRAM STATION

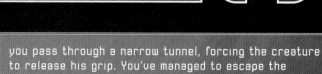

The infuriated network guardian suddenly appears as you ride down the elevator toward the tram station. He tries to attack you through the elevator's reinforced glass, but the glass holds, and you suffer no damage.

CAUTION

The elevator is tiny—don't try to return fire with your rocket launcher!

Realizing his attacks aren't affecting you, the network guardian grabs onto the elevator, grossly exceeding its weight allowance. The elevator begins to plummet faster and faster. Still in a rage and yearning to pummel you, the network guardian begins to bash the elevator's reinforced glass with his giant fist. He shatters the glass right before

you pass through a narrow tunnel, forcing the creature to release his grip. You've managed to escape the monster...for now.

You soon crash in a circular chamber near another elevator, none the worse for wear. Cross the chamber and collect the pair of small health packs near the locked door. Then use the chamber's central

elevator to continue moving down to the tram station.

This elevator brings you directly to the tram station. Run toward the tram car and then climb aboard to complete the "Return to Tram Station" objective and exit the level.

DATA NETWORKING TERMINAL

OVERVIEW

The tram car brings you directly to the entrance of the third and final security tower. The first half of this tower—Data Networking Terminal—is a relatively short level that features several tricky combat scenarios. You encounter a tough fight in practically every room you enter, so think ahead and save your progress often. Destroying the teleporters in each room is the most important thing to do here—otherwise, hoards of enemies will spawn in and overwhelm you. Raven Squad helps you through the first few rooms, but it's tough to ensure their survival. Take advantage of their assistance while you can.

ENEMIES ENCOUNTERED

- Berserkers
- Gladiator
- Grunts
- Gunners
- Light tank
- Sentries
- Strogg marines
- Tacticals

WEAPONS ACQUIRED

- Machine guns
- Railguns
- Shotguns

UPGRADES ACQUIRED

- None

AMMUNITION ACQUIRED

- Batteries
- Clips
- Dark matter cores
- Grenades
- Lightning coils
- Nails
- Rockets
- Shells

ITEMS ACQUIRED

- Armor shards
- Armor vest, large
- Health packs, large
- Health packs, small

OBJECTIVE: PROCEED TO TOWER ROOFTOP

START

- **AMMUNITION**
- **ARMOR**
- **HEALTH**
- **MEDIC**
- **A CONNECTION**

Strauss radios in as your tram car stops at the Data Networking Terminal entrance. He says you must reach this tower's rooftop to deactivate the third and final security system. This will allow you to enter the Nexus Core and destroy the Nexus. Collect the many pick-ups in the area (don't miss the dark matter cores!), then use the east elevator to reach the first waypoint.

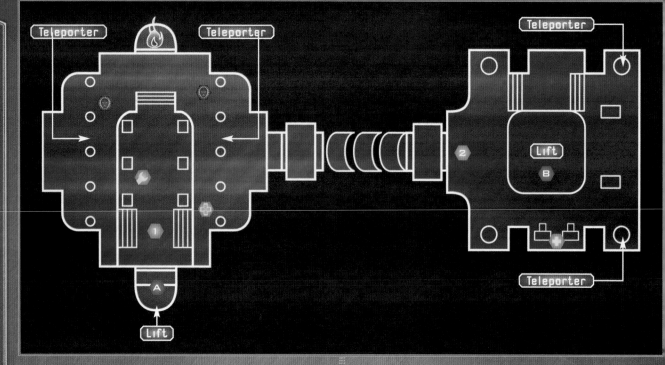

Teleporter   Teleporter   Teleporter

Lift

2

Lift

B

A

Lift

Teleporter

Legend

 HEALTH   ENEMY SPAWN

 MEDIC   1 WAYPOINT

TECHNICIAN   A CONNECTION

solid line = wall/object on upper floor
dotted line = wall/object on lower floor
small, thin rectangle = door

WAYPOINT #1

Raven Squad
finishes off a
small group of
Strogg marines as
you enter this
large chamber. The
chamber's lights
then shut off, and
two teleporters
become active,
one at either side
of the room. Two

sentries enter the chamber through openings in the
north wall as well. Let Raven Squad deal with the
sentries and use your machine gun to quickly destroy
both teleporters before too many Strogg spawn in. Help
Raven Squad secure the chamber and then continue to
the next waypoint.

WAYPOINT #2

This dark room is free of enemies—use the Strogg
Health Station to heal up, then call the elevator in the
chamber's center. Two walls slide away to reveal two
teleporters, one at the room's northeast corner and
another at the southeast corner. Immediately equip your
machine gun and fire at the teleporters to destroy
them. Help Raven Squad defeat the enemies that
spawned in, then use the central elevator to proceed.

ARMOR

HEALTH

ENEMY SPAWN

1 WAYPOINT

A CONNECTION

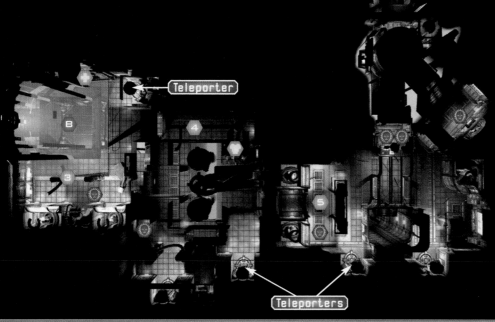

Teleporter

Teleporters

EXIT

WALKTHROUGH:
PART 3

DATA STORAGE SECURITY

DATA STORAGE TERMINAL (REVISTED)

TRAM HUB STATION

TRAM RAIL

DATA PROCESSING TERMINAL

DATA PROCESSING SECURITY

DATA PROCESSING TERMINAL (REVISTED)

DATA NETWORKING TERMINAL

DATA NETWORKING SECURITY

NEXUS CORE

THE NEXUS

WAYPOINT #3

Equip your machine gun as you ride up the elevator to reach this room. A light tank attacks you here, but ignore him at first—Raven Squad keeps him busy. Blast the room's teleporter and then help Raven Squad finish off the light tank. Kill any Strogg marines that spawned in and grab the room's large health pack. Continue to the next waypoint.

WAYPOINT #4

Tacticals spawn from the distant teleporter at this dark chamber's far end. Pepper the teleporter with machine gun fire and defeat the tacticals from range. A gunner ambushes you from an alcove as you move farther into the room—kill him, grab the room's large armor vest and proceed.

WAYPOINT #5

A berserker rushes you from the right as you enter this chamber. Avoid his first attack and fire your machine gun at the nearby teleporter. Quickly backpedal into the previous room and fire at the advancing berserker until you drop him.

Reenter the room and defeat the two tacticals that enter through the north door to attack. Move to the small health pack in the room's southeast corner and take cover behind the large pillar there—a gladiator soon stomps into the room from the northeast door. Quickly defeat the gladiator using powerful weaponry and then proceed to the next waypoint.

[Please refer to Map on pg. 173]

WAYPOINT #6

You encounter no more resistance on your way to this waypoint. Wait for the footbridge to extend, then go across it and into the teleporter to exit the level.

DATA NETWORKING SECURITY

OVERVIEW

The enraged network guardian has damaged much of the third and final security tower's higher floors, yet you still must find a way to reach the tower's rooftop and disable its security system. Fortunately, combat scenarios here aren't nearly as difficult as the ones you've overcome on your journey here—the network guardian's unfocused rage has killed many of the Strogg forces. Use lighter weaponry and conserve ammunition as you head to the roof—you'll need all the spare ammo possible once you reach the top.

ENEMIES ENCOUNTERED
- Berserkers
- Gunner
- Network guardian
- Tacticals

WEAPONS ACQUIRED
- Machine guns

UPGRADES ACQUIRED
- None

AMMUNITION ACQUIRED
- Clips
- Dark matter cores
- Grenades
- Lightning coils
- Nails
- Rockets
- Shells
- Slugs

ITEMS ACQUIRED
- Armor shards
- Armor vest, large
- Armor vest, small
- Health packs, large

OBJECTIVE: PROCEED TO TOWER ROOFTOP

[Please refer to Map on pg. 175]

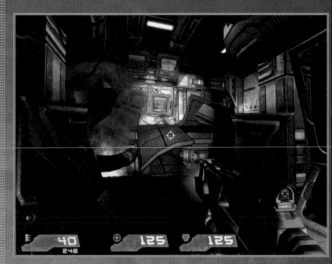

The network guardian has ruined most of this floor of the tower. As soon as you teleport in, watch him wreck stuff through the window, then turn left and jump up the bent steel plate to proceed.

WAYPOINT #1

This footbridge lies in ruins. Equip your shotgun and carefully proceed across. Defeat the gunner that

ambushes you from the right after you cross the footbridge. Use the nearby Strogg Health Station and continue into the next room.

WAYPOINT #2

A berserker charges at you from this room's far end. Avoid the berserker and destroy the room's far teleporter. Then defeat the berserker and proceed.

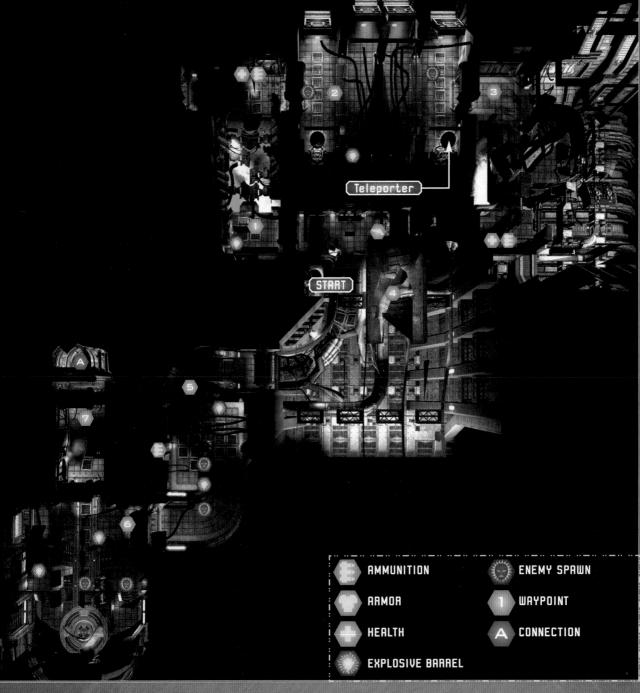

Teleporter

START

AMMUNITION

ARMOR

HEALTH

EXPLOSIVE BARREL

ENEMY SPAWN

1 WAYPOINT

A CONNECTION

DATA STORAGE SECURITY

DATA STORAGE TERMINAL (REVISITED)

TRAM HUB STATION

TRAM RAIL

DATA PROCESSING TERMINAL

DATA PROCESSING SECURITY

DATA PROCESSING TERMINAL (REVISITED)

DATA NETWORKING TERMINAL

DATA NETWORKING SECURITY

NEXUS CORE

THE NEXUS

Waypoint #3

The network guardian hovers just outside this damaged curved corridor. He begins to attack you from range as you navigate through the wreckage. Run through quickly to avoid taking much damage. The far door doesn't open all the way—crouch and crawl through.

[Please refer to Map on pg. 175]

WAYPOINT #4

Use the thick pipe here to proceed. Jump to your right when you reach the end and land on the ruined section of walkway near the door.

WAYPOINT #5

When you enter this room, fire at the far explosive barrels to weaken or kill the two tacticals that engage you. Finish them off if necessary and then continue onward.

WAYPOINT #6

Two berserkers charge you when you enter this room. Immediately fire at the yellow explosive barrel, then spray bullets at the berserkers to slow their advancement. Keep them pinned down until the barrel

explodes and weakens them, then backpedal into the previous room. Continue to pepper each berserker with your machine gun until you drop them both.

Reenter the room after killing the berserkers. Both

of the room's doors are sealed. Crouch and enter the crawlspace under the floor to proceed.

WAYPOINT #7

The short crawlspace spits you out here. Jump onto the bent portions of the floor above to exit the crawlspace. Use the north elevator to proceed.

WALKTHROUGH: PART 3

DATA STORAGE SECURITY

DATA STORAGE TERMINAL (REVISITED)

TRAM HUB STATION

TRAM RAIL

DATA PROCESSING TERMINAL

DATA PROCESSING SECURITY

DATA PROCESSING TERMINAL (REVISITED)

DATA NETWORKING TERMINAL

DATA NETWORKING SECURITY

NEXUS CORE

THE NEXUS

AMMUNITION

ARMOR

HEALTH

1 WAYPOINT

A CONNECTION

WAYPOINT #8

No enemies attack you on this small floor. Grab pick-ups from the floor's east and west wings before you use the northwest elevator to reach the tower's rooftop—you're about to face a monstrous opponent.

BOSS FIGHT: NETWORK GUARDIAN

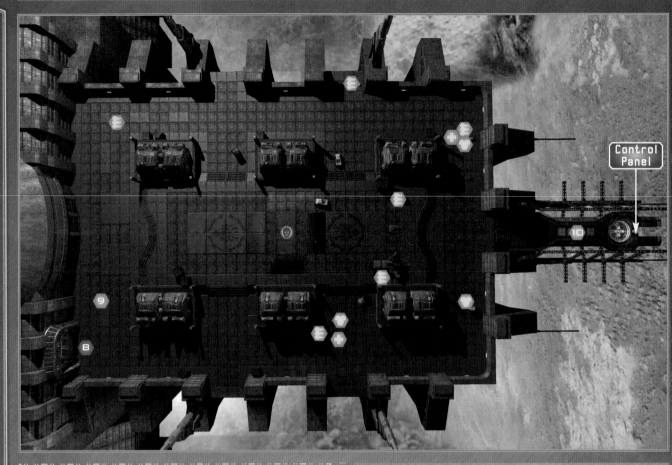

Control Panel

AMMUNITION		ENEMY SPAWN	
ARMOR		1 WAYPOINT	
HEALTH		A CONNECTION	

WAYPOINT #9

As you move across the tower's rooftop, the network guardian flies overhead and lands with tremendous force at the central area. Equip your dark matter gun, and follow the creature toward the roof's center as he moves through the air. Open fire with your DMG the moment he lands to inflict heavy damage; strafe to avoid his ranged attacks.

TIP

The network guardian is most vulnerable in the early stages of this fight. Hit him hard with your DMG.

The network guardian has only a few initial attacks:

Rocket Volleys: Most common attack, fired from his right arm. Rockets are fast but have no tracking ability. Circle-strafe to avoid direct hits. Jump and keep away from walls to reduce splash damage.

Heavy Tracking Missile: Second most common attack, fired from his left arm. Missile moves slowly but tracks you and inflicts severe damage on impact. Blast radius is wide and powerful—can hurl you through the air. Strafe as necessary to dodge missiles as best you can. Do *not* jump—impact aftershock can send you flying off the roof!

After suffering significant damage, the network guardian takes to the air and adds a new attack: He fires a powerful hyperblaster down at you from his left arm. Keep your distance and continue to strafe about as you combat the airborne network guardian. Use your machine gun to ensure that you score hits—its projectiles travel faster than any other weapon's.

The network guardian eventually lands, crushing a portion of the arena. (Don't get caught underfoot!) Switch back to your DMG or rocket launcher and continue to hammer him from range. If you're injured or low on ammo, move toward the arena's far end, where the best pick-ups are located.

Tip

There are rockets, clips, dark matter cores, and several armor- and health-restoring pick-ups at the arena's far end.

Eventually, the network guardian begins to fly about the rooftop at low altitude, attempting to burn you with the flames that shoot from his awesome jetpack. Though the damage from

this attack isn't too severe, backpedal and strafe to keep your distance. Continue to riddle him with your machine gun as you do so. Another good way to avoid him is to make a tight loop around the generator, avoiding his jetpack flames.

Caution

Don't accidentally backpedal off the roof!

After executing his jetpack attack, the network guardian lands and fires a missile straight up into the sky. The missile explodes high overhead, then several smaller rockets streak down toward you. Keep your eyes to the sky and avoid this powerful attack as best you can while you continue to chop away at the network guardian's health.

Objective: To the Core

Waypoint #10

You defeat the network guardian after you inflict enough damage to empty his Health meter. Collect the surrounding pick-ups and approach this waypoint. Use the nearby control panel to disable the third and final security tower. This completes the "Proceed to Tower Rooftop" objective. Strauss praises your efforts and tells you to use a now-active teleporter to reach the Nexus Core. Backtrack across the rooftop and use the lift to return to the floor below.

 AMMUNITION

 ARMOR

HEALTH

1 WAYPOINT

A CONNECTION

NEXUS CORE

OVERVIEW

The Nexus Core is the last true level of the game, and i by far the most difficult. You must call upon every ounce of gameplay knowledge and experience you've garnered up to this point in order to make it through the Core and into the Nexus chamber, where the final battle against the Makron occurs. Stay sharp and save your progress often—every combat scenario is extremel difficult from now on, and there are plenty of them.

WAYPOINT #11

The Nexus Core teleporter is located here. An unfortunate GDF marine tried using the teleporter against Strauss's advice, and his gruesome remains lie strewn about the floor. Strauss assures you that

your Strogglike physiology will allow you to teleport into the Nexus Core safely. Enter the teleporter to complete the "To the Core" objective and exit the level.

ENEMIES ENCOUNTERED

- Berserkers
- Gladiators
- Grunts
- Gunners
- Heavy tanks
- Iron maidens
- Light tanks
- Sentries
- Nexus protectors
- Strogg marines
- Tacticals
- Tele dropper

WEAPONS ACQUIRED

- Hyperblasters
- Machine guns
- Railguns
- Shotguns

UPGRADES ACQUIRED

- None

AMMUNITION ACQUIRED

- Batteries
- Clips
- Dark matter cores
- Grenades
- Lightning coils
- Nails
- Rockets
- Shells
- Slugs

ITEMS ACQUIRED

- Armor shards
- Armor vest, large
- Armor vests, small
- Health packs, large
- Health packs, small

WALKTHROUGH:
PART 3

DATA STORAGE SECURITY

DATA STORAGE TERMINAL (REVISITED)

TRAM HUB STATION

TRAM RAIL

DATA PROCESSING TERMINAL

DATA PROCESSING SECURITY

DATA PROCESSING TERMINAL (REVISITED)

DATA NETWORKING TERMINAL

DATA NETWORKING SECURITY

NEXUS CORE

THE NEXUS

OBJECTIVE: THE NEXUS

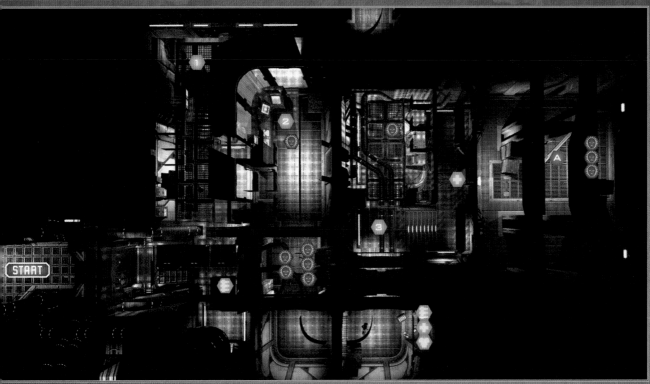

START

 AMMUNITION

 ARMOR

HEALTH

ENEMY SPAWN

1 WAYPOINT

A CONNECTION

Strauss radios in shortly after you appear inside the Nexus Core. He gives you your primary objective: Locate and destroy the Nexus so that the Strogg can be defeated once and for all. Proceed to the first waypoint.

[Please refer to Map on pg. 181]

WAYPOINT #1

Everything is quiet until you reach this waypoint. The door ahead slams shut and a railgun-armed tactical emerges from the far end of the hall you just came from. Equip your grenade launcher the moment the door slams shut, and lob grenades at the tactical to kill him fast.

A light tank storms down the hall to attack—pop it with

grenades as well. Switch to your nailgun if the light tank charges you; pelt it until it drops, backpedaling to keep your distance.

More tacticals pour into the hall. Defeat them all and then proceed to the next waypoint.

Activate the control panel near this waypoint to disable the security system, and then proceed.

WAYPOINT #3

You surprise a Strogg marine as you enter this area. Remain in the doorway and cut him down fast. Equip you grenade launcher, head into the room, and look right— two tacticals and a light tank ride up a large elevator. Lob grenades at them, aiming to hit the light tank—the splash damage kills the tacticals. Switch to your machine gun and finish off the light tank after softening him up with several grenades.

Step onto the elevator and activate its control panel to begin moving down. Waves of Strogg marines smash

through windows to attack you as you ride down. Equip your shotgun, run around, and blast each one as they enter. Keep moving and reload between waves.

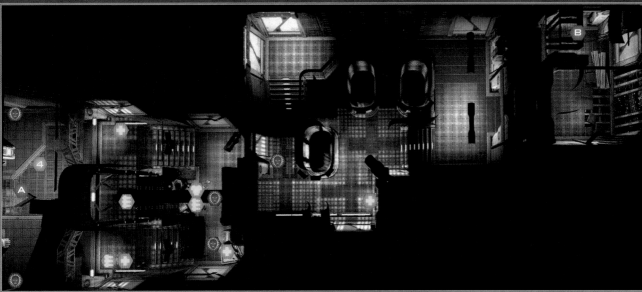

WALKTHROUGH: PART 3

DATA STORAGE SECURITY

DATA STORAGE TERMINAL (REVISITED)

TRAM HUB STATION

TRAM RAIL

DATA PROCESSING TERMINAL

DATA PROCESSING SECURITY

DATA PROCESSING TERMINAL (REVISITED)

DATA NETWORKING TERMINAL

DATA NETWORKING SECURITY

NEXUS CORE

THE NEXUS

 AMMUNITION

ARMOR

HEALTH

ENEMY SPAWN

1 WAYPOINT

A CONNECTION

⬡ =denotes item below or behind an object

Waypoint #4

The elevator stops in a large room. A gladiator attacks you from the room's far end, and two iron maidens materialize from the north and south sides of the elevator. Ignore the distant

gladiator and use your lightning gun or hyperblaster to defeat each iron maiden in turn. Then switch to your nailgun or rocket launcher and defeat the gladiator. Kill the lone tactical that rushes in after you drop the gladiator. Collect the many pick-ups in this room.

Objective: Find Elevator

Equip your grenade launcher and then open the room's west door. A tele dropper immediately ambushes you—backpedal and lob grenades at it until it dies. Use the Strogg Health Station in the next room to heal up. As you cross the room, you receive a new objective: Find an elevator that leads deeper into the Core. Equip your railgun and proceed to the next waypoint.

Waypoint #5

You enter this circular chamber's lower portion. Many tacticals spawn into the room from the central teleporter, one at a time. Stand behind the stacked barrels that are directly in front of you and rail each tactical that warps in.

[Please refer to Map on pg. 183]

Walk around the chamber and use the lift to reach the upper walkways. Use your railgun to quickly kill the tacticals that engage you. Proceed to the next waypoint.

Waypoint #6

Use this elevator to head deeper into the Nexus Core. This completes the "Find Elevator" objective.

[Please refer to Map on pg. 185]

Objective:
Scan Failed—Lockdown

Waypoint #7

A scanning device surrounds the elevator, and its inspection finds you to be a threat. A gladiator and two tacticals storm into the room, and the elevator doors open. The chamber's doors seal shut, however, locking you in.

Backpedal out of the elevator and move to your right. Quickly defeat the two tacticals with your railgun and then kill the gladiator. An iron maiden then smashes a hole in the chamber's floor and attacks. Kill her with your lightning gun and look down through the hole she created. You see several thick pipes below that lead into a crawlspace—drop onto the pipes and enter the crawlspace to proceed.

Waypoint #8

Use the ladder you find to climb out of the crawlspace and enter this room. Collect the room's pick-ups, equip your railgun, and then continue toward the next waypoint.

Waypoint #9

Several tacticals, a gunner, and an iron maiden ambush you as you enter this area. Backpedal toward the previous room, and use your railgun to kill the first few tacticals that chase you. Switch to your lightning gun and defeat the iron maiden, then use your railgun to defeat the rest of the tacticals and the gunner. Head into the next room afterward, and use its lift to reach the next waypoint.

Control Panel

DATA STORAGE SECURITY

DATA STORAGE TERMINAL (REVISITED)

TAAM HUB STATION

TAAM RAIL

DATA PROCESSING TERMINAL

DATA PROCESSING SECURITY

DATA PROCESSING TERMINAL (REVISITED)

DATA NETWORKING TERMINAL

DATA NETWORKING SECURITY

NEXUS CORE

THE NEXUS

 AMMUNITION

 ENEMY SPAWN

 ARMOR

 WAYPOINT

 HEALTH

 CONNECTION

=denotes item below or behind an object

WAYPOINT #10

Kill the lone tactical in this room and activate the nearby control panel to disable the Core's security system. This completes the "Scan Failed—Lockdown" objective. Backtrack toward the elevator chamber where you fought the gladiator a short time ago.

AMMUNITION		ENEMY SPAWN
ARMOR		1 WAYPOINT
HEALTH		A CONNECTION

WAYPOINT #11

Defeat the gunner and Strogg marines you encounter on your way back to the elevator chamber. Though you can't use the crawlspace to return to the chamber, deactivating the Core's security system has

unlocked the chamber's doors. Enter this hallway instead of the crawlspace and pass through its now-unlocked north door to return to the elevator chamber. Cross the chamber and use its northernmost door to reach the next waypoint.

WAYPOINT #12

This long chamber is a virtual deathtrap. Here you face several powerful enemies that spawn in two at a time from the teleporters at either side of the room. Break out the big guns and constantly run about or you'll never survive this assault. Circle around the chamber's pillars to keep your enemies guessing and unable to track you effectively.

Here's what you're up against:

Light tanks: Two spawn in. After you defeat one, a third spawns in. Use your rocket launcher to defeat each one in turn from range. If they close in, use your nailgun.

Heavy tanks: Two spawn in after you kill all three light tanks. After you defeat one heavy tank, a third spawns in. You *must* keep moving or their heavy tracking missiles will devastate you. Circle the pillars and try to keep track of the missiles they've fired. Kill the first two heavy tanks with your DMG—you cannot afford to mess around. Use your rocket launcher or nailgun to kill the third.

Nexus protectors: Two spawn in after you kill all three heavy tanks. Keep your distance from both and pound them with grenades. After you kill one, use lighter weaponry such as your machine gun or hyperblaster to finish off the other.

There are plenty of pick-ups in the chamber—take advantage of them. Nails and rockets are the most plentiful sources of ammo. You also find several small health packs at the room's far end. Proceed through the east door after clearing the chamber of enemies.

WALKTHROUGH: PART 3

DATA STORAGE SECURITY

DATA STORAGE TERMINAL (REVISITED)

TRAM HUB STATION

TRAM RAIL

DATA PROCESSING TERMINAL

DATA PROCESSING SECURITY

DATA PROCESSING TERMINAL (REVISITED)

DATA NETWORKING TERMINAL

DATA NETWORKING SECURITY

NEXUS CORE

THE NEXUS

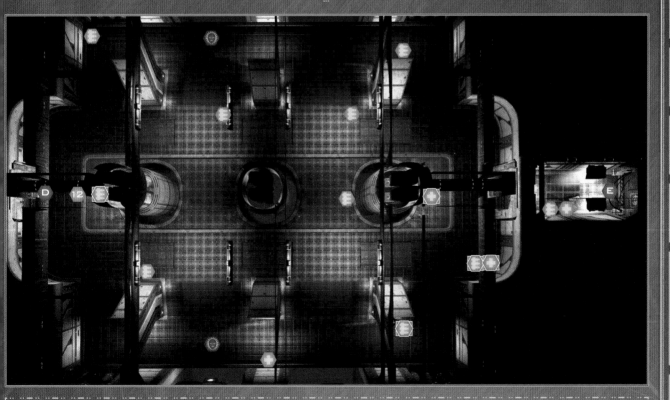

▣ AMMUNITION	♥ ARMOR	✚ HEALTH	1 WAYPOINT
⬡ =denotes item below or behind an object	⬡ ENEMY SPAWN	⬠ CONNECTION	

CHAPTER 1
WELCOME TO QUAKE 4

CHAPTER 2
BASIC TRAINING

CHAPTER 3
WEAPONS AND ITEMS

CHAPTER 4
VEHICLES

CHAPTER 5
CHARACTERS

CHAPTER 6
ENEMIES

CHAPTER 7
WALKTHROUGH

CHAPTER 8
MULTIPLAYER

CHAPTER 9
GAMERSCORE ACHIEVEMENTS

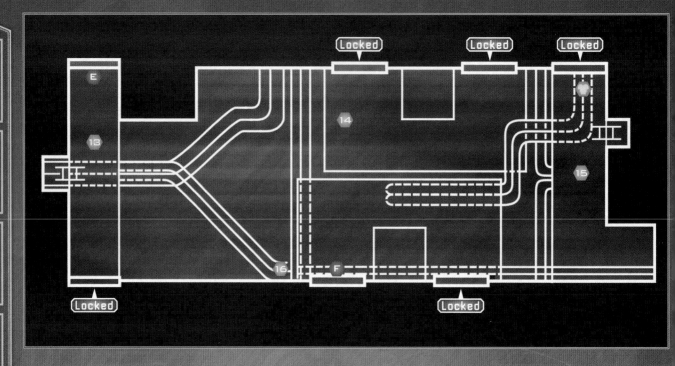

ARMOR

A CONNECTION

1 WAYPOINT

solid line = wall/object on upper floor
dotted line = wall/object on lower floor
small, thin rectangle = door

WAYPOINT #14

Cross the first set of pipes and fall to land on this lower balcony.

Carefully jump onto the lower balcony's railing. From there, jump to the set of pipes that travel upward.

WAYPOINT #13

You must navigate a series of pipes and beams in order to pass through this chamber. Falling means death, so move carefully and decisively. Your goal is to reach the highest balcony, which features an unlocked door. Start by climbing down the nearby ladder to reach the first set of pipes below the entrance walkway.

Tip

There's a small armor vest on the lowest set of pipes. Refer to the map for its location.

Tip

The repair bots occasionally pull out colorful sections of the outside wall. You can jump onto these and use them as platforms.

[For waypoints 15 and 16, please refer to Map on 188]

WAYPOINT #16

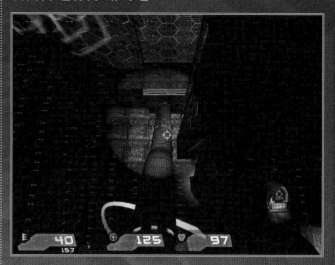

WAYPOINT #15

Move up the pipes to reach an alcove in the wall. Enter the alcove and climb the ladder to reach a higher balcony above.

A single pipe runs along the outside wall and passes below the highest balcony. Jump onto this balcony's railing and then drop to land on that pipe.

Cross the pipe to reach another pipe that runs upward. Move high up onto that pipe and then jump off to reach the highest balcony. Proceed through its unlocked door to continue.

WALKTHROUGH: PART 3

DATA STORAGE SECURITY

DATA STORAGE TERMINAL (REVISITED)

TRAM HUB STATION

TRAM RAIL

DATA PROCESSING TERMINAL

DATA PROCESSING SECURITY

DATA PROCESSING TERMINAL (REVISITED)

DATA NETWORKING TERMINAL

DATA NETWORKING SECURITY

NEXUS CORE

THE NEXUS

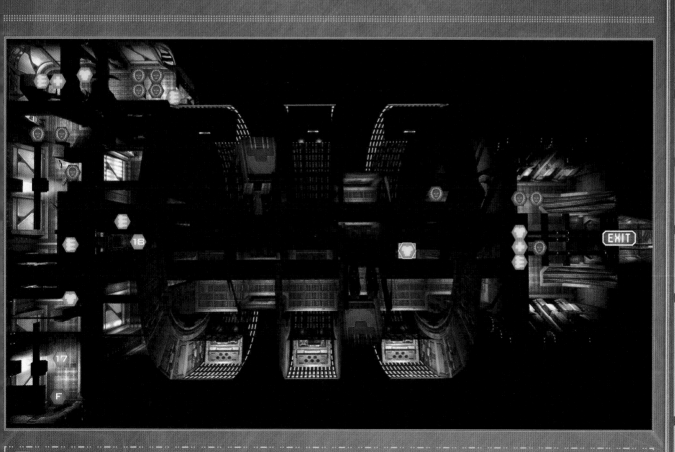

EXIT

AMMUNITION

ARMOR

HEALTH

1 WAYPOINT

=denotes item below or behind an object

ENEMY SPAWN

A CONNECTION

[Please refer to Map on pg. 189]

WAYPOINT #17

A large group of tacticals ambushes you as you head down this long corridor. Most of them are armed with railguns, so take cover behind a crate. Use your own railgun to pick each one off and duck for cover after each shot. Collect the many pick-ups in the hall as you continue to the next waypoint.

WAYPOINT #18

Climb down the utility ladder here to sneak underground and collect a small armor vest. Return to the ladder afterward and continue through the long chamber that follows.

A gladiator, a light tank, and a few tacticals attack you from the chamber's far end. Keep your distance and lure them all into one of the chamber's side halls. Unleash your DMG on them and strafe out of the side hall to avoid their fire. You can wipe out this whole group of enemies with two well-timed DMG shots. Collect pick-ups from the room's far end, then pass through the east door. Activate the control panel inside the door to exit the level.

THE NEXUS

OVERVIEW

This is it—you've breached the Nexus Core's defenses and have finally arrived at the chamber that houses the Nexus itself. This is the game's final level; here you must battle the supreme leader of the Strogg—the awesome Makron. There's no need to conserve ammunition anymore: throw everything you've got at the Makron and then destroy the Nexus once and for all. The fate of all mankind rests in your hands, Corporal Kane.

ENEMIES ENCOUNTERED
- Berserkers
- Gladiators
- Grunts
- Gunners
- Iron maidens
- Light tanks
- Makron
- Sentries
- Strogg marines
- Tacticals

WEAPONS ACQUIRED
- None

UPGRADES ACQUIRED
- None

AMMUNITION ACQUIRED
- Batteries
- Clips
- Dark matter cores
- Grenades
- Lightning coils
- Nails
- Rockets
- Shells
- Slugs

ITEMS ACQUIRED
- Armor vest, large
- Health pack, large
- Health packs, small

OBJECTIVE: THE NEXUS

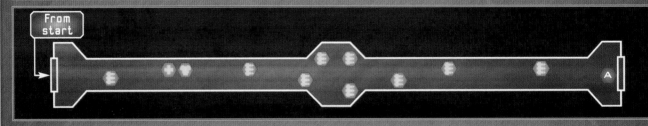

From start

A

 AMMUNITION	1 WAYPOINT
ARMOR	A CONNECTION
HEALTH	

solid line = wall/object on upper floor
dotted line = wall/object on lower floor
small, thin rectangle = door

Grab all the ammo you can carry from this first long footbridge—you're going to need it. Collect the health packs and large armor vest as well, then equip your dark matter gun and proceed through the far door to enter the Nexus Chamber.

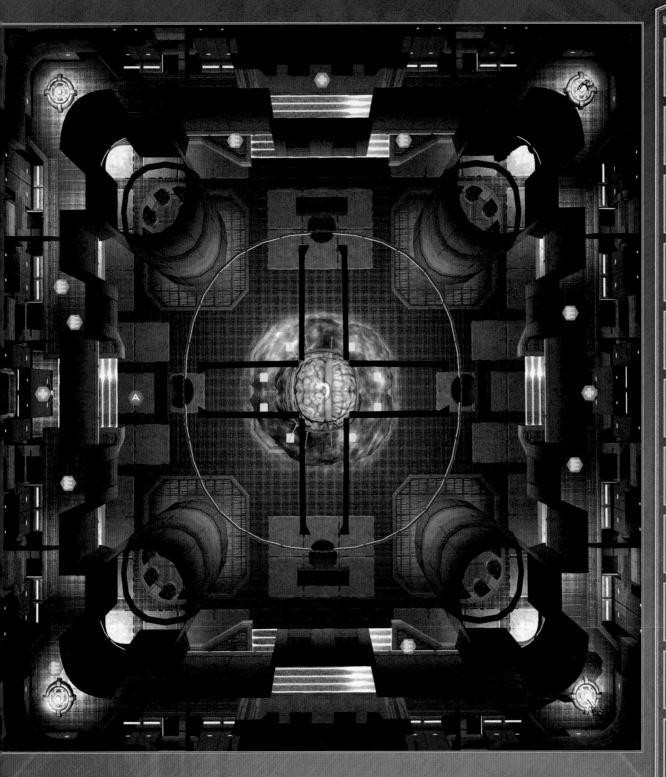

WALKTHROUGH:
PART 3

DATA STORAGE SECURITY

DATA STORAGE TERMINAL (REVISITED)

TRAM HUB STATION

TRAM RAIL

DATA PROCESSING TERMINAL

DATA PROCESSING SECURITY

DATA PROCESSING TERMINAL (REVISITED)

DATA NETWORKING TERMINAL

DATA NETWORKING SECURITY

NEXUS CORE

THE NEXUS

AMMUNITION   HEALTH   A CONNECTION

[Please refer to Map on pg. 191]

As soon as you enter the Nexus chamber, the center of the chamber's floor opens up and the Makron emerges from the pit below. The Nexus itself is nowhere in sight. The floor closes behind the Makron and the fight begins.

As soon as the Makron emerges from the pit, fire your DMG at him to immediately inflict heavy damage. Keep your distance from the Makron at all times to nullify his crippling melee blows. The Makron has a slew of powerful ranged attacks:

Triple Blaster: Most common attack, fired from his left hand. Strafe back and forth to avoid while you return fire.

Dark Matter Gun: Second most common attack, fired from his right hand. Circle-strafe in one direction to avoid as you return fire.

Dark Matter Beams: Rare attack, fired from his left hand. Strafe to one side and jump over one of the beams. Circle-strafe behind the Makron and continue to punish him.

Stomp: The Makron leans backward on his hind legs and then slams the ground with his front legs. Jump to avoid the resulting shockwave.

Hyperblaster: Rare attack, fired from his right hand. Circle-strafe in one direction to dodge as you return fire.

Dark Matter Grenades: Rare attack, fired upward from his left hand. Multiple dark matter grenades then fall about the room and quickly detonate. Watch them as they fall and move away to reduce splash damage.

The Makron collapses, nearly dead, after you erode his Health meter with your DMG. The chamber's four central pillars then open up to reveal four energy nodes. Streams of dark energy streak out from the nodes, strike the Makron and heal him. Revived, the Makron's lower body dissipates and his upper torso becomes airborne. The second stage of the fight begins.

Multiple enemies begin to randomly spawn in from the chamber's teleporters. Just about any type of enemy can spawn in—tacticals, iron maidens, and sentries are some of the most common. Immediately run to the nearest teleporter to reach the upper balcony—you're an easy target on the ground floor.

The Makron utilizes the same ranged attacks while airborne, but he's faster and tougher to hit. Continue to avoid his attacks as you drill him with your DMG.

Tip

When the fight's second stage begins, four teleporters appear, one in each corner of the chamber. Run into one to teleport onto the upper balcony, where several ammo pick-ups and three Strogg Health Stations are located.

Tip

Try to ignore the enemies that spawn. Kill them only if they get in your way.

After you've chopped away most of the Makron's health, he begins to draw energy from each of the chamber's four central pillars and heals himself. The Makron cannot attack you while he's healing, so switch to a rapid-fire weapon such as the hyperblaster, stand still, and pelt him repeatedly to quickly defeat him.

Fire a single rocket at the ceiling directly above the Nexus to destroy its energy shield. Switch to your DMG and strafe back and forth a bit as you wait for the energy shield to shatter; then fire your DMG at the Nexus itself. Quickly switch back to your rocket launcher and continue to pound the Nexus until its shield is restored—you don't have enough time to hit it with two DMG blasts. Repeat this process until you achieve victory.

Tip

Bring up your DMG right after you fire a rocket at the ceiling so the DMG can reload as you wait for the shield to shatter.

Move away from the chamber's center after you defeat the Makron for the second time—the floor opens up again to reveal a pit, and the Nexus rises into the room. Strauss radios in and tells you to destroy the Nexus while you have the chance. An impenetrable energy shield then surrounds the Nexus, preventing you from harming it.

After you destroy the Nexus, your fellow squad-mates radio in and congratulate you on your incredible effort. You're extracted shortly afterward and set to receive some well-deserved R&R, but it seems that you won't get the chance—General Harper receives a phone call with new orders for you just seconds after you arrive at HQ. Looks like you're headed back to the front, Corporal Kane.

MULTIPLAYER

MULTIPLAYER GAME MODES

The *Quake* series practically defined online multiplayer gaming, and *Quake 4* carries on that tradition with five killer multiplayer modes, each of which can be played via system linkage or over Xbox Live. Most of what you've learned in *Quake 4*'s single-player mode still applies in multiplayer, so make sure you've mastered the strategies and techniques covered in the Basic Training section at the beginning of this guide.

The biggest difference between single-player and multiplayer is the gameplay speed. You move much faster in multiplayer than you do in single-player, and you can fall farther distances without injury in multiplayer. The damage you take from falling is also scaled back in multiplayer play.

NOTE

This also means that rocket jumping is an option in multiplayer games, unlike single-player play [see the "Rocket Jumping" sidebar near the end of this section for more information].

Also, the gauntlet replaces the blaster as your default weapon in multiplayer. The gauntlet is a close-quarters melee weapon that cuts opponents down to size with a spinning buzzsaw. Few seasoned opponents will let you get close enough to use it on them if they know you're there, but pinning an opponent against a wall and slicing them up will earn you the "Humiliation" award [see "Multiplayer Awards," following].

Don't think of it as losing the blaster.
Think of it as gaining the gauntlet.

You also have the machine gun in your possession at the start of every multiplayer game and whenever you respawn after dying, so you'll always have a ranged weapon in your arsenal...unless you're careless with your ammunition.

MULTIPLAYER AWARDS

AWARD	REQUIREMENTS
Assist [CTF/Arena CTF only]	Help capture the flag by either carrying it within 10 seconds of scoring but not being the final carrier or returning your team's flag, allowing your team to score [within 10 seconds]
Capture [CTF/Arena CTF only]	Capture the flag in CTF/Arena CTF
Combo Kill	Hit a player with a rocket and then kill them within three seconds with a railgun shot; shots must be consecutive
Defense [CTF/Arena CTF only]	Kill an enemy who's close to your flag, or kill an enemy while you are close to your flag
Excellent	Score two kills in two seconds
Humiliation	Kill a player with the gauntlet
Impressive	Score two railgun hits in two seconds
Rampage	Score three "gib" [one shot, one kill] kills within five seconds

MULTIPLAYER MEDALS

MEDAL	REQUIREMENTS
Accuracy	Overall weapon accuracy is 50 percent or better
Brawler	Score the most gauntlet kills in the game; must be more than three
Critical Failure	Don't kill any other players
Frags	Score 100 or more kills in a game
Lemming	Suffer the most suicides in one game
Perfect	Score the highest number of kills among players who were not killed during the game
Rail Master	Score 80 percent of your kills with the railgun
Rocket Sauce	Score 80 percent of your kills with the rocket launcher
Sniper	Score 10 or more railgun hits and 90 percent railgun accuracy or higher
Team Player	Score the most damage but least kills

GAME MODES

There are five game modes in *Quake 4* multiplayer: Deathmatch, Team Deathmatch, Tournament, Capture the Flag, and Arena Capture the Flag.

DEATHMATCH

Deathmatch is the classic *Quake* multiplayer game mode. The object is simple: Run around a map and blast other players in an every-man-for-himself free-for-all. The player who reaches the frag limit first wins. Of course, it's a lot tougher than it sounds, which is why you're reading this guide right now.

TEAM DEATHMATCH

Like the name implies, Team Deathmatch is Deathmatch with teams. As a member of the Marines or the Strogg, it's your job to waste as many members of the opposing team as it takes to hit the frag limit, without letting them hit it first.

CAUTION

Some Team Deathmatch games are set up to allow for "friendly fire." If you're playing on one of these, be extra careful to avoid injuring or fragging your teammates—which makes the rocket launcher much less fun than it usually is.

TOURNAMENT

Tournament mode pits players one-on-one against each other in a single elimination tournament. If you win, you proceed to the next round and face the winner of another bracket until you're the champion—or a steaming pile of meat on the arena floor.

CAPTURE THE FLAG

Capture the Flag is a much more team-driven multiplayer mode. As a member of the Marines or Strogg, you must fight your way to the opposing team's base, take their flag (by running into it), carry it back to your base, and touch it to your own flag to earn a point. The first team to reach the capture limit wins.

NOTE

Your team's flag must be in your base in order for you to score. If you carry the opponents' flag back to your base and your flag isn't there, you'd better send your teammates out to get it back! In order to win, both your flag and the enemy flag must be in your base.

Most Capture the Flag arenas are larger than Deathmatch arenas, but they're simpler than they look. Each CTF arena is bilaterally symmetrical—one half of the arena is exactly the same as the other half. So when you're running toward the opponents' flag, it should feel exactly as if you're running back to your own base—except for, you know, the other team shooting at you and stuff.

Victory in CTF hinges upon your team's ability to function as a single unit. You must balance your manpower between raiding the opponents' base to get their flag with defending your own turf and preventing the other team from doing the same to you. Generally speaking, it's easier to play defense than it is to succeed on offense, so commit more manpower to seizing the opposing flag. Defending your flag is important, but bringing back the opposing flag is what scores points and wins the game.

TIP

Another reason not to leave too many players back at your flag is that players respawn near their flag when they die. So if your offense is unsuccessful, they'll effectively become defenders as soon as they die.

Also, send your offense out as a group to maximize their effectiveness. It's harder to take out three or four raiders than it is to pick off individual players making a rush for glory. But don't stay too close together, or a few well-placed rockets will wipe you all out!

ARENA CAPTURE THE FLAG

Arena CTF is exactly the same as regular CTF, with the addition of four power-ups in each team's half of the arena. Only one player can hold each power-up at a time. The power-ups remain in effect until that player dies, and they do not respawn until the player carrying it dies.

Teams that intelligently assign power-ups to their members have a huge advantage in Arena CTF. For instance, the Scout power-up is ideal for a player who's making a run for (or with) the enemy flag, while the Doubler and Guard power-ups are great for support players who must defend the flag carrier. And for the player who's sticking near his team's flag and defending it against enemy incursions, the Ammo-Regen power-up keeps him from having to leave the flag undefended while he searches for ammunition.

NOTE

The following Arena CTF power-ups can be stacked on top of other multiplayer power-ups, giving you both power-ups' abilities.

ARENA CTF POWER-UPS

POWER-UP	NAME	DESCRIPTION
	Ammo-Regen	Increases rate of fire for all your weapons and slowly regenerates ammo for all your weapons over time
	Doubler	All your attacks do double damage
	Guard	Increases your armor to 200 when picked up and raises your max armor to 200 without decreasing over time; regenerates 15 health/sec when your health is below 100 and 5 health/sec when it's over 100
	Scout	Increases your speed and rate of fire but prevents you from using armor

ENVIRONMENTAL OBJECTS

Be aware of the following three objects, which appear in multiplayer maps but not in single-player.

JUMP PADS

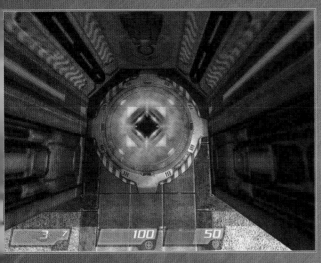

These pulsating red pads send you flying high into the air when you jump or run onto them. While in the air, you have a limited degree of control over your direction. When leaping off of a jump pad, try to land on a higher level to avoid suffering falling damage.

TELEPORTERS

Most multiplayer maps have teleporters placed in strategic locations around them. Entering into a teleporter either sends you to a corresponding teleporter elsewhere on the map or to a teleport location somewhere on the map. See the maps at the end of this chapter for the corresponding teleporters and teleport locations.

CAUTION

Don't hang around teleporters unless you're planning to use them. Other players can lob grenades through them and "telefrag" players near the destination teleporter!

ACCELERATOR PADS

![Accelerator pad screenshot with HUD values 3 7, 100, 50]

Accelerator pads give you a horizontal boost, similar to jump pads' vertical boost. Although they propel you in a predefined arc, you do have a limited degree of control over your movement while flying through the air.

WEAPON SPAWN POINTS

Every weapon in a multiplayer map appears at a weapon spawn point. When a weapon is picked up by a player, it takes a little while for the weapon to respawn. If you see an empty weapon spawn point, you know that the weapon will reappear there eventually and that another player has been there recently and is armed with the weapon.

MULTIPLAYER STRATEGIES

The following strategies are intended to complement the "Basic Training" chapter at the beginning of this guide. Learn them, use them, love them.

TEN KILLER MULTIPLAYER STRATEGIES

This chapter goes into detail on a wide variety of killer multiplayer strategies, but if you can't wait to jump into multiplayer combat, here's the quick and dirty low-down on the most important things to know:

10. **Learn the maps:** There's no point in becoming a crack shot with every weapon in the game if you don't know where to find them on each map. Before you can rise to the top of the rankings, you must do your homework on the maps you're competing on.

9. **Don't get tunnel vision:** Staring straight ahead in the direction that you're moving is the best way to get blasted into meaty chunks. You must be able to look in one direction while moving in another and keep looking every which way for threats.

8. **Keep moving:** This is a no-brainer. Moving targets are harder to hit. And if you're moving intelligently, you're also picking up all sorts of weapons, ammo, and power-ups.

7. **Master every weapon:** There are no lame weapons in *Quake 4*. There are only weapons you haven't mastered yet. You can't count on always having your preferred firearm at the ready, so make the most of what you've got. And yes, that includes the gauntlet.

6. **No, really—learn the maps:** If you can't instantly think of the shortest path to the quad damage or large armor vest from any spawning point on a map, expect to be fragged repeatedly by every player who can. There's nothing like a home-field advantage, so make sure every map you fight on is as familiar to you as the house you grew up in.

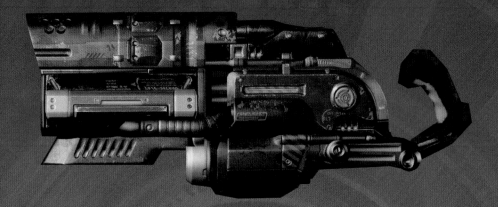

5. Hoard power-ups: If you see a weapon, pick-up, or power-up, grab it. Even if you don't plan on using it, you'll keep your opponents from getting it until it respawns.

4. Keep on fragging: In a Deathmatch, the only thing that really matters is the number of frags you've racked up. You can't win a bout without killing folks faster than anyone else. Even in a CTF match, fragging your foes is important—it prevents your rivals from gaining momentum and hinders their progress. And no matter which match type you're playing, blasting your enemies to bits causes them to drop whatever weapon they were wielding at the time you fragged them—a convenient way to bolster your supply of weapons and ammo.

3. Customize your control scheme: You can assign any button to any function you want, so don't just settle for the default control scheme unless it really is the best one for your play style. Experiment with a wide variety of schemes and get comfortable with one that lets you execute the maximum number of actions with the minimum amount of effort.

2. Avoid predictability: It's good to run a circuit around a map that lets you pick up the best weapons and power-ups, but change it up every now and again or your opponents will figure it out quickly. Likewise, don't just let a jump pad or accelerator pad shoot you in a direction—use the bit of control you have in midair and steer yourself to avoid turning yourself into a clay pigeon.

1. Seriously, dude, you've got to learn the maps: Get the point yet? Know where the power-ups and weapons are. Know where firefights tend to break out. Know three different ways to get from any location to any location on a map. Know. The. Maps.

CONFIGURE CONTROLS

The goal is to come up with something comfortable and versatile. In a game where victory is decided by tenths and even hundredths of a second, there's no such thing as too minor an advantage. At any given time, you must be able to attack an enemy, strafe to avoid his return-fire, adjust your reticle to keep it centered on your target, and jump to confuse your foe or avoid splash damage from rockets he/she may fire at your feet—and you must be able to do all of this simultaneously.

The first things to set up are your sticks, which you use to move and look about. Pick the setup that's most comfortable for you.

Next, view and edit the layout of your buttons. As we previously mentioned, you must be able to perform a variety of different actions at any given moment in order to succeed in multiplayer matches. Since your thumbs will always be tied up using Ⓛ and Ⓡ to move and look, the easiest buttons for you to reach are ⑬, ⑬, ⑬, and ⑬—the triggers and shoulder buttons. ⑬ and ⑬ are the next easiest buttons to hit because you just need to push down on the sticks, which you can do while looking and moving about. Unless you have extra digits or have developed a very unique way of holding your controller, pressing Ⓐ, Ⓑ, Ⓧ, or Ⓨ forces you to remove your thumb from Ⓡ. You should never be forced to release Ⓡ during the thick of battle, so don't set any vital controls to these buttons.

NOTE

You must edit your controls through the main menu in order to fully customize your buttons.

Finally, tweak the sensitivity of your "look" stick (default ⓡ). Generally speaking, higher sensitivity levels are preferred, because you can make faster movements and quickly react to attacks from any direction. However, you don't want your sensitivity set so high that you become unable to effectively target opponents. The goal is to achieve the perfect balance between being able to target your foes with pinpoint accuracy and being able to quickly spin around to combat threats from behind. The sensitivity sweet spot is different for everyone, and you'll instantly know when you've hit yours—tweak the levels and see how it impacts your game.

THE SOUNDS OF VIOLENCE

Sound is an often overlooked advantage in multiplayer games. Pay careful attention to it so that you can anticipate nearby situations. If you're low on health and armor, for instance, don't run toward the sound of gunfire or explosions. If you catch the distinctive sound of an opponent picking up items behind you, you know that they're right on your tail, so be ready. Was that the sound of some luckless sucker respawning near you? Take him out before he gets a chance to armor up! In some cases, your ears can be just as important as your eyes in *Quake 4* multiplayer.

And here's a tip for the sound-conscious: You don't produce footsteps when you walk instead of run. Is sneaking around silently worth not moving quickly? Not always, but it can be especially useful when you're trying to ambush an opponent.

MOVEMENT

In *Quake 4*'s single-player mode, you moved slowly, carefully, and methodically until enemies appeared. In multiplayer, that won't fly. Multiplayer is one giant battle, and he who hesitates is fragged.

CONSTANT MOTION

With *very* few exceptions, you must stay in constant motion if you want to succeed at multiplayer. Even if you're guarding an area or staking out a patch of turf, move around that area. A moving target is much harder to hit than one that's standing still and asking for a railgun slug right between the eyes.

Another reason to keep moving is you don't want to be standing still while your opponents are running around picking up weapons, ammo, health, armor, and power-ups. One of the worst things you can do in multiplayer is let yourself get outgunned, and that's exactly what will happen if you're twiddling your thumbs while your foes are gearing up for battle.

FACE ONE WAY, RUN THE OTHER

Another absolutely essential technique to master is the ability to run in one direction while facing another, because you can't expect your opponents to conveniently rush you from the front. Practice using ⓛ in conjunction with ⓡ until moving in any direction while looking in a different direction becomes second nature.

For example, if you want to keep running in the current direction but also look to see if anyone's behind you, you must instantly switch from ⓛ to ⓛ while quickly moving ⓡ in a 180 degree arch to spin yourself around. If you do it properly, you keep moving in the same direction you were moving in originally, but you can see if there's anyone behind you.

Another technique to master is looking to the right or left while running forward. To look right, switch from Ⓛ to ◀Ⓛ while gradually moving Ⓡ 90 degrees to the right. To look left, switch from Ⓛ to Ⓛ▶ while gradually moving Ⓡ 90 degrees to the left.

Tip

There are certain areas where enemies are more likely to appear, including blind corners, the ends of hallways, doorways, ledges, the tops of ramps, and the areas above jump pods and beyond acceleration pods. Constantly scan for these areas and be ready to get the drop on anyone who appears in them.

These are absolutely fundamental techniques that you should constantly incorporate into your gameplay. You shouldn't run in one direction for more than two or three seconds without backpedaling or side-strafing, looking around you for threatening enemies—or, if you're lucky, easy pickings.

KNOW WHERE YOU'RE GOING

Having stressed the importance of constantly moving, we must also mention that running frantically and blindly isn't going to do you any favors. Know exactly where you're going and why. You must control the map.

Controlling the map means that you are always running toward something you need, whether that's armor, health, a powerful weapon, or a power-up. You want to grab these things to use them on your opponents, and you want to make sure that they don't pick them up and use them against you.

In order to effectively control the map, you must know it inside and out. Know where all of the best pick-ups are, and know multiple pathways to each of them from any location on the map. There's no easy way to do this. You just have to play each map over and over until every detail of it is etched into your brain. Some players know their loved ones' birthdays better than they know their multiplayer maps. We call these players "losers."

MULTIPLAYER MODES

MULTIPLAYER STRATEGIES

MULTIPLAYER MAPS

JUMP PADS AND ACCELERATOR PADS

As mentioned previously, jump pads send you flying vertically, while accelerator pads fire you horizontally at high speeds. Both are great for moving quickly, but you can't just ride them out if you want to survive and succeed. Control your motion in the air to keep yourself from traveling in a predictable arc and getting blasted by an opponent who was just waiting for someone to use the pad.

Also, when you're in the air, look around in all directions. This keeps others from making an easy kill of you and lets you get the drop on unwary foes who weren't expecting someone to come up on them so quickly.

ESCAPING PURSUIT

Even if you master all of the preceding techniques, there will be times when an opponent gets the drop on you, and your options are limited to running and getting fragged. There's no shame in retreating if you're outclassed, but for frag's sake, do it under cover fire! There's no reason not to backpedal and return fire. You won't be moving any more slowly, and it's not like you're less of a target running backward and shooting than you are running forward with a "waste me" sign slapped on your back. Remember, the best defense is a good offense.

And while you're running, zigzag like crazy and jump around like you just stepped knee-deep into a beehive. Granted, it's not as easy to shoot your pursuer while jinking like this, but if you're having that much trouble hitting them, imagine how much trouble they're having hitting you!

No trick is too dirty when it comes to shaking an enemy off your tail. Here's one that won't catch many multiplayer veterans but is worth trying as a last-ditch effort: While being pursued, duck around a blind corner and wait for your opponent to hopefully rush on by. If they're stupid enough to take the bait, you might just frag them and save your own skin. If not, well, it was nice knowing you.

A quick change of vertical positioning is also a great way to escape a pursuer. Ideally, you want to move up quickly, not down (see the "Higher Ground" sidebar). But if dropping off a ledge is your only hope and you've got the health to survive it, do it. Every second you're out of your opponent's line of sight is a second that they can't shoot at you.

VEHICLES · CHARACTERS · ENEMIES · WALKTHROUGH · MULTIPLAYER · GAMERSCORE ACHIEVEMENTS
WELCOME TO QUAKE 4 · GETTING STARTED · BASIC TRAINING · WEAPONS AND ITEMS

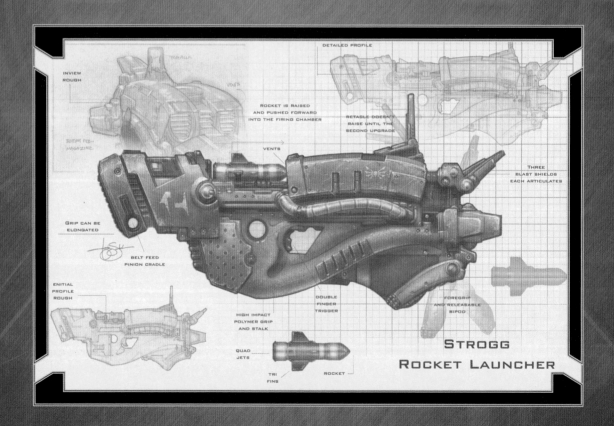

DETAILED PROFILE

INVIEW ROUGH

ROCKET IS RAISED AND PUSHED FORWARD INTO THE FIRING CHAMBER

RETACLE DOESN'T RAISE UNTIL THE SECOND UPGRADE

BOTTOM FED MAGAZINE

VENTS

THREE BLAST SHIELDS EACH ARTICULATES

GRIP CAN BE ELONGATED

BELT FEED PINION CRADLE

ENITIAL PROFILE ROUGH

DOUBLE FINGER TRIGGER

FOREGRIP AND RELEASABLE BIPOD

HIGH IMPACT POLYMER GRIP AND STALK

QUAD JETS

TRI FINS

ROCKET

STROGG ROCKET LAUNCHER

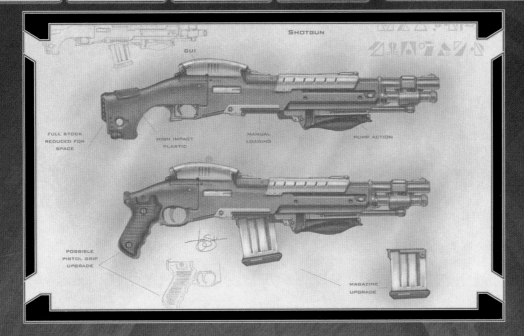

HIGHER GROUND

Generally speaking, the higher you get in a *Quake 4* multiplayer map, the better positioned you are to frag your enemies. It's much easier to hit a target below you than it is to hit a target above you. Also, if you're in a tight spot, it's much easier to come down from high ground than it is to jump up from a lower area.

Some players base their entire strategies around capturing and holding the higher ground, raining down death from a narrow perch. These players are called "campers." They suck, and everyone hates them. Do us all a favor and blast the hell out of anyone who engages in this lame tactic. You'll be fighting an uphill battle (literally), but consider this: Unless they've chosen their campsite well, they'll run out of health and ammo sooner rather than later.

RESPAWNING

So you got fragged. Well, it happens to the best of us...usually multiple times per game. When you respawn, you lose all of your armor, power-ups, and weapons (except the gauntlet and machine gun). On the bright side, you start with 125 health (which is more than you had a second ago) and machine-gun ammo.

The biggest mistake you can make is trying to avenge yourself by chasing down the nearest opponent. With no armor, no power-ups, and no powerful weapons, you're basically a free frag for just about anyone else. Swallow your pride and quickly move around the map, gearing

yourself up. Once you're loaded, get back into the game and prove that your last death was just a fluke.

PICK-UPS, POWER-UPS, AND WEAPONS

The importance of controlling the map cannot be overstated. You absolutely must know where the biggest and best power-ups and weapons are and constantly move from one to the next. Momentum is the key. Every pick-up you grab makes you that much more of a threat.

Keep picking up weapons, ammo, power-ups, health, and armor, fragging opponents as you go. You should be moving from pick-up to pick-up, not from enemy to enemy. Remember, snagging pick-ups denies them to your opponents while enhancing your own abilities, so keep collecting them!

HEALTH

As in single-player, your health is a measurement of how far from death you are. Your maximum health is 100, but there are power-ups and pick-ups that can boost you over that limit. If your health reaches zero, you're fragged, sunshine. There are four varieties of health pick-ups in *Quake 4* multiplayer. Each is represented by a different-color cross.

NOTE

Health shards and mega health boost your health to a maximum of 200, but it drops by one point per second until it reaches 100.

HEALTH PICK-UPS

PICK-UP	NAME	HEALTH POINTS
	Health shard	5
	Small health pack	25
	Large health pack	50
	Mega health	100

ARMOR

Armor in multiplayer works the same way it does in single-player. It's an additional layer of protection against mortal wounds. Each time you're hit, your armor soaks up some of the damage, reducing the attack's impact on your health. Your maximum armor value is 200, but it drops by one point per second until it reaches 100.

ARMOR PICK-UPS

PICK-UP	NAME	ARMOR POINTS
	Armor shard	5
	Small armor vest	50
	Large armor vest	100

POWER-UPS

In addition to the four Arena Capture the Flag power-ups (which only appear in Arena CTF games), there are also four additional power-ups that grant potentially game-winning abilities to whoever grabs them. Each power-up lasts for 30 seconds or until the player is fragged, whichever comes first. But seriously, if you snag a power-up and get fragged before it expires, we don't want to be seen hanging around with you.

NOTE

The following power-ups can be stacked on top of Arena CTF power-ups, giving you both power-ups' abilities.

POWER-UPS

POWER-UP	NAME	EFFECT
	Haste	Increases rate of fire and movement speed
	Invisibility	Makes you nearly invisible to other players
	Quad damage	Multiplies the damage from your attacks by four
	Regeneration	Regenerates 15 health/sec when you are under 100 health or 5 health/sec when you are over 100, up to a maximum of 200

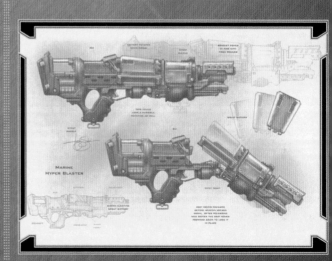

MARINE
HYPER BLASTER

WEAPONS AND AMMO

To be an imposing force in multiplayer, you *must* master every single weapon on the map, even the ones you don't like. The reason you don't like those weapons is because you haven't bothered to learn how to use them effectively. There are no useless weapons in *Quake 4*.

Also, be creative with your weapon use and find alternate applications for them. For instance, did you know that you can lob grenades through teleporters and potentially frag someone on the other side? Did you consider that you can use grenades and rockets to knock opponents into bottomless pits or off the map's edge for a quick frag? And have you fully explored the reckless thrill of rocket jumping? (See the "Rocket Jumping" sidebar.) If not, you need to sit under the learning tree for a little while longer, grasshopper.

ROCKET JUMPING

Rocket jumping is an alternative use for the rocket launcher that sends you leaping high into the air for pick-ups and ledges that would normally be out of reach. And all it costs you is a little health or armor (okay, a lot of health or armor). But if a rocket jump will launch you up to a perfect sniping post or a mega health, don't you think it's worth it? No pain, no gain!

Here's how to rocket jump: While running, look down at your feet, then jump and fire a rocket directly below you. The rocket's shockwave sends you soaring high into the air. When you land, find some health and armor—fast!

For weapons with a slow rate of fire, don't just hold down the Fire button. It gives your opponent a rhythm for dodging; they will know when the next shot is about to be fired and can jump or change direction. Holding down the Fire button with a slow weapon also practically guarantees that you won't have a shot at the ready when your reticle is lined up perfectly with an enemy. Ideally, you want to line up a great shot with a slow-firing weapon that does a lot of damage and then follow up with a fast-firing weapon if necessary.

TIP

Cheap Trick #1: Go after players who have just killed other players. Odds are, they suffered some damage in the battle and might be running low on ammo.

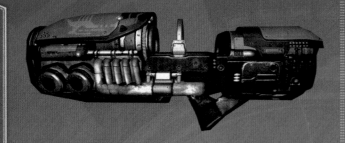

When fighting enemies in open areas, use area-effect weapons that do splash damage, like the rocket launcher and grenade launcher. Their blast radius is also why you never want to use them in confined spaces, unless you're an explosives genius. In nonteam play, throw a little chaos into the mix by dropping a rocket or grenade into open areas below you. Who knows? You might just frag someone.

The railgun is great for wasting distant opponents, because the instant you fire it, the slug hits whatever you've got targeted in your reticle. Its slow rate of fire makes it generally unsuitable for up-close work. And no complaining about how difficult it is to hit a distant target with the railgun—practice!

The hyperblaster is exactly the opposite: great for mid- to close-range combat but bad for long-range sniping. Its blasts don't instantly hit their targets, so a distant moving enemy can easily evade your fire.

When you're up close and personal, nothing beats a shotgun at very close range, but its lethality decreases quickly with range. The nailgun and hyper-blaster are better suited to mid-range combat.

Tip

Cheap Trick #2: If you see two or more opponents battling it out, fire a few rockets or grenades at them to waste them both and pick up two frags for the price of one!

The machine gun and gauntlet are less than ideal, but they're far from useless. Make a special effort to master them, because you always have them—and everything's a lethal weapon once you've picked up quad damage.

MULTIPLAYER MAPS

The following section contains top-down views of all 13 multiplayer maps in *Quake 4*, with every weapon, power-up, and pick-up labeled on each. These are enough to get you started, but having these maps alone won't make you a multiplayer expert. When you're in the thick of battle, you won't have time to consult this guide to find out where you are on the map.

Use these maps as a resource to locate the items that complement your unique play style and become familiar with the multiple ways to reach each of them. Success in multiplayer is a matter of practice. Expect to get your head handed to you the first few times you play on a new map; it's all part of the learning process.

Create circuits around the maps that take you past every power-up, every health and armor pick-up, and the weapons that you're best at using. Run those circuits and frag opponents as you go, reequipping yourself after each skirmish.

You must also be able to think on your feet and change your circuit so it doesn't become too predictable. If an opponent is running the same path as you but he's several steps ahead, change your path or you'll miss everything.

As you develop your skills and learn the maps, you'll climb to the top of the rankings. There's no substitute for experience, so get in there and get fragging!

QUAKE 4 MULTIPLAYER MAPS

MAP NAME	DM/TEAM DM	TOURNEY	CTF/ARENA CTF
Bloodwork	Yes	No	No
Death before Dishonor	No	No	Yes
The Fragging Yard	Yes	No	No
The Fragging Yard lvl	No	Yes	No
Heartless	No	No	Yes
The Longest Day	Yes	Yes	No
The Lost Fleet	Yes	Yes	No
No Doctors	Yes	Yes	No
Ice Edge	Yes	Yes	No
Relativity	No	No	Yes
The Rose	Yes	No	No
Sandstorm	Yes	No	No
Speed Trap	No	No	Yes

MULTIPLAYER MAP LEGEND

ICON	ITEM	NOTES
	Ammo-Regen	CTF Arena only
	Armor shard	–
	Small armor vest	–
	Large armor vest	–
	Guard	CTF Arena only
	Dark matter gun	–
	Dark matter core	–
	Flag	CTF/CTF Arena only
	Grenade launcher	–
	Grenades	–
	Haste	–
	Health shard	–
	Small health pack	–
	Large health pack	–
	Mega health	–
	Hyperblaster	–
	Batteries	–
	Invisibility	–

ICON	ITEM	NOTES
	Lightning Gun	–
	Lightning Coils	–
	Clips	–
	Nailgun	–
	Nails	–
	Regeneration	–
	Railgun	–
	Slugs	–
	Rocket launcher	–
	Rockets	–
	Scout	CTF Arena only
	Shotgun	–
	Shells	–
	Teleporter	If a pair of teleporters have the same number, entering one sends you to the other
	Teleport location	A one-way teleporter sends you to the teleport location with the same number
	Doubler	CTF Arena only
	Quad damage	–

BLOODWORK

CHAPTER 1
WELCOME TO
QUAKE 4

CHAPTER 2
BASIC TRAINING

CHAPTER 3
WEAPONS AND
ITEMS

CHAPTER 4
VEHICLES

CHAPTER 5
CHARACTERS

CHAPTER 6
ENEMIES

CHAPTER 7
WALKTHROUGH

CHAPTER 8
MULTIPLAYER

CHAPTER 9
GAMERSCORE
ACHIEVEMENTS

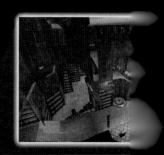

Bloodwork is a tight, complex Deathmatch map filled with narrow winding corridors that present end
nities for ambushes. Its two open areas are surefire locations for intense combat—try not to end u
of these zones.

DEATH BEFORE DISHONOR

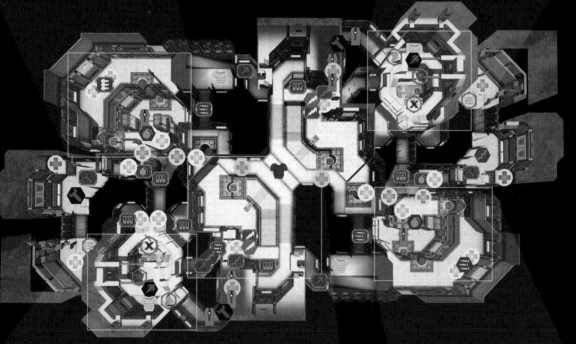

Death before Dishonor is a fast, multilevel Capture the Flag map with a plethora of jump pads that make it easy to bounce from the lower level to the upper level. If you want to get even higher, how about using some precision rocket jumping to reach the two vertical pillars on either side of the map? Even the most fervent anticamper will have to admit that the grenade launcher, nailgun, health packs, and small armor vest on the ledges near the pillars make these areas very tempting campsites.

THE FRAGGING YARD

CHAPTER 1
WELCOME TO
QUAKE 4

CHAPTER 2
BASIC TRAINING

CHAPTER 3
WEAPONS AND
ITEMS

CHAPTER 4
VEHICLES

CHAPTER 5
CHARACTERS

CHAPTER 6
ENEMIES

CHAPTER 7
WALKTHROUGH

CHAPTER 8
MULTIPLAYER

CHAPTER 9
GAMERSCORE
ACHIEVEMENTS

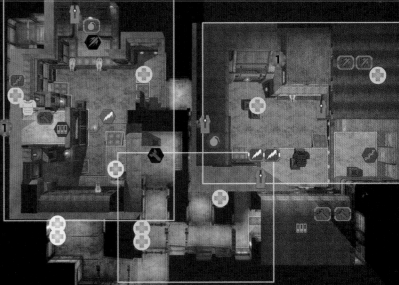

The Fragging Yard lives up to its name. If ever a map was designed to take advantage of every weapon in the game, it was this one. Wide-open spaces alternate with claustrophobic corridors, meaning you must be quick on the weapon switching if you want the right tool for the job. Make a special effort to memorize the locations of the teleporters and the pick-ups they lead to.

THE FRAGGING YARD 1v1

This special bite-sized version of the Fragging Yard is designed for Tournament and Deathmatch play only [no Team Deathmatch, though]. Most of the sprawl of the larger version has been eliminated, leaving only a lean, mean circuit. The small armor vest in the map's wide-open center is a tempting pick-up, but if your opponent is on the ball, he'll be waiting for you to make that exact move.

CHAPTER 1
WELCOME TO
QUAKE 4

CHAPTER 2
BASIC TRAINING

CHAPTER 3
WEAPONS AND
ITEMS

CHAPTER 4
VEHICLES

CHAPTER 5
CHARACTERS

CHAPTER 6
ENEMIES

CHAPTER 7
WALKTHROUGH

CHAPTER 8
MULTIPLAYER

CHAPTER 9
GAMERSCORE
ACHIEVEMENTS

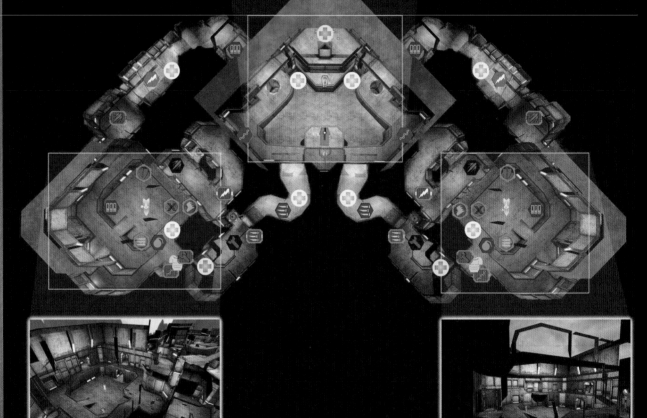

Heartless is one of the smallest and most straightforward Capture the Flag maps, but there's a surprising amount of complexity in its simple design. The open area in the level's center mirrors the open areas around each team's flag. Any player who's a crack shot with the railgun (found near either side of the map's center) will rack up the frags in short order. Controlling the central area is key, as it must be crossed in order to move from one base to the other.

THE LONGEST DAY

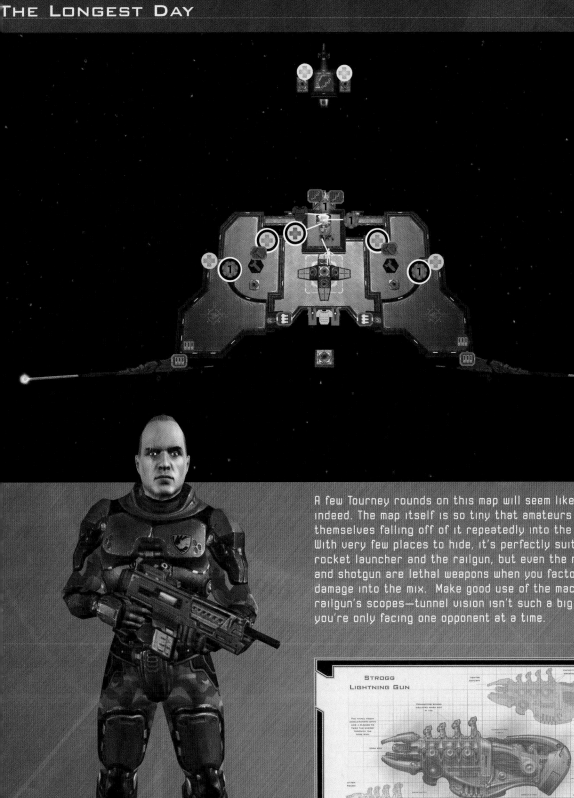

A few Tourney rounds on this map will seem like a long day indeed. The map itself is so tiny that amateurs will find themselves falling off of it repeatedly into the abyss below. With very few places to hide, it's perfectly suited to the rocket launcher and the railgun, but even the machine gun and shotgun are lethal weapons when you factor a quad damage into the mix. Make good use of the machine gun and railgun's scopes—tunnel vision isn't such a big deal when you're only facing one opponent at a time.

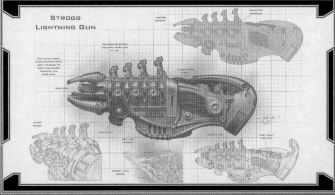

STROGG
LIGHTNING GUN

THE LOST FLEET

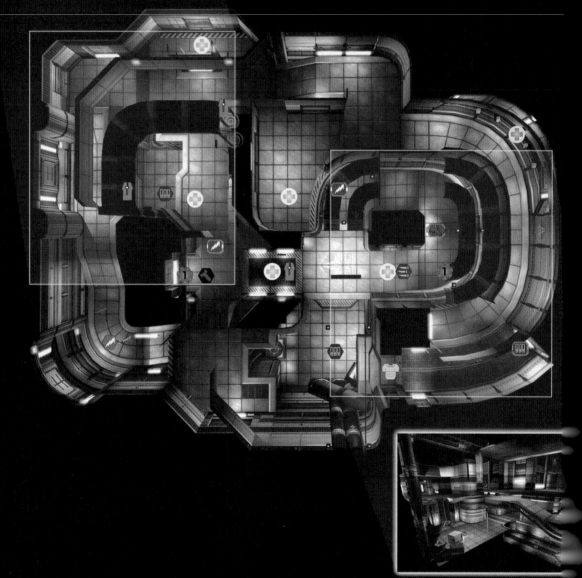

This tiny Deathmatch map favors those skilled in close-quarters combat. The looping corridors create natu
circuits through the map, all of which meet in the spiraling pathways at one end of the map. The shotgun an
lightning gun are the obvious choices here, but don't overlook the nailgun—the splash damage its nails crea
be quite effective.

No Doctors

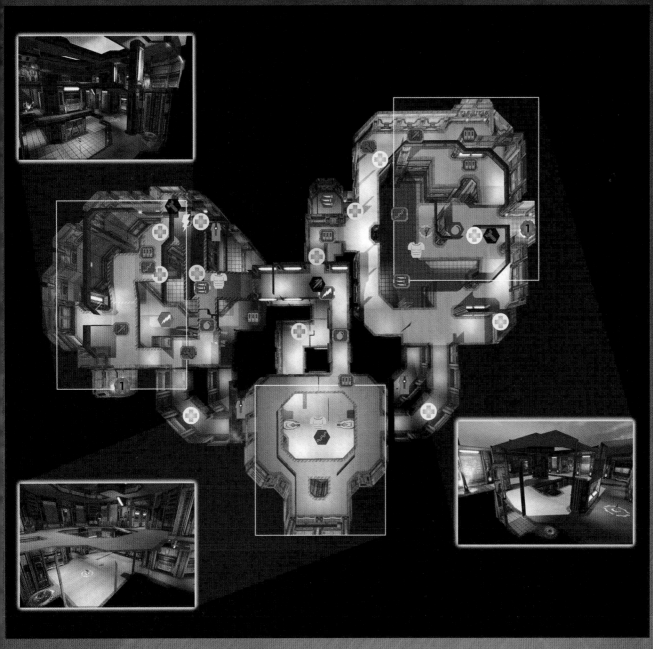

No Doctors is a Deathmatch map divided into three main areas, with two levels of pathways joining them. It's the ideal map for a novice to begin on, as it's a relatively painless introduction to all of the features of your typical multiplayer map, including jump pads, acceleration pads, and teleporters. It's also one of the easier maps to memorize and control, especially after you learn all of the ways to move from the lower level to the upper level.

QUAKE 4

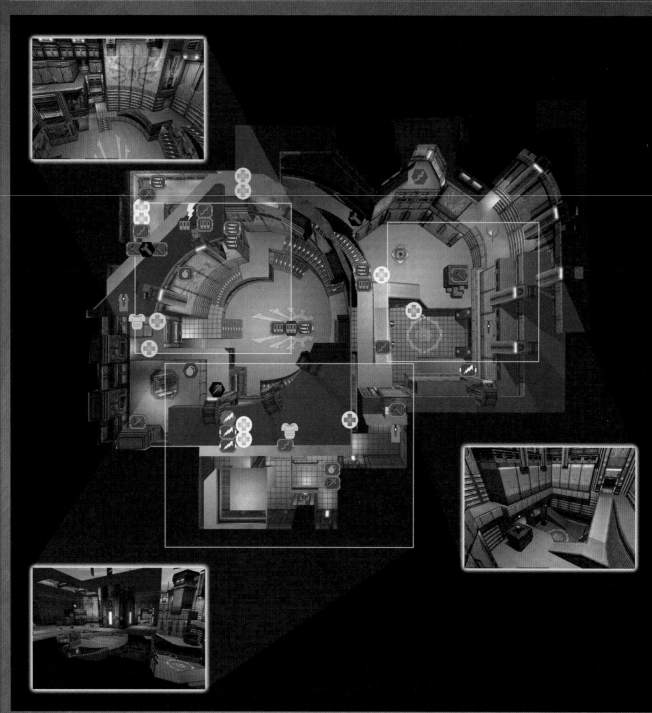

This Deathmatch map will warm the hearts of *Quake II* veterans, who will instantly recognize it as an updated version of the classic Deathmatch map, the Edge. If you're a newcomer, you might be overwhelmed by the complexity of this uncommonly vertical arena, and even veterans might have to play a few rounds before remembering where all of the twisting corridors lead. The giant circular area that dominates one half of the map is a sure-fire hotspot if you're looking for some frenzied combat—and if you're not, stay the hell away!

RELATIVITY

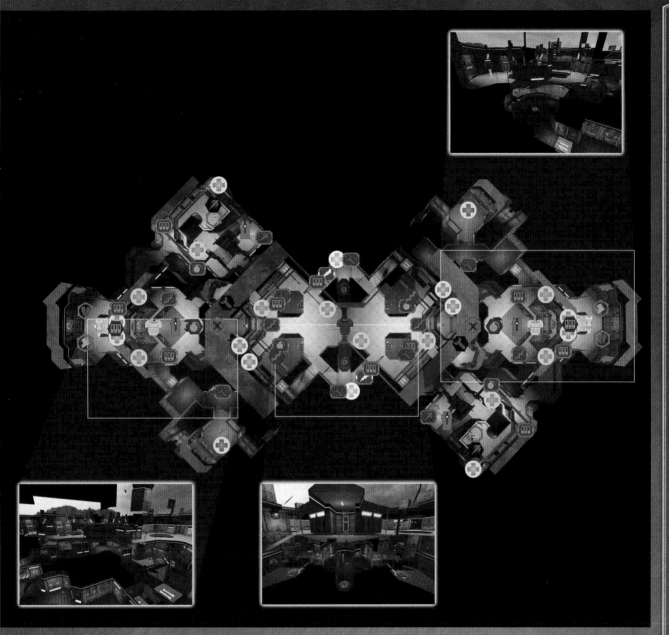

MULTIPLAYER MODES

MULTIPLAYER STRATEGIES

MULTIPLAYER MAPS

Relativity is one of the most complex CTF maps in the game. It is a maze of right angles and staircases, and most of it is three levels deep, making it very difficult to track enemy flag carriers. On the bright side, if you manage to snag the enemy flag, you can lose yourself in the map's complexity as well.

THE ROSE

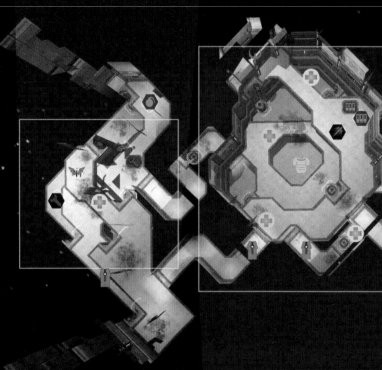

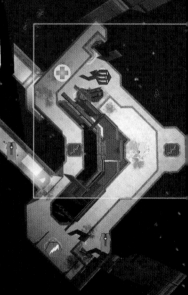

It's hard to say what exactly earned the Rose its name: the intricate pathways that resemble the delicate folds o the flower, or the crimson smears of blood that stain its every surface. There's no doubt that the Rose's winding pathways and multiple levels make it a confusing map to newcomers, but you should be more concerned that it's largely open to the void surrounding it. One well-placed rocket or grenade (and even a near miss) can send a play hurtling helplessly to their demise.

SANDSTORM

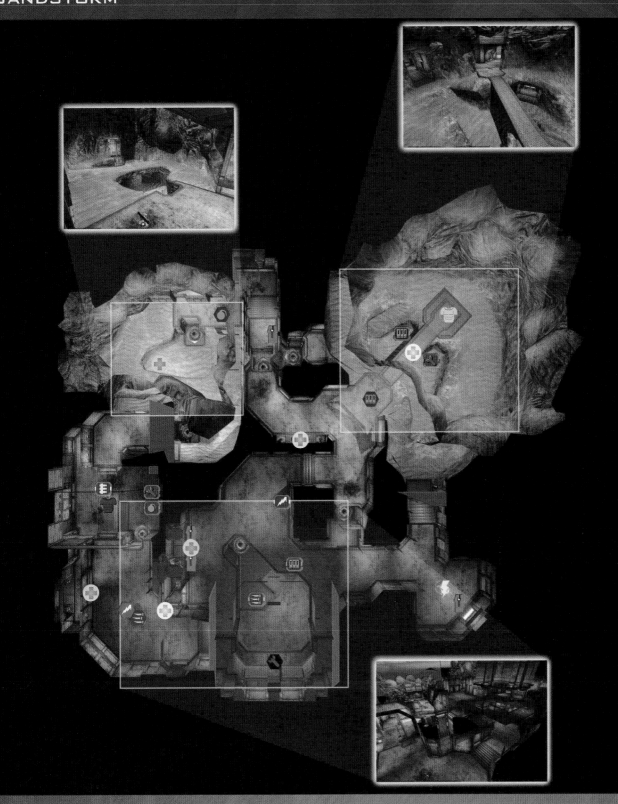

Sandstorm is a good test of your close-quarters combat abilities, and the nailgun and shotgun are your best friends in its tight corridors. The rocket launcher comes in handy in the two outdoor areas at the map's corners, but you might find that the splash damage does more harm than good anywhere else. Novice players should hone their skills on this map, as it's one of the easier maps to memorize and master.

Like the name implies, Speed Trap is one of the fastest CTF maps in the game. The "trap" part of the name becomes obvious when you realize that each team's base features a massive bottomless pit. Falling (or getting blasted) into either of them results in instant termination. Fortunately, once you've made off with the enemy's flag, it's fairly easy to give pursuing opponents the slip due to the map's many angled corridors and the fact that it's quite easy to move between its upper and lower floors. Defenders have their work cut out for them on this fast map.

GAMERSCORE ACHIEVEMENTS

There are fifty achievements you can complete in *Quake 4* to boost your Xbox 360 profile's Gamerscore. Some achievements are harder to accomplish than others, but completing all of them increases your Gamerscore by a total of 1,000 points, making it a worthwhile effort. Here we list each single-player and multiplayer achievement in the game, along with their point values, and the requirements to complete each one. Check off each achievement as you complete them to keep track of what you've accomplished and what you've yet to do.

NOTE

An icon appears at the bottom of your screen each time you complete an achievement. Press ⊗ at any time to view your total Gamerscore and number of completed achievements.

NOTE

To view the specific achievements you've accomplished, first press ⊗ to call up your profile blade. Then highlight your Gamerscore and press Ⓐ. Highlight "View Games" and press Ⓐ. Finally, highlight Quake 4 and press Ⓐ. Every achievement you've met in the game is then listed, along with their point values. You can view detailed descriptions of any achievement by highlighting it and pressing Ⓐ.

SINGLE-PLAYER CAMPAIGN ACTS

Certain single-player achievements are automatically met when you complete each "Act" in the single-player campaign on different difficulty levels. The single-player campaign is divided into three separate Acts, as follows:

Act 1: from the start of the single-player campaign to the end of the MCC Landing Site level.

Act 2: from the start of the Operation: Advantage level to the end of the Waste Processing Facility level.

Act 3: from the start of the Operation: Last Hope level to the end of the game.

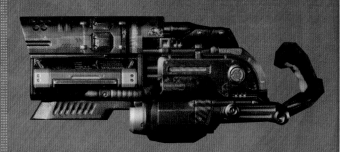

SINGLE-PLAYER ACHIEVEMENTS

ACHIEVEMENT	POINTS AWARDED	DESCRIPTION	COMPLETED?
Untouchable	10	Completed a single-player level without taking damage	☐
Private—Act 1	15	Completed Act 1 with the rank of Private	☐
Private—Act 2	20	Completed Act 1 and Act 2 with the rank of Private	☐
Private—Defeated the Strogg	25	Completed the game with the rank of Private	☐
Corporal—Act 1	25	Completed Act 1 with the rank of Corporal	☐
Corporal—Act 2	25	Completed Act 1 and Act 2 with the rank of Corporal	☐
Corporal—Defeated the Strogg	30	Completed the game with the rank of Corporal	☐
Lieutenant—Act 1	25	Completed Act 1 with the rank of Lieutenant	☐
Lieutenant—Act 2	25	Completed Act 1 and Act 2 with the rank of Lieutenant	☐
Lieutenant—Defeated the Strogg	30	Completed the game with the rank of Lieutenant	☐
General—Act 1	25	Completed Act 1 with the rank of General	☐
General—Act 2	25	Completed Act 1 and Act 2 with the rank of General	☐
General—Defeated the Strogg	30	Completed the game with the rank of General	☐
Full Arsenal	20	Landed a shot with every weapon in a full arsenal on a single-player level	☐
Blaster Master	15	Completed a single-player level using only the blaster	☐

CHAPTER 1 WELCOME TO QUAKE 4

CHAPTER 2 BASIC TRAINING

CHAPTER 3 WEAPONS AND ITEMS

CHAPTER 4 VEHICLES

CHAPTER 5 CHARACTERS

CHAPTER 6 ENEMIES

CHAPTER 7 WALKTHROUGH

CHAPTER 8 MULTIPLAYER

CHAPTER 9 GAMERSCORE ACHIEVEMENTS

SINGLE-PLAYER ACHIEVEMENTS (CONTINUED)

ACHIEVEMENT	POINTS AWARDED	DESCRIPTION	COMPLETED?
Blaster Master	15	Completed a single-player level using only the blaster	☐
Blazing Buckshot	15	Completed a single-player level using only the shotgun	☐
The Machine	15	Completed a single-player level using only the machine gun	☐
Pineapple King	15	Completed a single-player level using only the grenade launcher	☐
Hyperactive	15	Completed a single-player level using only the hyper-blaster	☐
Tooth and Nail	15	Completed a single-player level using only the nailgun	☐
Ballistics Expert	15	Completed a single-player level using only the rocket launcher	☐
The Sniper	15	Completed a single-player level using only the railgun	☐
The Dark Lord	15	Completed a single-player level using only the dark matter gun	☐
Enlightening	15	Completed a single-player level using only the lightning gun	☐
Solar Star of Courage	20	For courage in battle alongside Viper Squad, CPL Mahler has awarded you the Solar Star of Courage	☐
Sky Marshall's Medal of Valor	20	For rescuing PVT Lanier of Eagle Squad, you have been awarded the Sky Marshall's Medal of Valor	☐
Galactic Order of Heroism	20	For heroism in battle alongside Raven Squad, Technician Raffel has awarded you the Galactic Order of Heroism	☐

MULTIPLAYER ACHIEVEMENTS

ACHIEVEMENT	POINTS AWARDED	DESCRIPTION	COMPLETED?
The Bronze flag	5	Over 100 captures in ranked matches	☐
The Silver flag	10	Over 500 captures in ranked matches	☐
The Gold flag	25	Over 1,000 captures in ranked matches	☐
Viper Squad	5	Over 100 frags in ranked matches	☐
Warthog Squad	10	Over 500 frags in ranked matches	☐
Raven Squad	50	Over 5,000 frags in ranked matches	☐
Rhino Squad	75	Over 10,000 frags in ranked matches	☐
Basic Training	5	Played over 100 ranked matches	☐
First tour of duty	10	Played over 500 ranked matches	☐
Combat Veteran	25	Played over 1,000 ranked matches	☐
Seasoned warrior	50	Played over 5,000 ranked matches	☐
The Golden Gauntlet	20	Over 250 players have been humiliated by you	☐
Private—Multiplayer	5	Over 100 Win points in ranked matches	☐
Corporal—Multiplayer	10	Over 500 Win points in ranked matches	☐
Lieutenant—Multiplayer	25	Over 1,000 Win points in ranked matches	☐
General—Multiplayer	50	Over 5,000 Win points in ranked matches	☐
Perfect Win	5	Won a ranked match without being killed	☐
Number 1	20	Reached number one on the All Gametypes ranked leader board	☐
Top Ten	15	Was in the top ten on the All Gametypes ranked leader board	☐
The Best Impression	10	Over 250 Impressives in ranked matches	☐
Your Excellency	10	Over 500 Excellents in ranked matches	☐
Guts but no Glory	10	Over 100 Assists in ranked matches	☐
The Defender	10	Over 250 Defense awards in ranked matches	☐

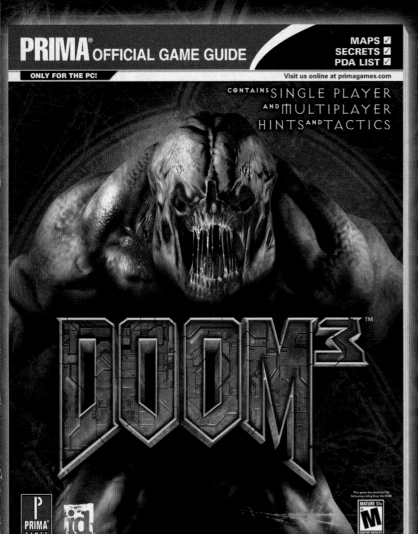
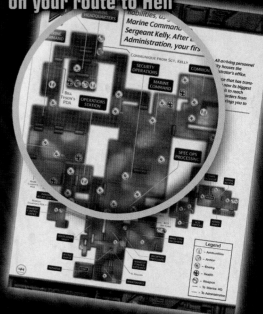
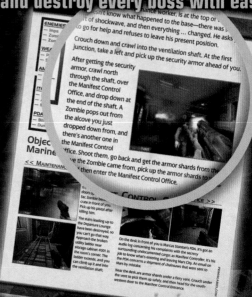